HANSARD SOCIETY SER
POLITICS AND GOVERN

Series Editor
F.F. Ridley

HANSARD SOCIETY SERIES IN POLITICS AND GOVERNMENT

Edited by
F.F. Ridley

The Hansard Society Series in Politics and Government brings to the wider public the debates and analyses of important issues first discussed in the pages of its journal, *Parliamentary Affairs*

Parliament in the Age of the Internet

Edited by
Stephen Coleman, John Taylor and Wim van de Donk

Series Editor
F.F. Ridley

OXFORD UNIVERSITY PRESS
in association with
THE HANSARD SOCIETY FOR
PARLIAMENTARY GOVERNMENT

OXFORD
UNIVERSITY PRESS

Great Clarendon Street, Oxford OX2 6DP

Oxford University Press is a department of the University of Oxford.
It furthers the University's objective of excellence in research, scholarship,
and education by publishing worldwide in

Oxford New York

Athens Auckland Bangkok Bogotá Buenos Aires Calcutta
Cape Town Chennai Dar es Salaam Delhi Florence Hong Kong Istanbul
Karachi Kuala Lumpur Madrid Melbourne Mexico City Mumbai
Nairobi Paris São Paulo Singapore Taipei Tokyo Toronto Warsaw

with associated companies in Berlin Ibadan

Oxford is a registered trade mark of Oxford University Press
in the UK and in certain other countries

Published in the United States
by Oxford University Press Inc., New York

A catalogue for this book is available from the British Library

Library of Congress Cataloging in Publication Data
(Data available)

ISBN 0–19–922422–6

Printed in Great Britain
by Headley Brothers Limited, The Invicta Press,
Ashford, Kent and London

CONTENTS

CONTRIBUTORS TO THIS VOLUME

Kim V. Andersen is at the Centre for Research on IT in the Public Sector, Copenhagen Business School (kva.inf@cbs.dk)

Christine Bellamy is Professor of Public Administration and Head of Politics at the Nottingham Trent University (chris.bellamy@ntu.ac.uk)

Eleanor Burt is Research Fellow at the Centre for the Study of Telematics and Governance in the Faculty of Business, Glasgow Caledonian University (e.burt@gcal.ac.uk)

Anne Campbell is the Member of Parliament for Cambridge and Parliamentary Private Secretary to the Minister for Energy and Industry

Matt Carter is at the Community Education Centre, OMB Watch, Washington DC

Stephen Coleman is Director of Studies and Head of the Parliament and the Electronic Media Programme at the Hansard Society, London (colemans@lse.ac.uk)

Mitja Decman is Researcher on Informatics at the School of Public Administration, University of Ljublijana

Sharon Docter is Professor of Communication Development in the School of Policy, Planning and Development, University in Thousand Oaks, California, USA (docter@robles.callutheran.edu)

William H. Dutton is Professor of Communication in the Annenberg School for Communication at the University of Southern California (wdutton@rcf.usc.edu)

Anita Elberse is Professor on the Future Media Research Programme at London Business School (aelberse@lbs.ac.uk)

Paul Gray is on the staff of the Scottish Parliament and Chair of its ICT Project Board (Paul.Gray@scotland.gov.uk)

Andrew Harrop is Research Assistant to Anne Campbell MP

Mateja Kunstelj is Researcher on Administrative Informatics and Information Science, School of Public Administration, University of Ljublijana

Karl Löfgren is a Researcher in the Institute of Political Science, Copenhagen (kalle@cbs.dk)

Campbell Lyons is at the Khululekani Institute for Democracy, South Africa (khuluct@zu.apc.org)

Tanya Lyons is Committee Clerk at the South African Parliament

Kirsty Magarey is a Research Specialist at the Library of the Australian Parliament, Canberra

Peter Mambrey is Senior Researcher at the German National Research Centre for Information Technology, St Augustin (mambrey@gmd.de)

Bert Mulder is Senior Information Advisor to the Second Chamber of the Dutch Parliament, The Hague

Hans-Peter Neumann is Coordinator for the New Media at the German Bundestag, Berlin (bt.neumann@t-online.de)

Charles D. Raab is Professor of Government in the Department of Politics, University of Edinburgh (c.d.raab@ed.ac.uk)

Kerstin Sieverdingbeck is on the staff of the Internet Services for the German Bundestag, Berlin (bt.sieverdingbeck@gmd.de)

Colin F. Smith is Lecturer in the Department of Business Informatics-Management and a member of the Centre for the Study of Telematics and Governance, Glasgow Caledonian University (c.f.smith@gcal.ac.uk)

Mette Frithiof Sørensen is Researcher at the Institute of Political Science, University of Copenhagen

John A. Taylor is Professor of Public Management and Dean of the Business School, Glasgow Caledonian University (jta@gcal.ac.uk)

Bill Thompson is Lecturer in New Media at City University, London (bill@dial.pipex.com)

Wim van de Donk is Associate Professor of Public Administration in the Centre for Law, Public Administration and Informatization of the Schoordijk Institute of Tilburg University

Mirko Vintar is Associate Professor for Administrative Informatics and Information Science, School of Public Administration, University of Ljublijana (http://www.vus.uni-lj.si/personal/mitjad/mitjad.htm)

Preface

BY SHELAGH DIPLOCK

This book is a welcome addition to the literature on how parliamentary democracies work. In an age of rapidly changing technological possibilities, it would be surprising if parliaments, as central institutions of democratic representation, were not to undergo change. In the chapters that follow there is a comprehensive account of that change—of its limitations in some cases and opportunities in others.

The Hansard Society exists to promote effective parliamentary democracy. That involves a constant examination of existing channels of democratic representation and a stimulation of creative new ways of making democracy work. Communication is at the heart of this. In our study of the first ten years of television coverage of the UK Parliament, we discovered that most people want there to be some parliamentary coverage on universally accessible TV channels, but at the same time only a minority of people actually watch parliamentary coverage on television. The broadcasters showed less of Parliament on News bulletins in 1999 than they had in 1989. The MPs feel that much of what they do is neglected or inadequately explained. (*Electronic Media, Parliament and the People: Making Democracy Visible* by Dr Stephen Coleman, Hansard Society 1999) There is clearly scope for more direct communication between parliamentarians and the citizens they represent.

As part of our new *Parliament and Electronic Media Programme*, we are running a number of experimental online discussions which allow citizens to debate parliamentary business as it is being considered in Parliament. Views expressed by participants in these discussions will contribute to the deliberations of relevant parliamentary committees. MPs are being invited to interact with these discussions. We will evaluate both the process and the outcome. Will such online discussions broaden the range of people who can participate in the national political debate? Will people regard these as channels of access to their representatives? Will MPs take them seriously?

At the same time, we are looking at ways of establishing online communication channels that will link MPs to their constituents. This is an exciting programme of experimentation and research for the Hansard Society. But before setting up these experiments we have first sought to map out the existing situation. This volume, the first to address the use of ICTs by legislatures, provides a valuable picture of the ever-changing map of parliaments in the age of the internet.

Shelagh Diplock, Director, The Hansard Society, 1999

Parliament in the Age of the Internet

BY S. COLEMAN, J.A. TAYLOR AND W. VAN DE DONK

Information for Parliamentary Democracy

The successful functioning of any parliamentary democracy is dependent upon efficient, multi-directional flows of information. Citizens need information before they can make sensible choices about who will represent them. Representatives within elected parliaments and assemblies, interest organisations, political parties and individual citizens need information about the activities of the executive so that between them they can pass effective legislation, scrutinise executive functions and generally hold government to account. Representatives need information from individual citizens and groups about those issues of local or national importance that they are expected to follow up. They do so in order to represent the public and thereby have a strong prospect of being re-elected. Citizens need information from and about their representatives so that politicians can be evaluated on the basis of their record and so that representative institutions are transparent in their activities. These are only some of the strands in the necessary lacework of information flows which make up a contemporary polity. It is not fanciful to suggest that, without information, democracy in any of its forms could not exist. Indeed, information coupled to effective communication provides the lifeblood of a democracy. The health of the democracy like that of the human body, is made more robust if that lifeblood flows richly and freely throughout the polity.

What would be the result if none of these information flows existed? We can envisage a situation in which no information is offered to citizens before they elect their representatives. Many would refuse to vote at all on the reasonable grounds that they could not make an informed choice. Others would vote blindly and their decisions would bring about a government that would have majority support but no degree of conscious endorsement. In such a 'non-information society', the executive would provide little or no information to the parliament elected to scrutinise it. If this were the case, then parliamentary representatives would support or criticise the government of the day on the basis of speculation, rumour and ideological prejudice, rather than any insight into the mysterious activities of this hypothetically secret executive. Representatives would receive no feedback from those who elected them: no surgeries would be held (or no constituents would attend them); there would be no mail from concerned citizens; there would be no scientifically-conducted polls to tell politicians what citizens are thinking. So, politicians would need to base their claim to be representatives upon an intuition that they know what their uninformed voters would want them to do. Equally, citizens and interest organisations would have no means of assessing how well their representatives' intuitions have served them. There would be no record of parliamentary debate, no coverage in the press or on television or radio, no way of gaining access to the deliberations of parliamentarians, and less still of interacting in any way with such deliberation.

Of course, we are engaging in reductio ad absurdum. Such a political scenario is hardly conceivable, not least because a political state that so rejected or was indifferent to the centrality of information to democratic processes would in effect have lost legitimacy and either collapsed or lurched into some non-democratic variant of governance. To regard such an uninformed political condition as an acceptable form of democracy would be utterly implausible, for flows of publicly available information are inherent to democratic representation. The stronger and clearer the flows of information between citizens and their representative arrangements, as well as between the legislature and the executive, the better is the health of liberal democracy.

Paradoxically, at the end of the twentieth century there exists both an increase in the capacity of societies, locally, nationally and globally to generate and disseminate information, and at the same time increasing disenchantment on the part of citizens towards many of the institutions and procedures of democracy. Political scientists have devoted much energy to explaining why citizens have been losing faith in government and democracy and their political cultural underpinnings which themselves find expression in different forms of democratic practice. One conclusion drawn by some commentators is that there is a 'crisis of political communication',[1] for the degree to which the public is exposed to high quality political information is dangerously low. Failure in this respect is variously attributed; to the media for its inattention to the provision of serious political information;[2] to politicians, and particularly party communications managers, for their tendency to blur lines between public information, propaganda and misinformation;[3] to parliamentarians for being too easily fobbed off by secretive and arrogant executives; and to citizens for their lack of civic engagement, discourse and insistence on being better informed.[4]

Information and communication technology in the democratic process

One response to this alleged 'crisis of political communication' is to examine the potential applications of new information and communication technologies (ICTs) to the political process. If the existence of efficient flows of information are as important for democracy as has been suggested, might not the immense developments in the means of communicating information, based upon digital technologies, the convergence of computers and telecommunications (telematics) and the extraordinary development of Internet technology, have a profound effect upon the way that democracy occurs?

Computer networks of many forms are enabling the virtually instantaneous transmission of information across spaces in unprecedented ways. As they do so new methods of working and organising are arising. Document handling systems are supporting the efficient production and storage of data; decision support, management and executive information systems are contributing to the search for more rational bases for decision-making; and many forms of 'teleworking' are emerging as 'working across the wires' provides new opportunities for the location of work. The internet is now emerging as the dominant ICT of the end of the twentieth century. Its potential impact is extraordinary, providing wide, even global, electronic access to vast information resources, to the prospect of 'e-commerce', to transactions that are non-commercial such as registering membership or application; and to a new and powerful public relations and marketing resource. Additionally, the web-site is used by many organisations for managing internal communications, supporting often complex organisations through the provision of an integrated, location-independent information resources.

How have scholars responded to questions about the impact of telematics?

Scholarly views have been far from unanimous, ranging from advocates of tele-democracy and the emergence of a new democratic polity which transcends the necessity for representation;[5] to those who have regarded ICTs as significant means of strengthening the representative process and democratic citizenship;[6] to those who see beyond the rhetoric of 'electronic democracy' to dangers of techno-populism,[7] Orwellian surveillance and the atomisation of social life.[8]

Whilst these and other issues are developed in some of the papers in this volume, our concern in this brief introduction is to take an altogether simpler proposition as our starting point: that ICTs are increasingly, for better or for worse, impinging upon the parliamentary process. Such effects have thus far been much more discernible and written about in the context of local democracy. However, ICTs are becoming more and more embedded into a variety of democratic forms[9] including processes of parliamentary democracy. In new and emergent parliamentary democracies, where there is a sense of 'blank sheet' structures being established, there is evidence of enormous enthusiasm for the incorporation of these technologies into the democratic process. In other long-standing parliamentary democracies too we are seeing a shift from ICT applications that derive from parliamentary library professionals and from individual enthusiasts and champions amongst the representatives, towards electronic systems that are aimed at producing greater administrative efficiency and democratic effectiveness.

Case studies

A number of questions recur in the following pages. How far are parliaments innovating around information and communication in response to capabilities resident within the new technologies? To what extent is such innovation enlarging, constraining or reducing democratic opportunity? Indeed, what understanding of democracy is revealed by the use of new technologies? What lessons can be drawn about the relationship between ICTs and parliamentary democracy? Not all of the contributors agree about the answers, with the different cases examined not presenting a uniform pattern of evidence, though there is a general if not unanimous theme that the use of new technologies is sub-optimal.

Democracy is made manifest in numerous basic forms and even more numerous variants upon them. Each one of these democratic forms is itself the subject of electronic innovation and associated techno-zealotry. For example, tele-democracy, a term usually reserved for ICT applications that seek to develop direct forms of democracy, is clearly a democratic form that has been substantially experimented upon. 'Push-button' democracy continues to beguile and deceive. Innovations and experiments come and go with regularity, but longevity is yet to become a central feature of any of them. Free-nets, HOST networks, Public Electronic Networks work with the grain of another democratic form, that of pluralist or associative democracy. Creating a public facility for citizen expression and discourse is one of their guiding principles, though in practice democratic application has often been superseded by commercial exploitation. In this volume such innovation and experimentation is examined only insofar as it impinges upon our core concern with representative, parliamentary democracy.

The central purpose of this volume is to look at parliamentary democracy, based upon the principle of political representation. Some argue the case in some circumstances for doing away with representative structures and making room for stronger forms of delegation and direct voting. Such an argument lurches into the kind of quasi-utopian zeal that emanates from the assumption that a better informed citizenry can become directly self-governing. The technocratic obsession with push-button democracy has tended to distract serious attention from the likely impact of ICTs upon the health of representative democracy. Moreover, we are careful to distinguish between parliamentary democracy and government. Governments are intensive users of ICTs pursuing their use for the delivery of public services, for the provision of information to service consumers, for acquiring consumer feedback about levels of satisfaction with services and for the efficient and effective production of public services. These are all interesting aspects of democracy in the information age, when seen at its broadest. In this volume, however, we are intent upon concentrating on parliaments, their inhabitants and their processes, as well as on the relationships that surround them that strengthen or weaken their democratic standing. What are the effects of ICTs upon all of that?

Representative institutions take many forms, so the papers which follow fall initially into three main sections, followed by a concluding section of analytical perspectives. Firstly, there is the established Westminster model, best exemplified by the UK Parliament. Some Westminster MPs have long complained at the technological backwardness of this ancient institution, while others have resisted new technologies as being disruptive to traditional practices. The chapters by Coleman and Campbell reflect this oscillation between the heady possibilities and the rather flattened down reality of technological life at Westminster. The Australian Parliament, though based on the Westminster model, is one of the most high-tech legislatures in the world: evidence, if it is needed, that political culture is at least as important as technological availability.

Secondly, there are new parliamentary democracies which seek to embody democratic representation in innovative ways. In the new Scottish Parliament there is a conspicuous effort to transcend the procedures of Westminster and to use ICTs to make legislators more efficient, transparent and accountable than those in older parliaments. In South Africa, where parliamentary democracy did not come easily, there is an understandable concern to connect legislators to those they represent — but 'infrastructural' inequality limits the value of such connectivity unless it is supported by public policy. In Slovenia there is a desire to use ICTs to foster a political environment of public transparency after decades of institutionalised state secrecy, though the hallmarks of state centrism are still to be found embedded in the design and practices surrounding the parliamentary web-site.

Thirdly, case studies of the effects upon representative bodies in Germany, Denmark and the USA indicate common threads as well as national differences in the ways that ICTs are employed.

In particular, there, is a concern about the sub-optimal design and development of web-sites that lead to their democratic usefulness being to support political elites at the expense of the wider citizenry. In the final section of this volume contributors have been invited to consider the likely effects of ICTs upon the future of representative democracies. These perspectives range from radical optimism about the democratic potential of ICTs to cautious scepticism of their alleged benefits to democracy. Both perspectives are valid. Had one set out in the 1930s to examine the effects of the new medium of television upon parliamentary democracy there would have been similarly mixed speculations, partly because all new technologies inspire both hopes and fears for the future, but also because technologies are not applied in a vacuum, but within specific political cultures. In this sense, the question is not about how parliaments will be affected by the internet, as if new technology is an irresistible extrinsic force, but how parliamentarians — and citizens — choose to use ICTs in the service of enhancing and evolving the process of democratic representation.

The editors are grateful to Sonja Grussendorf and Eleanor Burt, both of Glasgow Caledonian University, whose editorial assistance went beyond the call of duty.

1   J. Blumler and M. Gurevitch, *The Crisis of Public Communications*, London, Routledge, 1995.
2   D. McKie, *Media Coverage of Parliament*, London, Hansard Society, 1999; P. Riddell, *Parliament Under Pressure*, London, Victor Gollancz, 1998, ch. 7, pp. 162–79.
3   B. Franklin, *Packaging Politics: Political Communications in Britain's Media Democracy*, London, Edward Arnold, 1994.
4   I. Crewe et al., *Citizenship and Education*, London, Citizenship Foundation, 1996.
5   T. Becker, 'Teledemocracy: Bringing Back Power To The People' in *Futurist*, December 1981, pp. 6–9; M. Poster, 'Cyberdemocracy: The Internet and the Public Sphere' in D. Holmes (ed.) *Virtual Politics: Identity and Community in Cyberspace*, London, Sage, 1997.
6   S. Coleman, 'Cutting Out the Middleman: From Virtual Representation to Direct Deliberation' in B. Hague and B. Loader, *Digital Democracy*, London, Routledge, 1999.
7   P. Seyd, 'In Praise of Party' in *Parliamentary Affairs*, 51/2, 1998, pp. 198–208.
8   C. Bellamy and J. Taylor, *Governing in the Information Age*, Milton Keynes, Open University Press, 1998.
9   The Centre for the Study of Telematics and Governance [CSTAG] at Glasgow Caledonian University, *Telematics and the Scottish parliament: Transferable Democratic Innovations*, Edinburgh, The Scottish Office Stationary Office Bookshop, 1998.

Westminster in the Information Age

BY STEPHEN COLEMAN

Pre-history: when old technologies were new

The Westminster Parliament has witnessed at least two previous 'information revolutions' in its six-hundred-year history. First came the rise of the printing press, with the publication of the first printed Bill in the sixteenth century. Before then, Bills had to be read aloud in Parliament; hence the procedural terminology of Bills going through 'readings'. This was not only because of the inability to distribute written information but also because of the low-level of literacy of MPs. (One sixteenth-century Bill took two hours to read aloud to Members.) In 1786 the Treasury established His Majesty's Stationery Office in New Palace Yard; this had first been considered in 1783 as a result of extravagant costs being charged to the government for printed stationery. The culmination of the contribution of print to parliamentary information was the legal acceptance of the *Official Report*, printed unofficially since 1811 by Thomas Hansard and still named after him. The freedom to print a verbatim report of the proceedings of Parliament was not accepted without much resistance from MPs, who had long considered that 'every person of the Parliament ought to keep secret and not to disclose the secrets and things done and spoken in Parliament House to any other person, unless he be one of the same House, upon pain of being sequestered out of the House, or otherwise punished as by order of the House shall be appointed' (*Order and Usage howe to keepe a Parliament*, 1571). It was not until 1878 that a Select Committee examined the question of producing an official report of the House of Commons (The *Hansard* Reports, though tolerated were not official records.) Not until 1909 was the *Official Report* legitimised as a parliamentary service. With the official record came the rise of the press lobby in 1884, comprising a select group of accredited newspaper journalists who were granted special access to report from within Parliament. The respectable newspapers published verbatim accounts of important speeches in Parliament, but such reports have declined markedly in recent years, and this has been lamented particularly by the MPs whose predecessors were once so concerned to prevent such 'intrusion'.

The second 'information revolution' to face Parliament was the rise of telegraphy, followed by radio and then television. From the outset, Parliament had a curious relationship with the BBC, which was the sole broadcaster until 1954 when commercial TV was licensed. The BBC agreed not to broadcast discussion of any issue likely to come before Parliament within the next fortnight. This 'Fourteen-Day Rule' effectively gave Parliament priority to deliberate, closing off the channels of information and communication to the represented public until after their representatives had spoken. The establishment of ITV, with its less reverential approach to state authority, coincided with the Suez crisis: ITV covered the crisis as it happened, brushing aside the restrictions of the Fourteen-Day Rule, which was abandoned officially by all the broadcasters in 1958. Television had asserted its right to comment upon parliamentary affairs, but still the cameras were forbidden to enter the Commons and show the proceedings to the public. In 1978 radio microphones were allowed in and the public was permitted to listen in to debates; in 1985 cameras were allowed into the House of Lords; in 1989 cameras entered the Commons, initially for an experimental period, and have stayed there ever since, albeit under strict regulation. Parliament bowed to the power of the twentieth-century's most ubiquitous communication technology and the result was not only to strengthen the influence of the broadcasters, with their studios at 4 Millbank, serving as a magnet to publicity-hungry MPs, but to alter some aspects of Parliament as an institution (see *Electronic Media, Parliament and the People*, Hansard Society 1999).

From these two previous 'information revolutions' can be discerned a pattern of parliamentary response to new technologies of information and communication. At first, the new technology is distrusted and regarded as an intrusion into parliamentary business. Then, with some reluctance, the new technology is accepted and regulated rigidly. Eventually, the new technology becomes an inherent part of parliamentary activity and MPs realise that they cannot operate without it. At present the latest new technologies of electronic mail, the Internet and web-based discussion hover somewhere between the first and second stage of this process: the distrust of the unknown has diminished considerably as more MPs and their staff have become not only IT-literate, but PC-dependent. Parliament has come to accept the regulated use of ICTs.

Ancient history: computers in the Commons — the origins

According to Dr Jeremy Bray, giving evidence to a Select Committee in 1983, his secretary was the first person in Parliament to use an electric typewriter, twenty years earlier. When Mrs Thatcher's first government came to power in 1979 no MP used a personal computer in Parliament; word processors were regarded as being too costly and too technically demanding for most MPs to consider using them in their offices; no MP had an e-mail address, and hardly any had heard of electronic mail; there was no Parliament web-site and there were no party web-sites;

mainframe computers were still the size of the average MP's office. This was only twenty years ago.

In 1983 the Commons Select Committee on Services' Computers Sub-Committee, chaired by John McWilliam, conducted an inquiry into 'the Information Technology needs of Members, with particular reference to the relevant organisational characteristics of the House'. A report on Members' needs was commissioned from the Economist Intelligence Unit (EIU) and its findings and recommendations were the subject of the Committee's consideration of evidence and subsequent recommendations. The EIU report examined the average workload of Members and suggested ways that then existing technologies could diminish it. A list of 15 ways were identified in which IT could reduce time spent on routine office tasks. Members surveyed reported spending an average of five hours per day dealing with correspondence and secretaries spent an average of five hours per day, including sorting the post. Most Members reported that they spent some time redrafting material, such as speeches and correspondence, and one in five survey respondents 'expressed a desire to do more redrafting, saying that the time and nuisance factors were affecting them'. Only 6% of MPs responding to the EIU survey were using word processors, and 79% had no personal experience of using one, but 20% said that they would like to use a word processor for the purpose of redrafting. Other reasons for an interest in IT included file storage (each Member was officially allocated two four-drawer filing cabinets which were hardly sufficient to store all correspondence) and 'an electronic message system' whereby Members could communicate without making telephone calls, although the EIU report considered that 'the likely levels of use of such a network would not be great'.

The Committee took oral and written evidence from, amongst others, Paddy Ashdown MP, who had adapted microcomputer software for his particular needs — both he and Dr Jeremy Bray MP favoured the use of microcomputers by Members rather than simple word processors; Gordon Brown MP, who had established a computer in his Scottish constituency which was connected to his office at Westminster; the Commons Communication Manager, the House of Commons Library, the CCTA and Stuart Randall MP who had contributed to an earlier report by the recently-founded Parliamentary Information Technology Committee (PITCOM). In addition, the Committee visited North America: in the United States it observed congressional computers which had been in use since the 1960s; in Canada it saw the OASIS project which was about to provide video and data services to all members of the House of Commons via a local area network. The Committee's report, issued on 5 December 1984, recommended that Members should be provided with microcomputers with word processing facilities rather than just word processors. Learning the lesson from the Canadian House of Commons, which had centrally procured IT equipment for its members, the Committee noted that 'the technical disadvantages of encouraging a piece-meal development of terminals will severely restrict the future growth and use of the system'. Presciently, the report advocated the use of e-mail: 'Electronic mail could be used for messages now communicated by telephone or post. It could help overcome some of the problems caused by evening sittings and by the difficulties caused by Members not being able to spend time during office hours in their offices. House staff could also improve their services to Members if they had access to the system: short messages could be more directly delivered by this facility than via the Letter Board . . .' The report was debated in the House of Commons on 12 July 1984, on a motion for the adjournment, but no action was taken. Had Parliament voted to adopt its Select Committee's ambitious recommendations in 1984 there might from the start have been better coordination of the provision of Members' IT equipment.

By 1988 Members were discussing in the Commons chamber their concerns about Parliament's failure to embrace new technologies. Questioning why electronic mail had not yet been introduced in Westminster, allowing him to communicate with staff in his constituency office, David Wilshire MP stated that 'the technological revolution of which we are so proud in Britain seems to have passed Westminster by'.

The Services Committee revisited the subject of IT in its Fourth report in 1990 and this time, rather less ambitiously, it proposed that consultants be brought in to advise on the installation of a parliamentary video and data system. Following debate in the Commons, the House of Commons Commission approved this proposal in July 1991 and the consultancy study was completed by November of that year.

Recent history: the work of the Information Select Committee

After its Fourth report the Select Committee on House of Commons (Services) was replaced by five new domestic Select Committees. Domestic committees are primarily concerned with internal affairs of the House. Reorganisation of the domestic Committees followed the publication in November 1990 of a report of a working party chaired by Sir Robin Ibbs. One of its recommendations was to establish an Information Select Committee, to reflect Members' needs and wishes in relation to the provision of services by the Commons Library, provision of computer, TV and video services for Members, and provision of scientific and technological advice services, such as the Parliamentary Office of Science and Technology, which was established as an official office of Parliament in April 1993. The Information Select Committee was appointed in 1991.

The House of Commons Commission approved a pilot study on the provision of a video and data network, to be carried out in 7 Millbank (a parliamentary annex building.) The first task of the Information Committee was to assess this study. In the 1992–93 Session the Committee decided against central procurement of IT equipment for Members.

In February 1994 the Information Committee's report on *The Provision of a Parliamentary Data and Video Network* included a survey of all Members 'inviting their opinions on information technology matters and on the services they would wish to use on a data and video network'. Over half of all Members (327) responded to the survey, with 50% expressing a wish for direct reception of the 'clean feed' of proceedings in the House, 50% requiring direct access from their computers to the text of *Hansard*, and almost as many requiring direct computer access to the Parliamentary On Line Information System (POLIS) which then contained over a million name and subject-indexed parliamentary records. POLIS had thus far been only accessible via the Commons Library, but not directly from Members' own computer terminals. The survey found that over 91% of respondents already used IT in their offices and half of the remainder planned to do so in the foreseeable future. An appendix to the report compared the Westminster Parliament with assemblies in other European countries and found that only Turkey shared the UK's lack of a Parliamentary Data Network, while only Denmark, Finland, Spain and the German *Bundesrat* lacked video networks providing live feeds of proceedings to their members' offices. The UK Parliament was manifestly behind the times in this respect, and Members seemed to be in favour of remedying this. The Information Committee recommended 'the phased introduction of a full Parliamentary Data and Video Network', justifying this by observing that: 'It is a principal function of Parliament to oversee the actions of the Executive. Members have a responsibility to represent their constituents effectively. In both these key areas we consider the provision of a full network would increase the efficiency with which the House operates and the capacity of Members to cope with increasing workloads.'

The Committee proposed the introduction of the PDVN over seven years and that the service would include the provision of e-mail and outgoing faxes, as well as access to relevant CD-ROMS and POLIS. On 30 June 1994 the House of Commons approved the Committee's recommendations. The PDVN, which has since 1994 been linked to the Internet and an in-House intranet, has become a major resource for Members, particularly as a research tool.

Parliament's interest in new technology was initially solely related to easing the workload of Members and their staff. In 1996 the Information Committee turned its attention to the use of ICTs to provide citizens with better information about the work of Parliament. Since 1989 cameras had been in the Commons, providing for greater institutional transparency, and now the Committee turned its attention to broadening dissemination of information via the Internet — which by 1996 had reached a stage of exponential growth.

In 1995 the Board of Management of the House of Commons appointed an Electronic Publishing Group (EPG) under the chairmanship of Ian Church, the editor of the *Official Report*, to examine the possibility of making *Hansard* available to the public in electronic form via the Internet. The cost of *Hansard* was £11.70 a day and electronic access was only available commercially at prohibitive prices in the order of £2,500 a year. The Campaign for Freedom of Information complained that: 'The public is being denied access to *Hansard* and to Britain's laws on the Internet because of HMSO's policy of commercially exploiting Crown and Parliamentary copyright ... the Campaign wants HMSO to waive this unacceptable restriction and permit free on-line access to these essential materials', (press release, 16.10.95). The issue of Crown copyright dated back to the 1880s. In 1889 the Controller of Her Majesty's Stationery Office (HMSO) was granted Letters of Patent allowing him to decide what government materials may be published. Section 18 of the 1911 Copyright Act addressed specifically the right of officers or servants of the Crown to determine the cost of publication of protected material, including Acts of Parliament, Statutory Instruments, Command Papers, as well as the *Official Report*. A case could be made for wishing to protect such material from commercial exploitation, insofar as this would protect the general taxpayer against the use of official material, included value-added publications such as official photographs, statistical databases and mapping data, for private profit. On the other hand, the use of copyright privilege to restrict the dissemination of public documents, or to limit access to those with greater financial resources, could be regarded as undemocratic. The Information Committee, under the then chairmanship of Gary Waller MP, was particularly concerned to further the democratic principle of free dissemination of on-line information, following in the footsteps of the Australian, Canadian and New Zealand parliaments which had already adopted this principle.

The EPG concluded that 'Parliament as well as the public has a substantial interest in making its papers available in electronic form. As a law-making body, Parliament needs to ensure that those subject to its laws have easy access to them and the law-making process, and the group believes that there is a clear *public right* to unfettered access to this material', (emphasis added). This notion of a public right to information, which is in accordance with Section 19 of the UN Charter of Human Rights, was new for the UK Parliament. The EPG's report recommended 'that the full text of parliamentary publications be published free of charge on the Internet'. The working party did add two riders: firstly, that any external body wishing to use material published under parliamentary copyright for the purpose of added-value processing or selling-on could only do so under licence agreements which they would have to pay for; secondly, that parliamentary papers should be made available internally to Members before they are made freely available to citizens via the Internet. The Information Committee, in its report, *Electronic Publication of House of Commons Documents*, published in March 1996, welcomed the EPG's proposals and recommended to the House that they be speedily implemented. From the autumn of 1996 *Hansard* has been published on-line at 12.30 pm the day after the proceedings it records. There is no reason, apart from the desire of Members to correct the report, why an immediate record of the proceedings should not appear on-line; after all, there is already a direct audio feed from all proceedings in the Chamber and many of the Committees. But the *Official Report* is indeed a report rather than a record: the 1907 report of the Select Committee on Parliamentary Debates defined *Hansard*'s role as being 'though not strictly verbatim, (it) is substantially the verbatim report, with repetitions and redundancies omitted and with obvious mistakes corrected, but which . . . leaves nothing out that adds to the meaning of the speech or illustrates the argument'. So, immediate transcription of the parliamentary record would be performing a similar but not identical function to the present arrangement.

In the same report in which the Information Committee recommended the free electronic dissemination of parliamentary publications it also endorsed a proposal to establish a Parliamentary web-site. This has existed since the autumn of 1996 at www.parliament.uk and receives an average of approximately eight million hits per year, of which a considerable proportion come from outside the UK. The site performs a major role in providing a mass of freely available information, including the daily publication of the Commons' and Lords' *Hansard*, all Written Answers, Bills, Committee Reports, Weekly Information Digests and Explanatory Notes on Bills. Material can be searched for by name of an individual Member, by subject (including options for Boolean searches) and within specific date ranges. Since 1998 Library Research Papers, originally prepared to provide information on parliamentary issues for Members, have been placed on the web-site. Formidable though the achievement of the new information service has been, it has been open to some criticisms.

Firstly, the site is not particularly user-friendly for novice or lay users. Many people know that they need information, but lack the procedural knowledge to know what type of information it is that they require. The site has been constructed on the assumption that users possess such procedural knowledge and, although there is a very good three-web-page guide to 'Help with Searching', even this is formulated as if users possess some knowledge of how the parliamentary system works — and what separates it from other aspects of governance. The problem of organising metadata is central to the civic applications of ICTs: unless users can not only become informed, but become aware of what they need to know in order to be informed, the 'information revolution' may well empower the already knowledgeable at the expense of leaving the less informed even more confused. The parliamentary web-site has began to address this problem by providing simple routes to information, such as enabling users to find out who their MP is by typing their postcode. But navigational guidance in finding debate or legislation relevant to a particular theme, or the opportunity to enter Parliament as a virtual space, does not exist.

Secondly, the site lacks direct links to MPs. There is no list of e-mail addresses on the web-site. Links to MPs' web-sites do not exist, presumably because this would associate the parliament site with party campaigning rather than the simple supply of information. Users of the site, like letter writers and telephone callers to Parliament, will often want to contact not the institution as such, but their elected representative within it. Other parliaments have web-sites with direct links to members and, as Internet connectivity grows in the UK, there will surely be a need for such an official directory.

Thirdly, given the interactive character of ICTs and the broad uses of other web-sites to enable citizens to interact, the parliament site is conspicuously non-interactive. The site exists to provide raw information, but offers no scope at all for citizens to question the information, their representatives or the validity of parliamentary decisions.

Fourthly, the site is visually rather dull. It provides its service in a basic and reliable fashion, but it hardly seeks to attract or less still excite interest. Compared with some of the US legislative web-sites, particularly state-based ones, such as Florida, Massachusetts, Wisconsin and Arizona, the parliament site appears rather staid and user-unfriendly. Even local authority sites in the UK, such as Lewisham, Newham and Stirling, offer examples of what could be achieved in terms of graphics and navigation.

These criticisms should not detract from the high quality of the information service provided by the web-site. In 1999 a new educational web-site, aimed at young people, has been established (www.explore.parliament.uk) and this has a 'look and feel' much more likely to attract new users. Parliament's poorly-resourced Education Unit provides useful background material which is advertised on the site, including an introductory CD-ROM. The BBC, in collaboration with The Hansard Society, has also produced a CD-ROM about parliamentary government designed to be used by schools as an interactive educational tool. The inclusion of the study of citizenship within the national curriculum provides new opportunities for ICTs to be used to enable the next generation of citizens to practise the democratic skills of interacting with existing structures of governance. This is examined in appendix B of the Crick report on teaching citizenship and democracy in schools.

The present: how Parliament uses ICTs

Fifteen years ago, when the first Select Committee report on computers was published, few MPs possessed or used even word processors; only an advanced handful used computers. By 1994, when the Information Committee reported on PDVN, a survey of Members' use of information technology systems (to which 327 — or over half — of all Members responded) showed that the vast majority of Members used IT: 67% in their Westminster offices and 76% in their constituencies. Only half of the Members who responded used IT systems themselves: they were mainly used by secretaries and research assistants. The most common use of IT by Members within Westminster (76%) was for individual correspondence. Most Members did not use e-mail.

The 1997 general election witnessed a significant demographic change in the composition of MPs: more were from the generation that had become computer literate as part of their formal education or employment. In the summer of 1998 PITCOM and the journal, *Government Computing* carried out a survey of Members to find out about their IT use. 206 out of 659 Members responded. Approximately half of the MPs used a PC in their Westminster office, although most of their secretaries or PAs did. For MPs, the most common use for PCs was writing speeches; 78% of Members' offices used e-mail, but only 30% of Members used it themselves; 86% of MPs' PCs were used to access the Internet, but only one in five claimed to access the Internet themselves. Most used the Internet for research (32%) with only half that number using it for political projects or campaigns. Of respondents 43 had set up their own web-sites, but these were mainly used to provide information rather than as an interactive medium. Most of the sites were maintained by either secretaries or web specialists. Nearly a third of Members without a web-site stated that they were planning to set one up. The survey also asked Members whether they had ever worked in the IT field, but only 21 (9%) had done so.

In mid-July 1998 the Information Committee conducted a similar survey of Members, 54% responded giving a more representative picture than the PITCOM survey; 96% of respondents used some form of IT: 89% had PCs in their Westminster offices and 92% in their constituencies; 70% of Members' computer systems were connected to the PDVN. Approximately half of the respondents claimed to be experienced computer users or basically IT literate, while a third possessed limited or poor IT skills.

The Information Committee's survey was part of a wider policy inquiry into the procurement of IT by Members. As the 1984 Members Services Committee Report had noted presciently, the piecemeal procurement of IT equipment by Members would diminish the capacity of Parliament to provide universally compatible information systems. In a Commons speech on 7 March 1995 Graham Allen MP proposed that:

'We could do worse than use Parliament as our first model, symbolically to show that we in this place are committed to the information super-highway. Every Member of Parliament should be provided with access to the Internet, if they so wish, and facilities for sending e-mail just as they now send letters or use the telephone.' Although there has been a noticeable change of thinking on this subject since the 1997 election, there is still strong resistance from some Members to having centrally-provided IT. The reason for this is that Parliament is, in terms of office management, less like a corporate institution than like 659 small businesses, each run from separate small offices, each seeking to arrange the best deals for their own needs. Central procurement would only be likely to be adopted as a policy if Members' office cost allowances were effectively taxed to pay for them—and Members with their own IT equipment, often donated by their parties or other sources, would rather spend their office allowances on staff rather than information hardware. So, although the 1998 Report of the Information Committee reported that 73% of Members responding to their survey favoured 'some form of central procurement', 27% were opposed. The Committee concluded that 'the time is not yet right for the House to adopt central provision', but favoured the option of Members being given: 'The choice of a range of IT equipment and software together with associated maintenance, support and training, which could be supplied and installed by the House and claimed against the Office Cost Allowance.' Effectively, Members using IT equipment not within the range on offer will be denied the benefits of being part of the parliamentary intranet.

Another aspect of new technology should be mentioned, because ICTs are not simply about computers. Most MPs now possess digitally-operated mobile phones and/or message pagers. (There are no precise statistics regarding this.) This has had an important effect upon political communication, making them much more accessible to their staff, their parties and journalists wanting to set their agendas for them. This allows MPs to be more personally mobile: to arrange and alter meetings without returning to their offices; to be summoned for media interviews; and, most notably, to be kept 'on message' at all times. Members are not allowed to use mobile phones inside the Commons chamber or committee rooms. Pagers were being used inside the Commons chamber until the Speaker made it clear that pagers should be switched off and that elecronic devices could not be used as prompts to Members. The effect of mobile phones and pagers upon the workload of Members and the culture of parliamentary life has been arguably just as significant as the acquisition of PCs.

A further influence upon parliamentary culture has been the direct feed from the parliamentary chamber into Members' offices. The first parliamentary annunciator appeared in the New Smoking Room in 1891, an early benefit from the introduction of electricity. (The original annunciator is displayed still in the terrace corridor.) Before annunciator screens informed Members of what was happening in the Commons chamber Members were dependent upon rumours and personal messages delivered by stewards. As annunciator screens appeared throughout the parliamentary estate Members were able to know what was being discussed in the chamber without themselves having to enter it. With the entry of cameras into the Commons in 1989 there came a demand from some Members to be able to see and hear the proceedings in their offices. In the 1993 Information Committee survey prior to the introduction of PDVN one of the main benefits desired by respondents was the chance to receive a direct feed from the chamber. Opponents of live broadcasting had warned that this would be deleterious to Commons culture: Members, they argued, would sit in their offices and only bother to enter the chamber to speak or to vote. A Member quoted in the 1993 Report refuted this, arguing that live coverage direct to Members' offices was long overdue: 'The idea that it would keep us from the chamber is palpable nonsense. It is the sheer weight of constituency correspondence and related matters which keeps me from the chamber and then I feel cut off from what is happening. If proceedings in the chamber are the most important thing which happens here, it follows that our access to them should be improved.' Live feeds are now provided to Members via the PDVN; although some Members choose to view proceedings in a wider context by watching the BBC Parliament channel which includes coverage of the House of Lords, some committees and other assemblies as well as live coverage from the chamber. ICTs have had a particular effect in liberating MPs from the physical proximity of the chamber and this has enabled them to make more flexible use of their time.

Freedom from the chamber does not extend to voting. An archaic procedure of voting in person by filing through the Division Lobbies is still the only way that Members can register their votes. Divisions take twelve to fifteen minutes to complete and this is followed by a delay before names of the Members who have voted are made available. The Select Committee on Modernisation of the House of Commons, established by the government after the 1997 election considered in its Fifth Report (April 1998) options for electronic voting. All Members were consulted on a series of options, including the use of smart cards and non-contact readers, fingerprint readers, touch screens and infra-red handsets using remote detectors. Nothing like the push-button voting system adopted by the new Scottish Parliament (and already used in others) was offered for contemplation by the Modernisation Committee: 'Some electronic systems would in theory allow Members to vote without having to leave their rooms, or even to vote from their homes or constituency offices. However, we believe that the House would not wish to make such a radical departure from existing practice, so in all the options we put forward for consideration it is envisaged that voting will take place either in the existing division lobbies or in the immediate vicinity of the Chamber. This will ensure that . . . divisions will continue to be occasions when Members are brought together and backbenchers can meet leading figures in their party.' This latter rationale for the existing voting system is a factor of political culture which outweighs technological efficiency: the opportunity provided by divisions for Members to exchange information and approach senior colleagues with ideas and requests is too important to backbench Members to be sacrificed for the sake of a quicker, less congested voting procedure. The party Whips probably prefer the existing voting arrangements because they can literally shepherd their flocks through the lobbies without danger of straying; electronic voting could present a greater threat to disciplined voting behaviour.

In the event, most Members who responded to the consultation wanted to stay with the present voting procedure; 64% of all Members responded (419), and 70% of Members elected since 1997 responded (so there was no question of the responses being dominated by institutionalised Members); 53% gave the present system as their first preference and 70% said that they found it acceptable. Despite the high rate of IT use by Members and the broad commitment to creating a twenty-first century Parliament, the matter has been dropped and is unlikely to be raised again in the foreseeable future. In a Commons debate on ICTs back in March 1995 Peter Viggers MP observed that: 'It is sad that there does not seem to be as much interest in this subject in the House as there would be if the debate were taking place in a school or college.' It is certainly the case that the benefits of ICTs have not engendered much enthusiasm amongst MPs, except in relation to their own workloads. Few Members are particularly interested in issues of e-governance and e-democracy. The All-Party Internet Committee, established in 1998, represents an awakening of Members' interest in these subjects, and the 1999 inquiry by the Public Administration Select Committee into new forms of citizens' interaction with government suggests a commitment to rethinking ways of making democracy work. Most of the debates about the Internet in the House of Commons since it was first discussed in December 1988, however, have either been sparsely attended or have concentrated on such subjects as electronic commerce and on-line pornography.

Into the future: citizens and Parliament

So far, the use of ICTs within the UK Parliament has lagged behind similar developments in the corporate world. Unlike business corporations, however, Parliament exists to embody national democratic representation. If ICTs are being used to manage more efficiently the internal business of Parliament that is commendable, but has no necessary relationship to its competence as a democratic institution. In what ways might Parliament use ICTs to enhance democratic representation, and what steps can be expected in this direction? The following are likely aspects of future development:

Public consultations on draft legislation and issues being considered by Select Committees;

The use of new technologies to facilitate long-distance evidence by witnesses to parliamentary Committees;

An extension of MPs' use of web-sites and e-mail;

More transparent provision of information on-line by the executive which can be scrutinised by Parliament;

The development of interactive broadcasting and the effects of this upon the coverage of and public participation in parliamentary affairs.

The modernisation of Parliament, including new procedures in the Commons and a reformed second chamber, is ongoing. One aspect has been a reform of the legislative process whereby more Bills are coming before Parliament in draft form, to be considered thoroughly and opened to public consultation. Varied and imaginative ways of scrutinising such draft legislation have so far been used, including the establishment of Special Select Committees. Draft legislation, such as (currently) the Financial Services and Markets Draft Bill and the Food Standards Agency Draft Bill, can only benefit by public input, particularly from experts familiar with the technicalities and effects of proposed legislation. Diverse and conflicting interest-groups can rehearse their positions in the context of such pre-legislative deliberation and this will allow politicians to reflect more intelligently upon areas of conflict and to examine options for creating consensus, where possible. Such pre-legislative consultations can benefit from being conducted on-line: more people are able to participate than those able to spend time in London; the discussion can take place over a period of weeks rather than hours (as in the case of a hurried face-to-face meeting in a parliamentary room); participants in on-line discussion may well feel freer to set their own agendas, consider information and views presented by others and even change their minds; such discussions can be archived and looked at by politicians at their leisure, and summaries of the on-line discussion can be produced for them. A pilot on-line conference of this kind was run by The Hansard Society in the summer of 1998 when an expert group of participants considered their responses to the new Data Protection legislation. The report of that e-discussion can be found on the POST section of the UK parliament web-site. The Hansard Society is now running a series of pilot e-discussions relating to draft legislation, Select Committee inquiries and the work of the Royal Commission on the reform of the second chamber (these can be reviewed at www.hansard-society.org.uk). These e-discussions are intended to improve parliamentary deliberation, not to displace it; the objective is to strengthen representative democracy rather than intro-duce plebiscitary governance. Unless one accepts a strictly Burkean view that parliamentary deliberation is best when it is wholly autonomous, it would seem reasonable to expect that, in an age of increasing occupational and global complexity, citizen-input into the deliberative process is more likely to enhance rather than weaken or threaten democracy.

Although e-discussions would not constitute official evidence to parliamentary committees, witnesses called by committees could some-times give evidence without having to attend in person. Video-confer-encing has been used twice by Select Committees to question witnesses: the Foreign Affairs Committee questioned Chris Patten when he was Governor of Hong Kong, using a satellite link, but the link ended before the committee had completed its examination and it has been estimated that the cost of the satellite link was greater than it would have been to fly some of the committee members out to Hong Kong; the Trade and Industry Select Committee took video evidence at a special session held in the Queen Elizabeth II Conference Centre. Neither of these occasions were judged to have been particularly successful: web-based video was not as technically developed as it is now and will be as the technology improves, and some Members felt that the examination of witnesses suffered if they were not physically present. Nonetheless, as video-conferencing and web-based communications become increasingly com-mon practices in corporate life it is unlikely that Parliament will cease to experiment further with this possibility. It has already been adopted successfully by some legislatures, such as in Edmonton, Alberta. Indeed, as the UK Parliament finds it necessary to interact more frequently and more quickly with other, related assemblies, such as the Scottish Parlia-ment, Welsh and Northern Irish Assemblies and European Parliament, several of which will be using teleconferencing as routine procedures for the conduct of their own business, it seems likely that ICTs will increase the capacity to discuss issues of devolved responsibility via joint virtual meetings of committees from two legislatures. Barry Sheer-man MP has promoted a virtual European forum, Interparle, to serve the nearly 5,000 parliamentarians within the EU states. There are other ways in which committees can use ICTs to improve their work. At the BSE inquiry all members were provided with computers which carried instant transcripts of evidence, so that they could refer back to this at any point. This could surely benefit the work of Select Committees.

At present most MPs do not have their own web-sites and do not publicise their e-mail addresses if they have them. This contrasts sharply with members of the US Congress, the Canadian House of Commons and the Irish Dail. Even where MPs do have web-sites or e-mail addresses, it is a matter of luck to find them. There is no central directory; the parliament web-site contains no list of MPs' urls or e-mail addresses and direct links to none of them. There are current plans to create such a central network: a National Grid for Democracy. Some Members have complained that they will be overwhelmed by e-mail if they publicised their addresses, when they can hardly cope with their postbags at present. The response to this may lie in providing more appropriate office support for MPs rather than limiting convenient access to them. Another complaint is that too many e-mails would be sent to MPs from people who are not their constituents. One MP complained that when he publicised his e-mail address he was receiving countless requests from American university students who wanted him to write their dissertations. A solution to the problem of non-constituent e-mails would be to provide constituents with discrete passwords, perhaps one for each ward (this system has been tried with some success by Canadian MPs). The current position, whereby all Members have e-mail addresses, which can be worked out quite easily (surname + initial@parliament.uk), but only some use e-mail and only a few are prepared to respond to constituents' e-mails, is quite unsatisfactory. A net activist, Stefan Megdelinski, contacted 651 MPs by e-mail (he could not write to eight who had identical surnames and initials) asking them for their fax numbers and constituency surgery details; 145 (22%) responded of whom 111 (75%) gave details and 12 (8%) refused details and 12 (8%) proved to be wrong addresses. The 540 MPs who did not provide this simple information via e-mail would presumably be contacted more easily if one travelled to the Central Lobby, filled in a card and gave it to a physical messenger. MPs' web-sites tend to be dull, infrequently updated and non-interactive. This relates in part to resources for managing the sites. As the value of a political web presence becomes more evident, as may happen in some cases in the next general election, and is highly likely to by the following one when on-line penetration may have peaked, parties and individual politicians will wish to examine carefully best practices for on-line communication with those they represent.

If Parliament as a political institution is not to be further marginalised by the executive it needs to seek greater transparency from government departments. There has been a considerable use of the Internet by government as a means of placing information in the public domain. The effects of this may well be to enable backbench Members to be more personally proactive in scrutinising the executive and to allow opposition parties to be less excluded from the record of executive activities than has traditionally been the case. New legislation on Freedom of Information may well enable both representatives and citizens to place on the net material that has traditionally been confined to the inner circles. One effect of this could be to weaken the hand of those lobbyists whose 'expertise' lies in privileged access to information. This in turn could strengthen the hand of voluntary organisations and other citizens who have often been unable to afford to buy such access to information. Parliament possesses considerable power, through its democratic legitimacy, to open up areas of the executive that have existed in splendid isolation.

Parliament needs not only to be democratic and good at its job but seen to be so. Although it should not be exaggerated, there is some evidence to suggest falling public confidence in the work of Parliament. Citizens' main exposure to Parliament is through the media, and since the arrival of cameras in the Commons it has been via TV. MPs are the first to point out that the image of their work witnessed by TV viewers does not cast a positive light. There are several reasons for this public perception which have been discussed in a recent Hansard Society report. As the move towards digital convergence takes place new platforms for the provision of political information and communication will open up — perhaps digital TV, maybe web-casting, possibly both. Whichever technical platform dominates (in the UK DTV is expected to triumph, in the USA web-TV is seen as the more likely route), the future is likely to be much more interactive than the past. So far, interactivity has tended to be discussed in terms of teleshopping, telebanking and video-on-demand. It is unlikely that political interactivity will develop by being market-driven: public information and democratic deliberation are not commodity services. There is a strong case for the creation of a protected civic space within the new media for Parliament to be seen and discussed. At present one can either watch a Select Committee on BBC Parliament or read a Select Committee report obtainable from the parliament web-site. It is now technically possible to see any Committee that is archived by selecting it from a menu of available information and to receive its report from the same source. The feedback path made possible with digital communication will release the viewer from being a passive consumer of parliamentary deliberation and open opportunities for active deliberative engagement, between citizens, and with their representatives. This may mean that representation will itself become a much more interactive relationship; it will certainly limit the opportunity for citizens to dismiss parliamentary affairs as being nothing to do with them.

In the first extensive debate about the Internet, on 15 December 1994, David Shaw MP (an indefatigable proponent of the new technologies) argued that: 'The political debate will certainly be enlivened as more people have access to more information about the issues of the day.' The argument at this stage was that citizens could become better informed about Parliament and its deliberations by using the Internet. By 15 March 1995 Anne Campbell MP was envisaging a more interactive function for the Internet: 'Why not make Hon. Members' voting records available on the Internet? Why not make us more accountable and open to questioning from our constituents?' In a Commons debate on 13 January 1999 Robert Sheldon MP argued for electronic publication of all Select Committee evidence: 'When the evidence comes three or four weeks later, no one bothers with it. If one had the evidence from the Governor of the Bank of England, the Foreign Secretary or whoever the following day, it would become part of the activity of the House.' An institutional recognition is emerging of the need to expand both the volume and the speed of disseminated information as a means of enhancing the capacity of Parliament to perform its work effectively.

Where will this end? As Members become more IT-literate and the penetration of ICTs becomes more widespread, it is unlikely that parliamentarians will behave differently from other senior managers: they will become increasingly dependent upon ICTs, just as in times past they came (reluctantly) to depend upon print and broadcasting technologies. Such dependence need not in itself change the culture of parliamentary behaviour. A more likely force for change will be the effects of interactive technologies upon media coverage of parliament and citizens' relations with their representatives. Political journalists, who have traditionally reported and interpreted selected political events, may find themselves reporting less as more raw information becomes instantly accessible, and devoting more time instead to guiding interested citizens through information paths. Citizens may come to regard feedback as not only integral to the new technologies that they use, but to their rights as citizens within a democracy. These changes are dependent less upon the onward march of technology than the appropriation of existing and new ICTs in the service of what Benjamin Barber has called 'strong democracy'.

As Westminster edges slowly towards an accommodation to the latest 'information revolution', the most realistic conclusion to be drawn is that an internal institutional dependence upon ICTs is emerging, but the potential to employ these as channels of greater interaction between parliamentarians and those they represent has so far been relatively untested and regarded with traditional caution.

Towards the Virtual Parliament —
What Computers can do for MPs

BY ANNE CAMPBELL MP, ANDREW HARROP AND BILL THOMPSON

Introduction

Information and communication technologies (ICTs) have transformed our world, and new developments continue to transform business, domestic life, education and all other areas of activity. Politics is not immune from these changes, but while many Members of Parliament have adopted a range of ICTs to help them carry out their role more effectively, few visitors to the House of Commons would notice the impact of the digital revolution. Apart from the rare occasion when a Minister makes notes of a debate on his handheld computer, MPs seem at first sight to have decided not to use new technology to assist them.

However, this first impression is false: many backbench MPs make extensive use of personal computers, internet connections and web-sites to help them in their work. Their offices are filled with computers. They could not work without word processors, spreadsheets, electronic diaries, databases and e-mail. All researchers have internet access, and information and communications are everywhere. We shall explore here the many ways in which ICTs are being used and look at ways in which they could be used by MPs, and will discuss the current and potential impact of these technologies on the working practices and roles of the elected Members of Her Majesty's Commons.

ICTs and the roles of the MP

An MP has many roles and functions within our party-based parliamentary democracy, and new technologies impact on them in different ways. An MP serves four different groups: the constituency, the party, Parliament itself and the nation as a whole. Each of these groups has different expectations of an MP, and computers and their associated technologies can help (or hinder) in different ways.

Fulfilling all their diverse roles effectively is a demanding responsibility, which requires energy and commitment from Members. In order to be effective, MPs require and will increasingly require the support that information and communications technologies can offer. But these technologies are not just means for doing existing jobs better: they present opportunities for redefinition of the very way MPs act out their roles.

THE NEEDS OF MPS: MPs require tools for effective administration, efficient communications and comprehensive information management, both information gathering (research) and dissemination (publishing). Furthermore, MPs' responsibilities in their constituencies and in Westminster mean that most MPs Members choose to maintain two offices, to split their time as evenly as possible between the constituency and Westminster, and to have the capacity to work on the move or at other locations around the country. Being an MP is an active job. Speaking in parliament and attending meetings means that MPs do not spend as much time as they would like in any of their offices. When they do touch base they need efficient systems for organising their staff and dealing with business. With these constraints, MPs will only adopt new technologies, which can easily be fitted into their hectic routines. However, expectations are rising as response-times and speeds of information delivery speed up throughout society, and MPs are under greater pressure to act quickly in all their dealings.

While MPs may wish to adopt new technologies, they are constrained by a modest House of Commons allowance for employing staff and purchasing capital equipment such as ICTs. In 1999–2000 this Office Cost Allowance is £49,232. This figure is decided on following the recommendations of the Senior Salaries Review Board. The board has consistently underestimated the amount MPs need to spend on ICTs, because it has failed to take sufficient account of the need for duplication of equipment in their two offices. Many MPs do find some additional funds from other sources such as trade unions or their own other outside earnings. MPs are unlikely to be able to employ more than two members of staff from their OCA alone and have only limited funds for investing in new technology.

The House of Commons Information Committee considered both in 1993 and 1998 the introduction of the central provision or procurement of MPs' IT equipment. There would be three advantages in this centralisation. Bulk purchasing of hardware and software end-user licenses would bring economies of scale; the Parliamentary Communications Directorate (PCD) would be in a position to supply members with technical support and training; standardisation of equipment and software would reduce the cost and improve the quality of Parliamentary networking. The perceived disadvantage of central provision is a lack of flexibility. Firstly, MPs would have limited choice over what equipment and software they would be able to use. Secondly, centralisation would involve reducing the Office Cost Allowance by the value of the equipment being provided in kind; Parliament would be depriving MPs of their independence in deciding for themselves how they allocate their budgets between staff and office costs. The 1993 inquiry decided to continue with the status quo. The 1998 inquiry accepted that in the long term central provision was likely to be appropriate and that for the duration of the 1997 Parliament the PCD should introduce a voluntary system of central procurement. This will involve MPs having the option to choose their IT equipment from a small range presented in a catalogue. The price, which will be charged against the Member's Office Cost Allowance, is likely to include hardware, software, technical support and training.

HOW MPS CAN USE ICTs: An MP may use ICTs in a number of ways to help carry out their work. As stated, they use tools for administration, communications and information management, both information gathering (research) and dissemination (publishing).

An MP needs a well-organised office in order to work effectively. The main challenge each MP's office faces is handling and organising constituency casework and overcoming the difficulties of split-site working. MPs need to ensure that correspondence is replied to and followed up quickly, and that information concerning existing cases can be accessed instantly by MPs and their staff when necessary wherever they are. Although many MPs have successful paper-based or partially computerised casework record systems there are strong potential benefits in more effective use of ICTs in managing casework. There are the possibilities of reduced training times, of faster and more reliable case handling, of better cross-referencing with other databases such as electoral registers and, perhaps most importantly for MPs, of much improved distance and split-site working.

MPs need to effectively communicate with their colleagues and staff, with political interests and actors, with government, with the media, and above all with their constituents. Most MPs already have a huge mailbag and are reluctant to foster its growth. However, many acknowledge that existing communication systems revolving around written correspondence, telephone conversations, and interviews or surgeries are not ideal. ICTs can supplement these communication capacities mainly through e-mail but also through less exploited media such as web-site discussion fora and video-conferencing. The trend for MPs to split their time between Westminster and their constituencies and to work on the move poses fresh challenges for communicating, which ICTs can address.

INFORMATION MANAGEMENT: MPs need access to good factual information as a basis for all their activities in legislating, influencing government, assisting constituents or bringing together local organisations. MPs face the problem of being expected to know something about almost every area of public policy while they also wish to become genuinely expert in at least a few subjects in which they have chosen to specialise. In most cases rushed MPs will place a premium on being able to rapidly access accurate, concise information. Where they want detailed knowledge MPs instead expect to see a wide, fairly balanced range of detailed information. ICTs have immense potential in improving the quality and quantity of information MPs have access to. The world wide web, parliament's intranet and CD-ROM services and the greater ease of communicating with information providers by e-mail offers the capacity for far more, higher-quality information being made available. The vast amount of information available itself poses new problems for MPs with minimal time and few employees. ICTs however also offer solutions to the problem of gaining concise information quickly.

PUBLISHING: Campaigning and raising the profile of an MP, and his or her party, interests and achievements is obviously a priority for representatives who are always concerned with re-election. It is also however important in an effective democracy that constituents have the chance to see their MP clearly present information that promotes themselves and their parties but also offers assistance and information about their local community. Personal web-sites clearly offer one very convenient way of improving presentation and campaigning. MPs can face the challenge of share information with their staff and of mobile and split site working by developing local and remote networks. Again the practice Anne Campbell has developed may be an indicator of the networking most MPs will want to adopt in the nest few years:

I have three computers in my constituency office, one for each of my constituency staff and a third for a volunteer. The computers are networked and I can access the network through communications software from wherever I happen to be. My two assistants keep the diary and a list of contacts on one of the computers and I download this information at frequent intervals on to my laptop. Now I have discovered the joys of a palm top as well, so a duplicate copy of the diary and contacts list can also be transferred to this. The palm top is small enough to be carried in a handbag, so I always have this information close at hand.

The other aspect of the palm top, which I really appreciate, is being able to use it as a notebook with long lasting batteries. A section of this article is being written on a lengthy sea voyage on the palm top and will be transferred to the laptop at a later date. Like most MPs I am constantly on the move, the bits of paper on which I used to write reminders to myself get mislaid. Having everything organised electronically helps me to keep it all in one place.

Access to my constituency office network allows me to keep up to date with my accounts. The spreadsheet with details of current spending can be downloaded to my laptop and palm top, so financial decisions are well informed.

These networking arrangements, particularly those between the constituency and Westminster will be made considerably easier as Parliament's IT services are improved. At the moment Anne Campbell uses dial-up software independent of the internet. This means that although she can access the network in her Cambridge constituency, she, or the taxpayer, has to pay for a national rate call to do this. The number of computers that can access the network are limited by the number of modems and phone lines the Cambridge network is linked to so for example, at the moment Anne and her London researcher can not both access the Cambridge network at the same time. Finally when the modem is occupied for this dial-up remote networking Anne's Cambridge staff can not use the world wide web or send and receive e-mail. In practice this means that the networking can only be used by prior arrangement or at night. This will change as encrypted Virtual Private Networks for communications between MPs' and their offices are introduced. This networking technology works over the internet, in parallel to web and e-mail use, and provides secure but more flexible multiple user networking. Parliament is setting user standards rather than supplying equipment, which means that MPs will be able to use their networks for party political as well as parliamentary purposes. For example MPs will be able to establish networks with constituency party organisers and eventually with national party headquarters.

The survey evidence shows that many MPs are using e-mail for communicating with each other and with their staff; anecdotal evidence from the tea-room and cafeterias suggests that the numbers of members and staff going on-line is rising month by month. Many MPs have been criticised, however, for being shy about making their e-mail addresses public. Comments have been made that this is because Members are technologically illiterate or lazy or both. This is not a fair criticism. Many MPs from all backgrounds keep a close eye on new technological developments, when they can getting hands-on experience of new ICTs.

MPs are good at doing what works for them and their constituents. They are genuinely wary of gimmicks, which do not really improve the way they work. Many MPs, particularly those from less affluent parts of the country, do not feel that enough of their own constituents have access to the internet to make it worthwhile using e-mail as a form of communication. The same Members feel that opening up channels of communication to people who are not their own constituents is encouraging more work that they reasonably have the time or resources to take on.

Given the hectic, mobile lives MPs lead, trying to fit in a regular daily task such as downloading and answering e-mail is probably more than a busy MP will feel that there is time for, unless it genuinely helps them do the job more effectively. MPs who doubt whether e-mail will actually improve communications with the constituents with problems who they want to hear from can be forgiven for choosing not to incorporate public e-mail communications into the routines of their days. Of course, there are those who have embraced the new technology for its own sake and are determined to make it work for them. Those who have managed to incorporate information and communication technology into their daily methods of working will probably agree that it cannot be done without considering its effect on the office routine.

E-MAIL: Simply acquiring an e-mail address will win no new friends if the e-mail is not read and answered regularly. A day in the life of a wired MP must include an MP's staff, as new ways of communicating will only be effective if staff are on board. However, despite these hurdles an analysis of Anne Campbell's use of e-mail suggests that the costs can be more than outweighed by the benefits that it brings:

Staff in my constituency office begin the day as in every other office in the country. Two-thirds of correspondence still arrives by snail mail. It hits the office floor with a heavy thud, demanding attention. It has to be opened and sorted. Letters that are part of an ongoing correspondence are attached to an existing file. Invitations are checked against the diary. All new letters are date stamped and then sorted by one of my staff. Some will be replies from ministers, council officers or government agencies, a photocopy of which is passed on to the constituent on whose behalf the enquiry was made. I see the replies too and if I do not consider them to be satisfactory I will write again and say so. Questions about government policy are often dealt with by a pre-prepared standard reply. If no standard reply is available, then the inquiry will be passed to me to produce one. Other letters require some research and these will be posted to my researcher in London. If I am not in the constituency, all the sorted mail requiring my attention is posted on to me by snail mail again. After being posted, sorted, and posted again conventional mail can take several days to reach me.

The remaining third of my correspondence arrives by e-mail. This is probably a good deal higher as a percentage than most MPs receive, reflecting the hi-tech constituency I represent. The technology-saturation in Cambridge to some extent represents the position the rest of the country will reach in the next five years. My assistant downloads everything that arrives in my public e-mail address. He deletes the advertisements, the abusive messages and the round robins. The latter receive a polite message asking them not to clog my constituency mailbag by copying me into their internal electronic meetings. Several students each week send questionnaires, hoping that in providing answers I will inadvertently write their theses for them. Unless the survey is very quick to answer and it is a constituent who has sent it, they are told that regrettably I do not have time to reply. Standard letters are quickly e-mailed if that is an appropriate response. Those that need a Ministerial reply are printed out and sent with a covering letter by post. The remaining e-mails, which I need to see, are forwarded to my private e-mail address. I can pick up these e-mails on my laptop computer, wherever I happen to be. Since I work from home, from the office in the House of Commons, on the train and very occasionally from my holiday cottage in Brittany, e-mail has the great advantage of reaching me a few hours — rather than a few days — after it was sent, wherever I may be. I then send replies back to my assistant, who forwards them to the correspondent. This has the advantage of ensuring that he has an electronic copy of all correspondence on his machine and he can check that no omissions have been made.

This case study illustrates that, with a sensible routine established, e-mail can save time and resources. It also demonstrates that e-mail is still not a perfect communications medium. MPs offices do have to be geared up to dealing with junk mail. In addition, the usefulness of e-mail for MPs is limited when the people MPs deal with are not using e-mail. There are two important examples of this.

The House of Commons library — a major information resource for MPs — lacks any integrated e-mail reception system. Individual library researchers may or may not use e-mail for dealing with enquiries. However, MPs or their staff need to know which library researcher to approach. Even when they do send e-mail to the right person there is no guarantee that it will not sit in an inbox while the researcher is on holiday or working a half-week. The library urgently needs to consider introducing some centralised system for handling incoming e-mail. Even more importantly, the government is notoriously bad at dealing with e-mail. Many ministers do not have public e-mail addresses; those that do often do not appear to have systems in place that ensure a reply will be sent in an appropriate timeframe. This compares with the fairly slow but reliable responses to letters sent by MPs which are sent down a chain in departments for reply by civil servants but have their progress logged to avoid letters getting lost in the system. Few MPs are so far convinced that their e-mails would be treated in such a scrupulous manner. When these problems are resolved and MPs feel that they are embedded in viable networks of e-mail use the advantages of e-mail will really emerge. E-mails originating from a constituent will be forwarded to the House of Commons library or the relevant government department, replies will return by e-mail, and MPs will be able to forward these with their own comments to their constituents. Office time and resources will have been saved and a better, faster service will have been provided for the constituent.

The Parliamentary Communications Directorate will be helping to make e-mail communications work for MPs by providing them with better facilities through PDVN. Software introduced will make it possible for MPs to have multiple parliamentary e-mail addresses. With this system in place MPs will be able to adopt working practices similar to the techniques Anne Campbell uses with a commercial ISP's e-mail accounts. Introducing new technology alone is however of limited use. There is a need to raise awareness of how MPs could use e-mail, rather than just leave MPs to discover the technology for themselves.

RESEARCH: The wave of media-induced hysteria over genetically modified (GM) crops in February 1999 produced a rash of letters, telephone calls, faxes and e-mails to Members of Parliament. The government was taken by surprise. There had been no new policy developments since the last GM food had been approved for consumption early in 1997. No one had been taken ill, no one had died and no new authoritative research had been published to suggest GM food was unsafe. Some premature findings of poorly conducted research had been leaked to the press, though no reputable scientist was prepared to back the findings. In a country where the levels of scientific literacy are low, where the media thrive on sensationalism and where the opposition parties were desperate for an issue to dent the government's popularity, this was fertile ground for a scare story.

In these circumstances, the need to get authoritative information to Members of Parliament and to their constituents was paramount. New technologies played a key role in this. The Rowett Institute in Aberdeen published the work of the scientist, which had caused some of the anxiety, on the internet. The Labour Party e-mailed their Members of Parliament with a briefing produced by the Minister of Agriculture's Office. The Royal Society reissued their report on GM crops, first published some months earlier. ICTs provided a channel for factual information to penetrate the myths; the commotion began to subside. It is hoped that the debate will continue, but that modern communications will ensure that it is a debate, which is more balanced and knowledgeable.

Sourcing information

The world wide web, the parliamentary intranet and e-mail are revolutionising the way MPs can accumulate information. As the GM scare demonstrates the internet allows MPs access to relevant information first hand and find out the views of a range of organisations.

MPs firstly need information about parliament itself. Traditionally, MPs amass large piles of paper from the Vote Office, build up volumes of *Hansard* to refer to old debates and still need to refer to House of Commons library staff for much of their information about ongoing and past parliamentary business. The development of the parliamentary intranet has completely changed this. Almost all the day to day information MPs need can now be delivered to their desktops. The business agenda, bills, early day motions and written and oral questions awaiting answers are listed under current business. *Hansard* from 1988 to the previous day's proceedings is delivered on-line. Select Committee Reports and the proceedings of Standing Committees are also available. This is more than just a paper saving reform to the delivery of information. Presenting all information together in a format where desired information can be easily located means that MPs can take on more detail and so hope to do their job better. In addition, use of *Hansard* can be completely transformed by the use of search facilities so that every reference to a single topic can be traced. Over the past five years this same sort of work has been carried out by library staff using the POLIS database; before then only encyclopaedic memories could direct MPs to the parliamentary information they required. This technology is clearly being used. Since the 1997 General Election library staff in the Official Publications Room report that the number of enquiries has plummeted; a room once busy with MPs researchers and library staff is now usually near empty. This clearly has advantages for the House of Commons library as well as for MPs. When researchers and MPs can answer straightforward questions for themselves it means that the library resources are only need be directed at the tough questions which no amount of IT can answer without access to human expertise.

The other key information source MPs need to use is government. Government policy tends to be outlined in Green and White Papers, consultations, press releases, parliamentary statements and speeches. The details of policy are put together by directorates inside departments. In the past MPs had little chance of being able to find all the information they needed from this diverse range of sources. The problem was particularly acute when MPs or their staff were loosely trawling an area of policy to assess government activity rather than asking specific questions to which ministers, their private offices or experts in the House of Commons library might be able to give direct answers. Good departmental web-sites have completely changed this. As well as presenting the overall objectives of the department, they bring together in a single location all recent published documents including papers so specific they would never get drawn to the attention of MPs. Using a browser's word search and the still rather hit and miss departmental search engines an MP can find information in documents they did not even know to look for.

The Central Office of Information provides another amazingly useful resource, an archive of all government press releases since 1995. Using fairly basic internet search skills MPs and their staff can quickly identify press releases on the minor policy announcements and speeches that form the undercurrent of political life. These press releases usually point MPs towards more detailed information or at least furnish MPs and their staff with enough knowledge for them to ask useful questions. Some directorates within departments take the trouble to proactively publicise and raise awareness of a great deal of published information. One example of this is the DETR Local Government Finance Policy directorate which sends a weekly e-mail 'Direct2LG' to anyone who registers an interest. This is an ideal resource for MPs who want to keep up to date with the many diverse aspects of local government policy. Frequently the e-mails will point readers to relevant pages on the vast DETR web-site meaning that new developments need not go unnoticed in a quiet backwater of the public domain.

Closing information gaps

New technologies however could have the potential to have a more radical impact on the provision of information by government. Existing government web-sites, though many are extremely comprehensive (if on occasion not very user-friendly), only present information that the departments want the public to see. Department web-sites have moved beyond being mere PR vehicles as government has developed a culture of publishing every document issued onto its web-sites. However, this still leaves MPs with gaps in available material where information seems trivial or where no policy has been released to the public. It is areas that government is not talking about that may be of most interest to opposition and government MPs alike. At one extreme, some MPs may feel that they will have more chance to influence policy development prior to any formal pronouncements that set government thinking in stone. At the other end of the spectrum, the information an MP seeks may be too specific or trivial to be worth publishing on a web-site. Many MPs, conscious of the advent of a government culture of Freedom of Information, would like the opportunity to gain direct information from civil servants in departments. At the moment access to civil servants is usually only available to MPs through Ministers' private offices, as these are the only departmental phone numbers to which MPs have access. Practice is slowly changing. Some Departments, such as the DETR, do publicise e-mail addresses for civil service directorates and sections. In the future it will hopefully make clear sense for MPs to e-mail civil servants directly for non-controversial information. However, one example demonstrates that there is someway to go before this working practice can be adopted.

A Cambridge constituent whose cat had just been run over phoned to complain that the law treated the killing of cats and dogs on the road unequally. Running a dog over needs to be reported to the police; running a cat over does not. Anne Campbell promised to find out what the law was, the reasons for the law and whether there were any plans for change. A quick phone call to a House of Commons library researcher established the broad basis for the law. Some dogs are still working animals of commercial value, so killing a dog is considered qualitatively different from killing a cat. To find out what plans there were to review the law Anne's researcher decided to carry out an experiment and e-mailed his question to the published e-mail address of the DETR road-safety directorate. There was no response for several days so losing patience he instead phoned the private office of the Roads Minister, Lord Whitty, asked his question and was phoned back with a detailed reply the next day after the private secretary had spoken to a civil servant in the road-safety directorate. Weeks later, after a sympathetic letter had been written and posted to the constituent, an e-mail reply emerged. Its content was identical to the previous explanation, but it had taken ten times as long to be delivered. This was despite the fact that e-mailing the relevant official should in theory have been the most time and resource-efficient method for accessing civil service information.

Part of making open government a reality must involve making such direct official-MP communications work. New technologies clearly offer the most viable way for this to happen. As the culture develops many

MPs must hope that government to MP e-mail can develop into a two-way information channel with officials equally happy listening to the ideas of MPs as they are providing them with timely, authoritative information.

Publishing

Web-sites clearly offer an excellent opportunity for profile raising, campaigning and serving constituents. They are only effective, however, when MPs and their staff have spent a considerable amount of time considering what they want to get out of them, and are then prepared to maintain them on a regular basis.

The benefits and burdens a web-site brings an MP can be illustrated by the example of the use of Frequently Asked Questions (FAQs). Anne Campbell takes all the standard letters she has written outlining her position on specific policy areas and posts them on her web-site. There is evidence that some constituents do read these and as a result decide they do not feel the need to write or e-mail to Anne about a policy issue. The FAQs page has saved time for both Anne and her constituent. However such a system can only work when these FAQs are kept up to date. On fast changing issues such as the Gulf situation or the GM foods debate it is worse to publish an out of date position than no position at all. In the height of the GM food scare several people e-mailed Anne to tell her that the standard letter on GM foods on her web-page was out of date. This was an incentive to update it as quickly as she could. She has now adopted the practice of reviewing FAQs and current standard letters at the start of each week.

Another major use of Anne's web-site is the posting of her public engagements for the week ahead. This draws attention to her work in the constituency and publicises the activity of the organisation or business Anne's visit is there to highlight. At the beginning of each week Anne discusses with one of her staff, who has the responsibility of updating her web-pages, which of her diary engagements should go on the site. If she can, she likes to arrange a link to the web-site of a firm or an organisation that she is visiting. The web-site also carries copies of her press releases. These are not issued as frequently as might be expected. The local press keep up with Anne's activities in the House by personal contact, by reading *Hansard* and by picking things up through the Parliamentary channels. But they also read Anne's web-site, so the detailed public engagements information gives them the news they need without the press releases that she used to send. This means more labour saving.

Once again centralised provision of ICT services will be a huge step boost in getting MPs on to the world wide web. Parliament is planning to provide each MP with web-space. This will have the huge advantage of giving MPs' web-sites standardised, memorable addresses, which will ensure higher hit rates for all MPs' web-sites. With some training, perhaps technical assistance and the provision of web-site templates, parliament could assist MPs' staff without an IT background build or at least maintain a web-site. Before an MP sets up his or her own web-site the parliament could set up a generic single-page web-site for each member. These could perhaps consist of the photograph and Dod's biography of the MP. Where MPs wanted it the site could also provide a link to a public e-mail address. This central provision of a single, crude web-page would act as an incentive for MPs to arrange for a personalised web-site as a replacement, at the same web address; seeing other MPs on the parliamentary site displaying well-designed personal web-pages, web-sites would hopefully be a competitive spur for MPs to develop their sitepages.

Web-sites and e-mail in combination have immense potential for MPs' campaigning activities. The most vivid example of the potential ICTs have for this sort of work is the Louise Woodward campaign. Louise's local MP, Andrew Miller, set up a campaign web-site with a register of support form. Using this register he was able to e-mail the thousands of people who had contacted the site with up to date information on the case and news about new information on the web-site. This kept the maximum number of people informed and drew them back to the site again and again. It is perhaps the most successful example so far of how ICTs can help MPs carry out tasks they would never before have been able to take on.

Towards the virtual MP: advanced use of ICTs by MPs

There are a number of areas in which the impact of ICTs will be felt. MPs may be expected to cope with a larger caseload of constituency issues, or to perform more effectively in committee thanks to their access to internet-based research. They may feel obliged to offer performance guarantees to constituents, promising a reply to any enquiry within a fixed time period, or publish performance statistics and be ranked in league tables.

Using ICTs to do an existing job better is not however sufficient. MPs must respond to the use of ICT by those outside Parliament, including developments such as on-line democracy. The whole area of on-line politics is growing in importance, and MPs are increasingly required to engage with and participate in debate in the virtual realm. We may never see the on-line equivalent of the stump meeting in every constituency, but few MPs (and prospective MPs) will escape an on-line grilling at the next election.

Perhaps the biggest impact is likely to be in the role MPs play in the wider political process, and it is the internet and its associated technologies which will create this changed environment. Whatever valuable impact improved diary management may have on the daily routine of an MP, it is the widespread availability of internet access that will force them to rethink their role, as the political process moves on-line. We are not referring here to electronic voting, although that is a welcome development, but to the increased use of the internet as a medium for political activity of all kinds.

On-line politics: the beginning

The rapid growth of the Internet over the last five years has created a medium for debate, which is unparalleled in history. Tens of millions of people—the latest estimate for global internet use is 133 million connected—can be reached from a single web-site, and electronic mail provides a means of engaging with any one of them, whatever their interests. Although most of the attention given to the internet and its principal publishing medium, the world wide web, has focused on its use for entertainment, commerce and pornography, the net has also been used as a space for political debate and even decision-making. Most political parties now have web-sites, and the governments of most industrialised countries have official web-sites.

The Internet has always been a forum for the exchange of views, with a number of technologies available. Electronic mail, and the use of multi-addressee mailing lists, provided the first debating tool. USE-NET, IRC_, a multiplicity of web-based chat services have augmented it, and proprietary chat tools from AOL, CompuServe, MSN and others. These tools were used throughout the 1970s (on ARPANET) and 1980s (on the internet, established 1 January 1983) but they were not part of the political process and were certainly not taken seriously in any way by the major parties, even in the US where internet use was most prevalent.

One of the earliest examples of a successful attempt to use ICT for formal political debate, which directly influences the 'real-world' political process is the Minnesota e-democracy mailing list. This was set up in 1994 to promote debate within this US State. The Minnesota Electronic Democracy Project was founded in July, 1994 by Steven Clift, a 25-year-old student at the Hubert H. Humphrey Institute of Public Affairs in Minneapolis, Minnesota. Clift was interested in the impact of new communications technologies on governmental organisations and the political process, and he set up the list as a way to give the public access to information from and about the candidates running for office in the November 1994 state and national elections. However, it rapidly became the centre of a much wider debate. The list, distributed to several thousand readers and available as a mail archive on a web-site, has provided people within Minnesota (and those with connections to the State who live elsewhere) with a new public space in which they can engage with each other and, increasingly, with candidates for office and elected representatives. It is one of the earliest and most successful examples of electronic democracy, or e-democracy, the application of information and communication technologies such as the internet to the democratic process. It also demonstrates that it is not the 'coolest' technology, which necessarily succeeds: the list is based around text-only e-mail, archived to a web-site.

Another important example of the use of the internet in debate is the series of debates hosted by the *Guardian* newspaper in early 1996. The 'LiveWire' debates were a joint project between the *Guardian*'s New Media Lab and CompuServe, and used the (proprietary) CompuServe forum, with all contributions mirrored onto the *Guardian* web-site. These debates were carefully managed to ensure that contributors were not swamped by too many questions. The chair (broadcaster Vincent Hanna) controlled the event, inviting contributors to place questions and passing them to the participants. The participants (who included Tony Benn MP, David Trimble MP and Paddy Ashdown MP) were given time to compose answers and to take supplementary questions, in a format very similar to *Any Questions* and *Question Time*. This format was also used successfully during the 1997 General Election when a number of politicians, including Anne Campbell, took part in similar debates on the Microsoft network site.

The on-line space created here serves a campaigning or debating function. While the debates are of interest, they are very much 'set-piece' events and cannot really be said to influence policy-making. In this respect MN–e-democracy is far more important as a model since it allowed practising politicians (and candidates for office) to engage directly with constituents, think-tanks, activists and others.

On-line politics in the UK

In the UK a number of organisations came into existence to explore this space. Nexus was set up in 1996 by Stewart Wood at Oxford University and David Halpern at Cambridge University following discussions with the Labour Party (then in opposition) about the need to involve academics in the policy making process.

Around the same time UK Citizens On-line Democracy (UKCOD) was launched to promote the use of the internet in the democratic process at all levels. It has been particularly successful in running on-line debates and consultations on behalf of local and national government. UKCOD has run debates for Brent Council and hosted the public consultation on the Freedom of Information White Paper (www.foi.democracy.org.uk).

For MPs, the 1998 Nexus Third Way debate marked a significant shift in the way that ICT was used in policy-making. For the first time the Policy Unit at Number 10 endorsed an on-line debate on a key policy issue — the nature of the 'Third Way' — and the results of that debate were fed directly to the Prime Minister via a written paper and a policy seminar. The debate was described by the Prime Minister as 'a unique experiment in political debate, [which] has shown the potential of the new medium to be serious, constructive and imaginative'. The contributors to the Third Way debate and the resulting seminar at

Number 10 have almost certainly had more influence over Blair's thinking on this key issue than most government backbenchers. This raises the wider issue of access and accountability within electronic politics. Policy formulation in the UK has long been based on closed meetings, invitation only seminars and private contacts. It would be a tragedy if the closed mailing list replaced the smoke-filled room as the locus of political manipulation, particularly if MPs were excluded through lack of understanding of the technology involved.

The importance of on-line debates

Events such as the Third Way debate are important not just for what they achieve but for the model they present. In the longer term we will see more and more policy formulation taking place using information and communication technologies. Nexus points the way to a new form of 'wired' political activity, one that has the potential to be more inclusive, more open and more effective than current practice. It is a form of political activity with which MPs will have to engage if they are to remain central to the political process. Just as most MPs now receive some form of media training so that they can cope with an appearance on *Newsnight*, so they will have to learn how to participate on-line. Intellectuals and researchers can make a contribution not only to debates on specific policy issues, but also, in the longer term, by winning arguments over ideas and by changing the political and intellectual terms of debate. It is vitally important for this process that the debate is listened to by senior politicians — those who will actually write and implement policies — and so Nexus has tried hard to ensure that as many MPs, think-tank researchers and senior policy staff are on the lists or are kept informed of what is happening on the lists.

In the UK the distinction between this sort of consultation and the nation-wide public participation encouraged by pressure groups such as UKCOD seems likely to grow, with electronic politics and e-democracy emerging as separate threads of the larger digital universe. The 1998 launch of the government intranet, providing a secure network for ministerial and Civil Service collaboration across departments, and the encouragement of interactive technologies in local government mark other important developments, suggesting that digital governance is here to stay. It is something, which MPs will be require to engage.

Conclusion

The ability of new technologies to breakdown old barriers has been observed many times in industry. As computers have become smaller and more powerful so the tools they provide have been used to challenge assumptions, decentralise enterprises and shift the balance of power. The use of electronic mail in many organisations has contributed directly to shifts in the way that organisations work.

Within Parliament MPs are only just beginning to realise the implications for their own way of working. It is not just that the library is empty because researchers are sitting at web-browsers: the physical constraints on information dissemination and the need for physical proximity that created the need for a parliament — an assembly of representatives — may be being challenged by the capabilities of the new information and communication technologies. As more and more businesses experiment with teleworking and telepresence, MPs may start to question why they are forced to attend the Palace of Westminster in order to carry out their business. If the 'water cooler effect' is all that can be claimed in favour of the assembly then perhaps it is time to consider a virtual parliament.

The economist Schumpeter has distinguished three stages of technological innovation. In the first stage, when a new technology is first introduced, organisations use the technology to replicate their existing processes: fax replaces letters; or e-mail messages replace memos. In the second stage they realise that the technology permits new and more efficient ways of carrying out the processes that underpin their business. It is not until the third stage that they reengineer the business around the technology, which has become core. ICTs are already central to many companies but they are not yet core to the operation of our Parliament or to the role of the MP. In the market, those companies that do not adapt to use the new technologies often find themselves challenged for market share by new entrants, smaller rivals who do not have an investment in older technologies and can take advantage of the new tools. With the increased use of ICTs and the Internet by the roads-movement, single issue groups and policy-making organisations that appeal directly to the executive, MPs may have to start taking computers a lot more seriously.

The Internet and Australian Parliamentary Democracy

BY KIRSTY MAGAREY*

The Australian Federal Parliament's use of ICTs

While the Australian Parliament as an entity is making contributions to enhancing access to parliamentary information by utilising information and communications technologies (ICTs), Parliamentarians as a group have yet to fully exploit the opportunities offered by these technologies. One commentator has put it plainly when he commented that '[t]he role of the Internet in Australian politics is relatively minor . . .'.[1] Despite the fact the Australian population has an unusually high take up of Internet technology it will be some time before ICTs are used creatively to embellish Australia's democratic processes. In 1982, Barry Jones, a former Minister and social commentator, complained that 'the Australian Parliament [has] proved almost totally incapable of taking any collective position on the social impact of technology . . .'.[2] Since Mr Jones' comment remarkable strides have been taken by the Parliament, but there is still a paucity of academic reflection on these issues. One of the areas that has received scant attention is the question of how ICTs may impact on Australia's democratic process. Unlike the US, Great Britain and some other countries, Australia has not conducted in-depth research into 'e-democracy'.[3] This may reflect the fact that suggestions for direct democracy have not fared well in Australia. Proposals for Citizens' Initiated Referenda have not been widely embraced and, from the Constitution down, systems are not designed to be particularly responsive to an unmediated majority.[4] However, while Australia has not pursued issues of e-democracy so enthusiastically, it has been a leader in the publishing of public sector information. Research institutions and enthusiasts have led both the government and the Parliament down this path, and these institutions are now beginning to embrace the benefits of publishing on-line with greater vigour.

PARLIAMENTARY INFRASTRUCTURE: The Australian Parliament has a fairly sophisticated information and communications infrastructure. The primary providers of the information technology (IT) infrastructure within Parliament House are the Department of the Parliamentary

---

* The author recently spent 15 months as a Research Fellow at the University of New South Wales Law Faculty. The views expressed here are her own, not those of her employers, either past or present.

Reporting Staff's Parliamentary Information Systems Office, the Departments of the Senate and the House of Representatives (the Chamber departments) and, in respect of constituency offices located in all States and Territories across Australia, a non-parliamentary department, the Department of Finance and Administration. Another parliamentary department, the Department of the Parliamentary Library, (DPL) while not directly involved in the provision of IT, plays an important role in the provision of information management to the Parliament. It chairs the Parliamentary Internet Publishing Coordinating Group and is a primary source of information for Members and Senators.

The bureaucratic arrangements behind the service provision of IT can sometimes be complex. For example the question of who was responsible and capable of providing and financing desktop Internet access for Members and Senators took some time to resolve. Desktop access to browsing facilities and external e-mail only became universally available to Members' and Senators' parliamentary offices in 1997, although other Parliamentary Departments had been on-line for longer, and the Parliamentary web-site was already well-established.

The Parliament House computing network provides networked PC's using Microsoft operating systems and applications, as well as specialised parliamentary applications, including database and news services.[5] The 250 geographically diverse electorate offices have locally networked computers with dial-up access to Parliament House. The electorate offices have a significantly lower bandwidth available than the Parliament House offices. Most do not currently have access to Internet web-browsing, although they do have access to Internet e-mail, and can access some of the corporate applications across the 'extended parliamentary network'. Some electorate offices are currently participating in a trial of Internet browsing access. The telecommunications infrastructure is extensive and well-established, and fax services are provided from both stand-alone fax machines and a fax gateway server, (allowing them to send to pre-programmed multiple destinations). Mobile and digital phone services supplied by commercial carriers are available within Parliament House. The Sound and Vision Office of the Department of the Parliamentary Reporting Staff provides the House Monitoring Service (HMS) which delivers radio and television coverage of the parliamentary proceedings throughout Parliament House.

In a recent examination by the Department of the House of Representatives on the impact of new technology on the operation of Parliament House it is reported that while '[w]ireless technology is in place to give full access to the Parliamentary computing network from the Chamber . . . [t]here are . . . a number of implementation issues including the costs for the central base station, notebook computers and wireless cards, and the potentially major impact of the technology on the character of proceedings in the Chamber'.[6] The option to implement these facilities has not yet been taken up.

ELECTRONIC PROCEDURES: Despite the fact that Parliament House itself is thoroughly 'wired up' neither Chamber relies on electronic voting and the prospects of this option being pursued currently seem distant. In the Senate there has been some discussion of electronic voting to speed up the process of Divisions, however a paper tabled by the President in 1990 argued that it would not be useful, 'assuming that senators would continue to vote in person in the chamber, very little time would be saved because four of the approximately seven minutes spent on each division consists of the time taken to ring the bells to summon senators to the chamber'. The paper also pointed out that electronic voting would have significant disadvantages, including that:

— it would remove part of a pause in the proceedings, which is often convenient;
— activities, which now take place during the count, may be transferred to other components of the time spent on divisions, so that little time would in fact be saved;
— the current practice of senators sitting to the right or left of the chair has some advantages which would be lost; in particular, it makes the act of voting immediately visible and public;
— more divisions may be called.[7]

It also argued that electronic voting is only an advantage with large houses, suggesting it would become economical with houses of 300 or more members. This position was supported by selected overseas examples, such as the United States House of Representatives (435 members), which adopted electronic voting while the Senate (100 members) did not, and the French Senate (320 members), which rejected electronic voting while it was adopted by the National Assembly (577 members). The matter has not been re-considered since 1990, and there seem to be no immediate prospects for it to be raised again.

There has, however, been a recent revision of the rules regarding the meetings of Senate Committees. Committees have been authorised to hold 'electronic meetings', that is, meetings at which the members and other participants communicate by electronic means. These meetings are subject to prescribed conditions, principally that the participants can all hear each other and communicate contemporaneously, including communications with any witnesses who may be 'appearing'.

Parliamentary use of ICTs in the broader community

BROADCASTING: At a federal level Australia was a pioneer in the radio broadcasting of the proceedings of Parliament. According to the Report of the Select Committee on Televising in 1991: '[Australia was] the second national parliament of the Commonwealth to introduce the broadcasting of proceedings of the House of Representatives on 10 July 1946.'[8] However it was not so quick off the mark with television broadcasting. The technology was available to it during the 1950s but the Parliament did not, generally, allow televising of its proceedings until the early 1990s. While there had been earlier broadcasts for special occasions, the Senate only started televising in 1990 and the House of Representatives in October 1991. The permission to broadcast was subject to various conditions and guidelines.

The 1993 review of the arrangements for televised proceedings in the House of Representatives suggested the reasons for the delay in the uptake of the medium were that there was a 'recognition of the pervasiveness and power of television as a medium'. The Review pointed out that these characteristics have both attracted politicians and made them apprehensive. 'The attraction has been the recognition of the capability of the medium to project the parliament to the broader community that has become increasingly reliant on television as a source of news and information. However, the power of the medium also has made politicians apprehensive about whether television will portray parliament in an appropriate perspective.'[9]

The conditions imposed on the broadcast of televised proceedings, the feed for which can only be supplied to broadcasters by the Sound and Vision Office, include that they must only be used for 'the purposes of fair and accurate reports of proceedings,' and prohibit their use in (a) political party advertising or election campaigns; (b) satire or ridicule; or (c) commercial sponsorship or commercial advertising. Furthermore the conditions provide that 'reports of proceedings shall be such as to provide a balanced presentation of differing views'.[10] The tensions in the Parliamentary attitudes to the broadcasting of proceedings have been explored by Miller.[11] He concludes that the decision to broadcast was an institutional response to three related perceptions: a 'putative' lack of public familiarity with Parliament and its distinctness from the Executive, a putative lack of public knowledge of citizenship, sovereignty, democratic participation, and related concepts; and, 'overlapping with these, the additional problem of how to form channels of communication between the public and politicians that avoided the mediation/determinations of media owners and professionals'.[12]

Miller highlights certain tensions inherent in this process and argues that it constructs contradictory accounts of the 'citizen' through presuming both 'that it is the work of a parliament to tell the people why they should be interested in and faithful to it, while at the same time claiming their considered acceptance and support as the grounds for its own existence'.[13] Photography in the Chambers is also regulated, although the then Prime Minister, Mr Keating, gave a Personal Explanation in 1995 in which he denied the accuracy of press reports that he had intervened to use the regulations to ensure his bald spot was not photographed.[14]

INTERNET PUBLISHING: With the advent of Internet technology, it would seem that the Australian Parliament is once again taking a more proactive position. Possibly the capacity to control its own publishing process lessens the concerns that were raised at the prospect of televised proceedings being at the 'mercy' of journalists and media enterprises, although Parliament House has not always been the provider of the publishing service, with the initial availability of *Hansard* provided through the Advanced Computational Systems Co-operative Research Centre within the Australian National University (ANU).

From the beginning of 1995 the PASTIME project (Parliament Sound and Text and Image Environment) run from ANU provided on-line access to *Hansard*. This project not only looked at providing access to *Hansard* but also at how to link the text into a multimedia framework including audio-visual resources. Tom Worthington, an influential IT policy commentator, has reflected that the process of the government's entry to the on-line environment amounted to a process of 'reconciling traditional bureaucratic culture to accept the anarchic ways of the Internet'.[15] The interaction between tertiary institutions and 'official' sources of information represent one such interaction. At about the same time that PASTIME was being launched through ANU, another tertiary institution, the Australasian Legal Information Institute (AustLII) was negotiating with the Commonwealth to make its database of legal information freely available over the web, including the full text of Commonwealth legislation. The involvement of the tertiary sector in this on-line publishing hastened the processes considerably, however this also resulted in some discomfort for the bureaucracy. The 1995 Senate Select Committee on Community Standards relevant to the Supply of Services Utilising Electronic Technologies was another example of some steep learning curves for both bureaucrats and parliamentarians.[16]

From mid-1996 the Department of the Parliamentary Library has been publishing the full text of its wide ranging research publications: Research Notes, Current Issues Briefs, Background Briefs and the Monthly Economic and Statistical Indicators, Bills Digests, along with excerpts from the Parliamentary Handbook and other Library publications. It also provides research guides to Internet resources, such as the Guide to Australia's Political Parties on the web. The Parliamentary Education Office, with its brief to 'encourage students to become active and informed citizens through developing an understanding of Australian parliamentary democracy' now runs a site which includes a virtual tour of the Parliament. The Parliamentary web-site started out as a disparate number of sites reflecting the structure of five parliamentary departments, but has now been unified. It offers a significant amount of useful material to those interested in the workings of the Parliament itself, as well as material on the substantive issues being dealt with by the Parliament.

Senate Parliamentary Committee Reports are available in full-text, as is *Odgers Australian Senate Practice*. The most recent edition of *Odgers* comments that '[i]t is now considered that the electronic text *is* the book, while the printed version is only an offshoot of that primary text, a still picture, as it were, taken from a moving film'.[17] The Senate also provides a wide range of information regarding its functioning — it provides inter alia tables of sittings, guidelines for official witnesses, notes to assist in the preparation of submissions, the order of business, the Notice Papers and other Senate publications (including the Senate Briefs). There are also guides about the meanings, significance, standing and inter-relationship of many of these documents.

The House of Representatives provides inter alia its *House of Representatives Practice*, a straightforward guide to frequently asked questions, guidelines regarding Committees, information on business before the House, a Disallowable Instruments List (an informal listing of tabled instruments for which disallowance motions may still be moved) and information on the Work of the Session. Unfortunately, only some Committee Reports are available on-line.

Both Houses now supply each member with a 'home page' providing basic biographical information, a copy of their maiden speech, information about the Member's/Senator's term of office and links to the appropriate Party site or externally based home page. A decision has been taken not to host parliamentarians' 'personal' home sites on the Parliamentary servers, in part because this would be likely to involve utilising Parliamentary resources for party political purposes and in part because of a lack of resources. In case there should be any confusion about this, the parliamentarians home pages remind users when they are leaving the Parliamentary site.

In November of 1998 the Australian Broadcasting Corporation's (ABC) web-site began audiostreaming the Parliamentary and News Network, a network which carries the parliamentary debates live during sittings. An internal pilot is now being run through the Parliament House 'intraNet' whereby live audio-visual broadcasts are being streamed to approximately 2000 PC's. The Parliamentary Information Systems Office is hoping that these audio-visual broadcasts will be available through the Internet sometime in the near future, although they will look to an external organisation such as the ABC to provide the necessary server capacity and bandwidth.

Much of the parliamentary information now on-line was previously difficult to identify, and obtaining it also presented a challenge — the Parliament has a complex and sometimes obscure structure. By increasing access to this information the Parliament has, in an immediate and practical way, enhanced its democratic processes which, in order to flourish, depend on the availability of information. During 1997–98 there were '2.254 million direct Internet access requests for *Hansard* material, nearly twice as many as in 1996–97'.[18] However hazardous it is to rely on log records, there is a clear and growing demand in the community for this information. Greg Taylor, the Vice President of the

Electronic Frontiers Australia (EFA), comments, 'as far as Parliament goes, the site is one of the best in the world in terms of government information availability. *Hansard* is available early the next morning after sessions in both houses, and there is a host of other useful information there. Before the Net, *Hansard* and the Parliament was more or less inaccessible to the population at large without considerable effort. Now it's all accessible in an amazingly timely fashion. EFA couldn't research issues properly without it.'

The EFA is a lobby group formed to 'protect and promote the civil liberties of users and operators of computer based communications systems' and is understandably enthusiastic regarding on-line access to information. However lobbying groups dealing with non-digital issues have also found the Parliamentary site useful. For example, Alison Aggarwal, a spokesperson for Australians for Native Title and Reconciliation (ANTaR), a major lobby group dealing with indigenous issues, has commented 'the capacity to get up-to-date information on the Native Title Bill's progress through the Parliament was crucial to ANTaR's work as we followed the Bill through the Senate. Access to the Joint Committee's Reports on indigenous heritage protection has also been critical in the preparation of our submissions to the Committee.'

Accessibility of the Internet in Australia

The Australian population is generally regarded as being quick to take up new communications technology, although they are, arguably, discriminating in this process.[19] Certainly Internet technology has been taken up with a high degree of enthusiasm. While it is hard to find comprehensive figures, the US based Internet Industry Almanac estimates that on a numerical basis, in the year 2000 Australians will be among the top 10 users of the Internet world-wide. For a country with a relatively small population, this is remarkable. Use per capita figures indicated that Australia ranked in the top five countries of the world. Domestically the Australian Bureau of Statistics (ABS) reported in August 1998 that 32% of Australia's total adult population had accessed the Internet in the 12 months to August 1998, while *The Bulletin*'s Morgan poll estimate, reported in February 1999, was even higher — 41% of those aged 14 and over.[20] The percentage of regular users is smaller, with the ABS estimating that 26% of adult users have general access, and the Morgan poll estimating 28% of adults are regular users (accessing it at least once a month).

Some of Australia's demographic features have impacted upon our comparatively widespread adoption of these technologies. The distances involved — Australia is a large country with a widely dispersed population — mean that the Internet offers particular utility as a form of communication. A large immigrant population also means that as a nation Australia depends heavily on ICTs to maintain connections with families and friends overseas. The enthusiastic adoption of the technology by some Australians should not obscure the reality that a large majority of the population do not have access to the Internet and that patterns of access reflect the socio-economic status of users — those who have access are generally more affluent. The exacerbation of pre-existing social inequalities between the information 'haves' and 'have-nots' has been the subject of some comment, both by government and others. The commentary has not, however, always translated into effective action being taken by governments to remedy the problem.

BANDWIDTH: In late 1994 the Final Report of the Broadband Services Expert Group was issued and included an examination of equity issues in the context of Internet technology. It recognised that: 'The ability to communicate and the right to have access to information are fundamental to a democratic society. Access to digital information and the ability to communicate electronically may become just as fundamental in the future.'[21] However the Group held back from recommending that broadband Internet services should be defined as part of a telecommunications carrier's 'universal service obligations' (USOs), concluding that the 'massive cost' meant that the traditional 'universal service' approach was not appropriate. Nor did it specify the need to ensure that narrow band digital access to the Internet should be part of the USOs.

Australia's telecommunications regulatory framework has for a long time incorporated a principle regarding USOs, or, as they once were, 'community service obligations'. USOs are designed to ensure that basic levels of telecommunications service are provided to all Australians at an affordable rate. The obligations are a recognition that, while economies of scale are available to major population centres in the provision of telecommunications services, the regional population should be protected from the forces of an unregulated market. USOs are designed to rein in what could otherwise be prohibitive costs in telecommunications infrastructure to certain sectors of the community.

In 1996 the incoming government commissioned a Review of the Standard Telephone Service which recommended that, given digital data was of increasing importance to all Australians, the USO should be upgraded to include a data communications requirement. It identified that problems were being experienced, particularly by rural and remote Australia. The government then had the Australian Communications Authority conduct a review, which concluded that the cost of upgrading Telstra's network to 28.8 or 14.4 kbps would exceed the benefits. The government committed to an upgrade of the USO which requires 96% of the population to be covered by ISDN access and for the other 4% to be given access to an 'on demand Internet-based asymmetric satellite service that delivers a satellite down-link service comparable' to the 64 kbps service mandated in the USO, with 50% of the cost of the necessary satellite receiving equipment to be reimbursed by the government. The problems with rural bandwidth are continuing, as the government recognised when instituting its latest inquiry into 'National Bandwidth'.

AFFORDABILITY: People in metropolitan Australia may also experience difficulties in accessing the Internet due to the costs involved. The previous government gradually developed a policy regarding the need to provide subsidised access to the community, and various ad hoc programs to supply access to the community were run by different agencies. One of the largest and most heavily funded of these was the Community Information Network, a pilot program offered through the Department of Social Security, which, had it continued, may have offered some of the benefits of studies of 'e-democracy' which took place overseas. This program was part of a larger Departmental research project aimed at discovering ways to help people on low incomes improve their standard of living. It was also designed to enable access to 'government services and information' and to create links within the community, which would allow the exchange of ideas and information. Generally resources have been slow to follow policy articulations of the need to broaden access. One of the reasons for this has been on-going tensions between State and Commonwealth governments about who should be funding public access initiatives. The Community Information Network was de-funded before it produced much of lasting value.

Prior to the 1996 election both the major parties had adopted similar policies regarding the need to provide equitable access to on-line services. The Australian Library and Information Association (ALIA) reported that there had been bipartisan support for the funding of over $11 million to supplement public access to on-line information through public libraries, but go on to comment: 'it is history now that this was one of the much publicised "broken promises" reduced to $2.2 million in the first Costello budget of [the new Government]'. (ALIA did, however, go on to point out that $2.2 million, while not $11 million, 'is better than a poke in the eye with a burnt stick'.) Responsibility for policy objectives of 'equitable access' is spread between a number of agencies under the current government. A number of electronic lobby groups have recommended the formation of a dedicated cabinet position addressing IT issues.

One of the stated key areas of activity of the National Office of the Information Economy (NOIE) is to develop 'strategies to facilitate community access to and participation in the information economy'. NOIE has issued a 'strategic framework for the information economy' which discusses the need to improve the infrastructure available to rural and remote areas, and which gives policy recognition to the need to ensure general public access. However a recent submission to the

Parliament's Joint Committee on Publications pointed out that some people accessing State Library Internet terminals might have to wait three days to secure a one-hour booking.[22]

Equity issues and access to information

The questions of broader government policy regarding the fostering of Internet access are, generally speaking, beyond the purview of the Parliament. The executive government will choose its policy path with or without input from the Parliament. However the question of how to ensure equity in access to information published by the Parliament itself is very much a concern for the Parliament.

Gary Chapman, a US based commentator on IT has said that: 'No other industry is as self-absorbed, arrogant, insular or in love with itself and its products as high tech.'[23] After suggesting that inequalities are being entrenched by the 'technology revolution' Chapman goes on:

But inequality appears to be of little interest to most high-tech industry leaders, as a recent article in the National Journal, on the link between technology and inequality, illustrated. Not one of the high-tech executives interviewed for the article expressed any concern about income inequality.

The need for training in IT to include some 'basic ethics' and 'social policy' has also been recently discussed on Australia's Link list (referred to earlier), and the Australian Computer Society is considering conducting its own survey of IT professional's ethical attitudes. However the ethics of publishing should not be left to IT professionals because it raises issues that the broader community needs to comprehend. Important policy questions regarding the inclusion or exclusion of otherwise marginalised members of the community are involved in technical issues of publishing.

The impact of Internet technology on particular communities has been summarised in two ways. The first suggests that '[i]t will become possible to site any screen-based activity anywhere; and to tap into all sorts of information and advice — from crop prices to university courses to medical help — from anywhere in the world. The further a country or a town is from the main centres of economic activity, the more it will gain as a result.'[24] In stark contrast to this prediction, there is another: 'Basically, almost all of our technology has enabled us to amplify the centre at the cost of the periphery.'[25]

Internet technology does have the potential to enhance access to information for otherwise marginalised groups. If properly utilised it could help satisfy the 'ultimate' test of democracy which has been propounded by Australia's Governor-General, that our 'worth as a true democracy' is defined by how we treat 'our most vulnerable and disadvantaged'.[26] However implementations of the technology which force users into ever higher cost markets, which close off user options and which require a bandwidth that will exclude areas with inferior infrastructure are likely to 'amplify the centre at the cost of the periphery'.

Parliamentary publishing practices: hardcopy

A primary premise when publishing parliamentary information must surely be that, given access to the Internet is still limited, there is a need to retain hardcopy publishing and the move to utilise ICTs must be made cautiously. The future of the Parliamentary Papers Series was recently the subject of an enquiry by the Joint Committee on Publications. There had been a suggestion from the Presiding Officers that the Series should be discontinued, essentially due to its costs. The Presiding Officers suggested that the electronic publication of many of the papers in the series was further reason to cease the series. The Joint Committee firmly concluded that the series should continue in its present form until there is a viable replacement either in electronic or printed form (or both). It commented, 'publication in electronic form does not necessarily guarantee appropriate distribution or accessibility of documents'.[27]

The Committee also explored various hazards in the process of Internet publication, particularly the question of archiving materials, and concluded that:

When the Chief Government Information Officer has standardised the electronic output of publications across government departments, and has provided a suitable publicly available Internet search facility across all government departments, then will be the time to review the production of the . . . series.[28]

Any cursory examination of a few Commonwealth government sites would show that such a time is a long way off.

Parliamentary publishing practices: digital

Questions of equitable access are important not only with respect to the choice of electronic or hardcopy publishing, but also with respect to the form of electronic publishing. If Parliaments are to pursue the opportunity offered by Internet technologies to provide access to information for all, including marginalised members of the community, then the question of web design and choices of format cannot be sidelined as an arcane technical decision. In fact the accessibility of the format is as important as the decision to provide the information in digital form in the first place. From an early stage of the Internet's history there have been ideological issues of open access, which have been central to the development of Internet technologies and standards. The very process of setting standards for publishing was, in some ways, a central innovation of the web. HTML publishing initially represented an implementation of open standards developed by the CERN research institute. The world wide web consortium, a group of experts who provide a 'collective voice of over 300 industrial members', now provides standards for HTML. The open standards mean that a specification is stable and will contribute to web interoperability. A recommendation by the consortium means that the standard has been reviewed by the consortium membership, who favour its adoption by the industry. This means that no particular industry source dominates directions of a particular technology, nor do they directly derive a market benefit from this domination.

By comparison Portable Document Format or 'PDF' files are coming to represent a de facto standard for publishing in a hard copy like format. The PDF publishing format is not an open standard. It is a proprietary publishing format, which is closed and belongs to Adobe Software. While Adobe distributes PDF readers freely, the capacity to generate PDF files requires the purchase of specific software and the technology required to extricate the data is also the property of a proprietary company. Furthermore data embedded in a PDF file is not transparent but is encoded in a binary format. It is, in effect, as if the text has been included in a graphical picture of a print page. Tony Barry has commented, 'PDF takes the electronic genie and puts it back into the print bottle'.[29]

A large number of government sites in Australia use the PDF format, including the Parliamentary web-site. PDF is easy to use and solves some problems with presenting and printing information in HTML. When information is offered in both PDF and HTML formats, PDF files can function as an enhancement for those with the technology to access it. However when information is *only* offered in PDF format it will exclude many users. The use of PDF as the only publishing format for information squarely raises issues of standards and accessibility on the Internet. The publication of information in digital form has opened up access to information for people with vision impairments. Synthetic speech screen readers allow them to access information that would have previously been inaccessible. HTML can be browsed by non-graphical browsers, which means the web offers new opportunities for engagement. But these vistas of inclusion are always in danger of being cut off by technologies once again excluding those at the margins. This has included PDF publishing, which has been inaccessible to screen readers.

Other accessibility problems raised by PDF files are the size of a document in PDF. PDF files are often significantly larger than a file in HTML. This means that users with low bandwidth—those in regions where the market will not support the provision of an adequate service —are also excluded by PDF publishing. The other public which is excluded by PDF is those who simply have inferior or old hardware. While non-graphical browsers can be run on older computers in many instances they will not support PDF software. Finally, PDF thwarts most search engines and does not allow hyperlinking, one of the useful features of the HTML publishing.

There are, however, reasons why PDF is adopted as a format. It produces a high quality printout and allows the publisher to specify the appearance and formatting of pages. It is widespread and the browser is freely available. More recently Adobe have begun to provide mechanisms to enable access to PDF files for users who cannot effectively access PDF readers. They provide a free service of translation of PDF files into HTML. This is a slightly cumbersome process but it provides some method of accessing the information. Furthermore, as a proprietary company, Adobe has an interest in ensuring their technology moves with the times and is up to date. The other side to this advantage, however, is that the decisions taken are dictated by market forces rather than a concern for equity and access. So, for instance, recent reports indicate Macintosh users' concern that many of the features of Adobe's PDF producing software would only be available in a Windows version.[30] While this issue may come to be dealt with over time if the market forces are favourable, it illustrates the difficulties of allowing a proprietary company to determine standards.

Open standards have been developed, and these now include cascading style sheets, which offer many of the same benefits of PDF and the advantages of reusable information and large-scale information management. Admittedly one of the reasons formats such as Adobe's become widespread is that the standard setting process may take a long time and can lag behind technological developments. However these issues need to be understood and considered by the Parliament as it launches into digital publishing. Publishing exclusively in a PDF format is not the only practice which may contravene principles of inclusion. Another good publishing process, which is honoured more in the breach than in the practice, is to ensure that a site itself is accessible to different browsers, including non-graphical browsers. As mentioned above, non-graphical browsers can be used by those with vision impairments, low bandwidth and/or comparatively low levels of technology. At the moment a large number of sites on the web, including some areas of the parliamentary web-site, do not bear up to this test.

Parliamentarians usage of information technology

In 1998 the Department of the Parliamentary Reporting Staff (DPRS) conducted a research study into client perceptions of DPRS services. The research was based on 33 in-depth, individual interviews with Senators and Members, along with a pro forma survey of 33 others. The survey involved some examination of the role that IT was playing in the work of Senators and Members and concluded that while 'the Internet and e-mail were widely recognised as the future communication and work management technologies of choice' and 'there is a shift in the level of computer-awareness and literacy amongst Senators and Members,' this shift 'is far from universal'.[31]

In order to gauge the use that Parliamentarians are currently making of the Internet technology available to them, a small survey of Senators and Member's offices was conducted for the purposes of this article. Telephone interviews were conducted with 76 offices—covering a third of the Parliament's 224 Members (there are 76 Senators and 148 Members). The participants reflected, broadly speaking, the Party make-up of the Parliament. The interviews were conducted with staff members nominated as having the best levels of understanding or use of the technology, rather than with Senators and Members themselves.

When analysing the poll its limitations must be borne in mind. First, it should be emphasised that the interviews do not necessarily reflect the views held by parliamentarians themselves, but rather reflect a staff member's perceptions. Secondly, without a more comprehensive exercise it would be unwise to draw any elaborate statistical conclusions from the sample. Thirdly, the staff members were drawn from both electorate and Parliament House offices, and, as the levels of available technology differ according to the primary location of the staff member, this will be reflected in the results. Finally, many of the questions asked were seeking qualitative evidence of the views of staff and parliamentarians regarding the role of e-mail communication rather than statistically quantifiable data, so the analysis will be more in a narrative mode than a statistical one.

Just as the DPRS survey suggested, the range of responses varied as widely as conceptually possible, from those offices where e-mail is not used and there is no current interest in it, to those where there is enthusiasm about the possibilities for wider communication and where the technology is already heavily relied on. Some features, which emerged from the interviews, were:

— Use of the technology to interrogate the public regarding policy questions is minimal. Certainly any theoretical anxieties that representatives may become mere ciphers at the whim of continuous polling are not currently relevant to the use being made of the Internet in Australian federal politics. The primary impact of the Internet technology has been in terms of intra-office efficiencies and information accessibility and communication. The ease with which policy queries can be answered by referring to a website address was frequently noted, and the general ease offered in the dispatch of information also featured in responses, however there were very few suggestions that the technology could be put to dynamic interactive use.
— There was a strong awareness of the limited nature of the audience. Many of the staff interviewed referred directly to the unrepresentative nature of the socio-economic profiles of Internet users, frequently noting the inequities involved in giving undue weight to the information 'haves', at the expense of those without the means to access the technology. Many staff identified their particular electorate as having features, which meant that Internet

communications were limited in their area. This did not necessarily manifest itself in any uniform manner — for instance some
rural electorates identified their constituents as relying more
heavily on Internet communications due to the geographical
features of the electorate and the distances involved, while others
pointed out that Internet access was limited in their regional rural
area. A more uniform response was received from electorates
where the population was identified as working class — the sense
that the technology was exacerbating existing inequalities in these
areas was frequently articulated.

— Another strand of thought regarded e-mail as 'unreal' or suspect.
It was not regarded as an official communication in the way that
hard-copy communications would be. While this was not a
universal concern, it was distinctive. Another drawback to the
consideration of e-mail communications was that e-mail was seen
as 'too easy'. There was an awareness that automation may play
a role in the sending of e-mails, and consequently they were seen
to carry less weight than a hard copy letter. (Parliament House
was the subject of an e-mail 'bombing' campaign from Turkish
lobby groups during 1998.) Many offices identified coordinated
campaigns that had been run through e-mail as carrying less
weight than 'genuine' communications. The campaigns against
the Multilateral Agreement on Investments and a proposed ura-
nium mine at Jabiluka were often cited as examples of this.
Another strand that came through here was the extent to which
people on the Internet have 'nothing better to do with their time'
than send e-mails, or that e-mailers are in some sense isolated
from the wider community.

— A number of offices identified e-mail as allowing different voices
to be heard, particularly young people who would not otherwise
communicate.

— A major drawback in the possibilities of using e-mail as a method
of communication with constituents was seen to be the fact that
e-mail correspondents may not fall within the geographical area
of the Member. An Australia-wide audience (or even an international audience) was identified as having less relevance to the
work of particular members. Interestingly there was a slight
preponderance of upper house members who were keen to utilise
the technology, and this may reflect their different electoral base.

— E-mail was almost inevitably identified as increasing workloads
in terms of the increase in communications arriving from the
public creating more work for the office, although the possibilities
for automating responses sent from the office were being
explored. There was, however, a concern that automating the
responses could alienate people — in fact one attempt to send
standard form responses foundered when it was discovered the

same response had been sent to replies from the constituent who had responded to the initial standard form response.

— There was an almost universal affirmation amongst users that e-mail assisted in efficient intra-office and party work.

— Only a few parliamentarians have their own personal web-pages, as distinct from parliamentary pages. Ten of the 76 hosted their own, while a Party web-site covers others. Ministers will often be supplied with a page by their Departments.

— There was frequently a sense that Internet communications were the way of the future, although this view didn't stem from current practices. There was a belief that it would become more and more central, despite the fact it currently is not.

— There was an idea that the immediacy of the medium affects the temper of communications. 'It's quickened the process and height-ened the process,' was one response. The sense that receiving communications on a topic currently under discussion had a more immediate impact was sometimes mentioned. The amount of e-mail received clearly increased enormously when sittings were happening, and this was not simply due to an increased level of office activity so much as increased levels of public interest.

— E-mail was only infrequently seen as a tool to be used during election campaigning. While campaigns seem to lead to increased constituent enquiries by e-mail, there was a frequently expressed hesitancy over utilising parliamentary supplied technology for essentially party political purposes. However the Party structures did use web-sites and e-mail during the last few elections.[32]

— There was a clearly discernible difference in attitude to utilising the Internet to communicate with the public among the parties. The larger parties utilised e-mail more for intra-party communica-tion whereas the smaller parties and the independents rely on Internet communications to reach the public more often.

It is possible to categorise the respondents who had strong opinions on the questions into three schools of thought. While this is a crude model, the 'types' were frequently repeated:

— Those who focussed on the efficiencies of e-mail and Internet publishing for themselves as well as the increased communications and representations made possible for constituents. The expanded opportunities for different 'voices' to be heard was also a feature.

— Those who see the technology as 'more trouble than it's worth'. In this strand e-mail communications from the public were seen as largely disingenuous attempts to lobby. Furthermore the bur-den or risk of overload due to the ease of e-mail communications loomed large. A sense that the technology could be subject to illegitimate practices or fraud was also prevalent.

— Those, a smaller group, who were more conscious of the limited distribution of the technology to date, reflecting that it had not yet had much of an impact and that an inordinate amount of attention was being paid to a technology which was not yet proved to be particularly important.

The clearest conclusion that could be drawn from this poll is that there is certainly no Internet revolution in Australian politics at the moment. The Internet is becoming one more medium of communication and information processing, most particularly a new way of publishing, but is yet to be utilised in innovative ways on a large scale. There is, however, a strong sense that the technology will be of growing significance.

Case study: the Native Title debate, lobbying and on-line activism

'I believe the ultimate test of our worth as a true democracy is how we treat our most vulnerable and disadvantaged . . .'

Sir William Deane, Governor-General of Australia
Annual Australia Day Lunch, 22 January 1999

While the interactive aspects of the Internet are in no way central to Australia's parliamentary processes, the technology is nevertheless having an impact. During 1997–98 one of the most central events in Australia's political and parliamentary scene was the passage, or non-passage, of the government's Native Title Amendment Bill 1997. The role of the Internet in this debate was not directly critical, however community opinion did play a significant role in the outcome of the debate, and the Internet was a critical tool contributing to the activist community's capacity to organise and be heard.

In his introduction to a special edition of *Media, Culture and Society* looking at electronic democracy, Colin Sparks comments: '[t]he problem is that the technical changes which have made opposition easier have also further empowered the already powerful.' He goes on to explain that, because the technology is available both to those who would oppose and to those who are already powerful, technical change 'does not shift the balance of forces either for or against democratisation'.[33] However the outcomes of the Native Title debate may suggest otherwise. By providing access to low cost mechanisms for organising, the new technologies may actually benefit those who have to rely on their organisational efforts rather than their economic resources in order to be effective.

BACKGROUND: The debates over Native Title were some of the largest and most animated social policy debates Australia has had in recent history. The debates were highly polarised, centring on a perceived conflict between the interests of rural land-holders and mining concerns on the one hand and the Native Title interests of indigenous communities on the other.

The introduction of the Native Title Amendment Bill 1997 in response to a High Court of Australia case on Native Title generated unusual levels of interest in the parliamentary process. The debates on the Bill in the Senate were the longest in Australia's parliamentary history, and at various stages a double dissolution election was threatened over passage of the Bill. The government did not hold a majority in the upper House, rather Senator Harradine, an Independent, held the balance of power.

Prior to the introduction of the Bill, the Prime Minister, Mr Howard, declared that the pendulum of the law had swung too far to the side of the interests of indigenous people and that his government would act to rectify the imbalance. On the other 'side' there was a strong reaction in the community which sought to support indigenous interests and rallied around the National Indigenous Working Group (the primary indigenous negotiating body). A 'people's movement' for reconciliation found expression in a plethora of fora and opposed the government's proposed amendments with great energy, using a range of methods, including a number of on-line initiatives. One of these initiatives was the first on-line petition accepted by the Federal Parliament. This was an event, which, in the grand schema of the debate's conduct, attracted little attention. It was nevertheless a significant event, both because it represented a progression in the Parliament's acceptance of Internet communications, and also because it had played an important role in promoting the community activism which was engendered during the debate. The actual tabling of the petition was only one part of the process of the activist community's use of electronic communications.

The interests arrayed against the holders of Native Title were significant and well-resourced, which makes the partial success of Native Title holders and their supporters all the more remarkable. Although the final outcome of the debate was called a 'day of shame' by the National Indigenous Working Group, those opposing the Bill had some successes along the way. The Bill was delayed over a lengthy period, it was heavily amended in the Senate and the government had to compromise significantly. The community support, which arose in support of Native Title holders, was also important, and the Internet represented a valuable opportunity to organise and channel this groundswell of support. Obviously there were voices and organising forces which were also using these technologies to organise against Native Title holders, however this case study looks specifically at the role played by the Internet in the 'pro-Native Title' side of the debate.

The mechanics of the on-line petition

The on-line petition was tabled by Senator Natasha Stott Despoja, who had earlier tried to table an electronic petition regarding timed calls, but had been prevented from doing so because the petition did not follow the precise form of the wording stipulated in the Senate's standing orders regarding petitions. The interpretation of these standing orders has been strict, with many petitions having been ruled as unacceptable. It was, therefore, surprising to many that the Senate was prepared to accept electronic petitions without much soul searching regarding their validity, although Senator Stott Despoja commented that '[t]he Standing Orders are not compromised and the words have been applied so as to meet the meaning and spirit of the rules.' She went on to point out that an electronic petition is, 'in effect, no different from the old style of hand writing on parchment'.

The Clerk of the Senate scrutinises the initial process of tabling and will table documents only where s/he can be sure that the petitioners have actually signed the electronic document and conformed with the Senate rules. The tabling Senator must supply the Senate with a printed hard copy of the electronic document, an assurance that the petition was published electronically and an assurance that the signatures were appended electronically.

The petition regarding native title provided background information on the issues involved and also allowed signatories to choose whether to give their contact details to the network supporting the National Indigenous Working Group (otherwise all the data was only to be used for the purposes of generating the hard-copy petition). Signatories were also given the option of making individual comments and of choosing whether to display their name, state and comment on the site.

The primary control mechanism introduced to monitor fraud was a record of the Internet computer through which the signatory was communicating. This record could be of some use in checking for illegitimate multiple entries, although, in the final analysis, it was, by force of circumstance, a non-rigorous process. Until current proposals for the regulation of electronic signatures are implemented it will not be possible to require reliable forms of identification.[34]

It should be noted here that the question of fraudulent entries need not be of greater significance in the case of electronic petitions than it is with hardcopy petitions. A determined individual with a number of pens and some creativity could currently come up with fraudulent entries on a hard copy petition. While the potential *volume* of fraudulent entries could be enhanced in the electronic medium, particularly because databases could be transferred, these risks could to some degree be countered by control mechanisms in the tabling, starting with the extant requirement in the petition tabling process that the tabling Senator must be satisfied due process was followed.

Certainly the signatures coming in to this petition did so with a timing and flow which gave no indication that the anarchic hordes on the Internet were abusing their anonymity and displaying anti-social, fraudulent behaviour. The topic of the petition was possibly too sober to attract truancy, although there were a few patently false entries, from individuals such as 'whitey brown' and 'Eddie Mabo',[35] however, these were not numerous—eight out of the 7,026 signatures received (7,018 were submitted to the Parliament). The opportunities for 'spoiling' results were limited by the presumed desire of any intending spoiler to minimise the numbers who could be quoted as signatories, i.e. false entries could simply add weight to the legitimate signatories. Entries with patently false details and offensive commentaries were simply expunged.

The tabling of petitions may not be one of the most effective forms of lobbying. They are commonly used and easily ignored. By-products of the on-line petition process, however, were significant. As well as the broad-based reach of the e-mail database, the opportunity offered by the petition for individual comment was frequently taken, with well over 900 of the signatories adding their personal reflections to pages published at the site. These comments formed the basis of a submission to the Parliamentary Joint Committee on Native Title and the Aboriginal and Torres Strait Islander Land Fund, which enquired into the provisions of the Native Title Amendment Bill. The comments make dramatic reading, ranging from the plebeian to the impassioned, although in the end it is partially the sheer volume of personalised responses which leaves the strongest impact. A sample of the nine hundred comments are reproduced here:

> This a time for genuine reconciliation not for protracting the suffering of the people who have been dispossessed. It is a time for compassion, contrition and sincere sharing. May the Parliament be guided by wisdom, not greed or fear.

> I strongly urge acceptance of and action on the above petition. It is central to transforming the rhetoric of Australia as a 'democratic and socially just nation' into reality . . .

> We will pay so that some of the richest people in the world can upgrade their titles—but not for children taken from their parents: what sort of a country are we becoming?

> The world's oldest and therefore presumably most mature culture is to be reduced to a squiggle on a tea towel in an airport shop.

> When your 68-year-old mother (from a pastoralist family) tells you that for the first time in her life she's ashamed to be Australian you just know something terrible is happening to your country. Just tell me what can I DO to help?

> The opinion I express here in no way reflects the views of my employer.

> Thanks for the petition. We both signed it and participated as consenting adults in the wonders of techno-democracy in the privacy of our own home.

Some of the comments were from people who may not have otherwise participated in the debate, including a number of younger people. During the Native Title debate the Council for Aboriginal Reconciliation sponsored a project to link remote indigenous communities to the Internet.[36] People who signed the petition during this process commented that there would have been no other way of feeding into the parliamentary debates. The petition details were also passed around the schools network as a tool to be used to illustrate the workings of Parliament.

Details of the petition were passed around tertiary educational institutions, although responses were not initially as numerous as the academics' letter regarding native title. The academic's letter was an e-mail campaign which generated more than 6,300 signatories to a strongly worded open letter to the Prime Minister regarding the importance of the Wik decision. These signatures were collected from university staff around the country in just nine days. The on-line petition only received 2,000 signatures in its first two weeks. A few reasons which could explain this difference in initial momentum may be that the on-line petition did not have the same levels of institutional backing, in fact there were only two individuals who initiated the promotion of the petition, whereas the academics' e-mail had the backing of the National Tertiary Education Union, whose organisers actively sought signatories on each campus. Furthermore the on-line petition required people to use the web rather than e-mail. E-mail is still the application, which is the most popular and available form of on-line communication. While the on-line petition was initially offered both on-line and by e-mail, the difficulties of automating the data processing with the non-standard data received through e-mail meant that entries were eventually restricted to the web interface.

Electronic networking during the Native Title debate

The data generated by the on-line petition was used in a number of ways. The most immediately memorable expression of community opposition to the Native Title Bill was known as the 'Sea of Hands'. This was an installation artwork consisting of thousands of large coloured plastic hands planted in the ground, each bearing the name of a person opposed to the passage of the Bill. These names were predominantly collected via a traditional, hard-copy process in which people signed an 'Australian Citizens' Statement on Native Title,' however the dissemination of this Citizens' Statement was assisted by its electronic distribution. Furthermore a number of the initial 100,000 signatories had been collected through the on-line petition. Five thousand of the names were those of people who had signed the petition and had chosen to have their names and contact details passed on to the network supporting the National Indigenous Working Group.

The role of e-mail was sometimes central to the coordination of campaigning at a national level. In the lead-up to the first Sea of Hands a National Day of Action supported Native Title. When a mass e-mail was sent to signatories of the on-line petition regarding actions in the different States and Territories, there were strong reactions in support of the exercise. The ease of duplication and reposting of messages to a number of e-mail discussion lists meant that a large number of people were contacted speedily and simply. People around the country volunteered their labour in response to this e-mail message, and some of the key organisers were put in touch with each other after responding to this message. Indeed in one State where no action had been planned and which did not previously have an organised structure, the e-mail message was the catalyst for the formation of a coalition which organised local events.

As well as the on-line petition, a range of initiatives by different groups in support of native title were pursued on-line and allowed activities to take place at local, national and international levels. A number of public advertisements in the press regarding the issue were made possible by financial support gathered electronically. Local networks made particularly good use of the asynchronous communications offered by e-mail. As a voluntary network many members of ANTaR had full-time occupations and were working to support Native Title in their 'spare' time. E-mail made communications possible between volunteers with different demands on their time. This was particularly noticeable in the Australian Capital Territory (ACT), which, given its location, was in the front line of campaigning around the parliamentary debate, staging the Sea of Hands twice and organising tactical events designed to exert pressure during the course of the debates. The ACT has the highest usage of the Internet in Australia,[37] and the availability of e-mail to this community was vital to its functioning.

It is interesting to note here that in *Asleep at the Wheel: Australia on the Superhighway*, John Nieuwenhuizen expressed a concern that e-mail lobbying and 'rallies in cyberspace' will lead to alienation and a 'community of fortresses' being built.[38] He speculates that the Internet may lead to increased isolation, and may be destructive of 'commonality' as people scatter 'into a million mediated communities'. The practical experience of lobbying on Native Title illustrates some flaws in this thesis. E-mail was a tool for 'real' people to organise 'real' events. Internet users have an incarnation in the community and are as likely to use the technology to enhance their contact with others as they are to isolate themselves. Nieuwenhuizen also worries that Internet technology will lead to a loss of a communal 'national dialogue' since people will create their own individually comfortable discussions and interactions.[39] However, in so far as the participants in the 'virtual world' are also likely to participate in the 'national dialogue' these media can feed each other rather than operating as an isolating force. Nieuwenhuizen scoffs at the idea that voters would have the time or inclination to utilise on-line Parliamentary information.[40] However, this is precisely what did happen during the Native Title debate. The issues involved in Native Title are technical and complex. The law involved is difficult, and informed commentary was vital to support the community campaign. Parliamentary information and e-mail were key features in the passing on of analyses and the transmission of information which could be used in the preparation of submissions, briefings and summaries.

Towards the end of the passage of the Bill through Parliament, the outcome was negotiated privately by Senator Harradine and the Prime Minister outside the parliamentary forum. The scrutiny and opportunity for public comment were limited at this stage (although Senator Harradine has commented that at one stage of the debate he was receiving up to 400 e-mails in the space of an hour). The agreement, which resulted in the passage of the Bill, is a feature of representative democracies — decisions may be left in the hands of a few individuals. The positions of the parliamentary players meant the matter was resolvable through these private negotiations. The closed nature of this final process frustrated those in the community who wanted greater transparency, with indigenous leaders commenting that they had been once again left out in the 'woodpile' while their fate was decided by their white 'governors'.

This final process had however, not been universally representative of the debate, much of which was carried out very publicly. The opportunity for comment had been given, and was taken up by a large number of people in the community. The networking that took place between the indigenous community and their supporters was a feature of the debate's process. In fact the 'people's movement for reconciliation' found unusual levels of support during the parliamentary debate, which has fed into on-going policy discussions regarding the position of Australia's indigenous people.

One of the benefits a parliamentary democracy may offer is the possibility that its processes of deliberation may build community and engender civic involvement. In fact John Stuart Mill, Carole Pateman and Pericles have all suggested that participation in the democratic process will itself 'breed virtue'.[41] To the extent that electronic communications assisted in a process of community participation in the parliamentary debate on Native Title, Internet technology arguably contributed to a fulfilment of these broader aspirations for Australian democracy.

Conclusion

The Australian Parliament has access to fairly extensive ICTs, which are being used to publish and/or broadcast through a variety of media. In launching into electronic publishing the Parliament must grapple with the ideological issues inherent in electronic publishing processes. One of these current issues is the extent to which Internet technologies are including or excluding the marginal in our community. In particular whether the technologies used are as open as possible. Parliamentary use of ICTs is still largely confined to the dissemination of information about Parliament, its deliberative processes and their outcomes. The interactive possibilities of Internet technologies have yet to be explored and raise some concerns in Parliamentarians offices, both with respect to its limited availability and because it may create demands on resources which cannot be met.

Within the activist community the interactive possibilities are being utilised more extensively, and offer opportunities for networking, which would not otherwise be available, particularly to organisations with limited resources. The Internet offers both enhanced access to parliamentary information and a broader potential for community involvement in Parliament's deliberative process. These features proved useful to the community supporting the interests of Native Title holders during the debates on the Native Title Amendment Bill and contributed to that community's capacity to participate in the debate more fully.

1   B. Robertson-Dunn, 13.10.98, on the Link list (quoted with permission). The link list was established in 1993 as a forum to discuss emerging issues related to the development of the Internet in Australia. The membership initially came from the library, networking and standards community and now includes a number of academics, journalists and industry professionals.
2   *Sleepers, Wake!*, Barry Jones, OUP, 1982, p. 243.
3   Some of these studies are document in *Media, Culture & Society*, 18/2, 1996. See also G. Scott Aikens case study on Minnesota at http://aikens.org/phd/toc.htm.
4   The Australian Constitution is entrenched in such a way that any modifications require a referendum to be carried first through both Houses of Parliament, then a majority of the voters, and a majority of voters in a majority of the States. These provisions have meant that only eight of the 42 proposals for constitutional amendment put to the Australian people have succeeded.
5   Further information is available in the *Joint Information Technology Plan between the Parliamentary Departments and Department of Finance and Administration 1998–2000*.
6   Paper to the Society of Clerks at the Table in Commonwealth Parliaments, *The Impact of New Technology on the Operation of Parliament*, R. McClelland, Clerk Assistant, Department of the House of Representatives, October 1998, p. 2.
7   Reported in *Odgers'* Australian Senate Practice, eighth edn (rev), 31.10.98, Chapter 11, Voting and Divisions, p. 7.
8   New Zealand was apparently the first, commencing broadcasts in 1936, while the UK did not start regular sound broadcasts till mid to late 1970s. *The Eyes Have It: Inquiry into the Televising of the House of Representatives and its Committees*, Report of the House of Representatives Select Committee on Televising, August 1991, p. 2.
9   Ibid., p. 1.
10 *House Practice*, Chapter 10, 'Parliament and the citizen'.
11 T. Miller, *The Well-Tempered Self: Citizenship, Culture, and the Postmodern Subject*, John Hopkins University Press, 1993. 'Political Institutions and Broadcasting' in *Stay Tuned: An Australian Broadcasting Reader*, A. Moran (ed.), Allen & Unwin, 1991.
12 1993, pp. 131–2.
13 Ibid., p. 134.
14 *House Hansard*, 20.9.95, p. 1343.
15 *Internet in Government — for IT Practitioners*, Australian UNIX and Open Systems User Group Canberra Conference, 15.2.95.
16 Some of the exchanges in this Inquiry show that new modes of communication were being thrust on Senators and members of the public service quite rapidly. See in particular the exchange at *Committee Hansard* 201, where a member of the government admits to having been 'extremely ignorant and unsophisticated' with respect to the technology, while one witness points out that it was he, rather

66   *Parliament in the Age of the Internet*

than the government, who had ensured messages were disseminated over the Internet asking for submissions to the inquiry.

17 http://www.aph.gov.au/senate/pubs/Html/httoc.htm.
18 Department of the Parliamentary Reporting Staff, *Annual Report 1997–98*, p. 22.
19 The slow uptake of pay TV is sometimes remarked upon as a contra-indication of the common thesis that communications technologies are embraced rapidly in Australia. However it is arguable that this response has been due to a resistance to paying for what has previously been a largely free-to-air product, rather than a resistance to the technology itself.
20 *Use of the Internet by Householders*, (No. 8147.0), Australian Bureau of Statistics, August 1998 and 'Bosses Log On to the Net', *The Bulletin*, 9.2.99.
21 *Networking Australia's Future: The Final Report of the Broadband Services Expert Group*, December 1994, p. 60.
22 Future of the Parliamentary Papers Series: Report by the Joint Committee on Publications, AGPS December 1997, p. 22.
23 'Microsoft Trial Obscures Larger Inequality Issues', G. Chapman, *Los Angeles Times*, 12.10.98.
24 'The revolution begins, at last', *The Economist*, 30.9.95.
25 From John Seely Brown, Chief Scientist of Xerox and Director of its Palo Alto Research Centre. I am indebted to Peter Morris of the Link list for the identification of these quotes.
26 Sir William Deane, Governor-General of Australia, Annual Australia Day Lunch, 22.1.99.
27 Op. cit., p. 21.
28 Ibid., p. 22.
29 http://www.anu.edu.au/mail-archives/link/link9808/0046.html.
30 *Net News*, 19.2.99, A. Farrelly, *News Interactive*, Australia. http://www.newsclassifieds.com.au/ni/netnews/archive/19Feb1999.htm
31 Department of the Parliamentary Reporting Staff, *Annual Report 1997–98*, AGPS, p. 124.
32 For further information on this process see generally, P. Williams, *How the Internet is Being Used by Political Organisations: Promises, Problems and Pointers*, Research Paper No. 11, 1997–98, Department of the Parliamentary Library, Australia.
33 *Media, Culture & Society*, 18/2, 1996, p. 182.
34 The government is exploring options for the establishment of a 'National Authentication Authority'. See, for instance, *Establishment of a National Authentication Authority: A Discussion Paper*, 19.8.98 at http://www.noie.gov.au/docs/naadp.htm.
35 Eddie Mabo was the, now deceased, successful claimant in the first successful Native Title claim before the High Court in *Mabo v Queensland [No 2]* (1992) 175 CLR 1.
36 For further information on this project see 'Indigenous people's legal issues via Internet', *The AustLII Papers*, Moore, Magarey et al and see generally, http://www.austlii.edu.au/au/special/rsjproject/.
37 Australian Bureau of Statistics, *Household use of Information Technology*, 8146.0, 1998, p. 12.
38 Nieuwenhuizen, *op. cit.*, see generally Chapter 3.
39 Ibid., p. 112.
40 Ibid., p. 95.
41 *Democracy and New Technology*, I. McLean, Polity Press, 1989, pp. 28–30.

The Scottish Parliament: [Re-]Shaping Parliamentary Democracy in the Information Age

BY COLIN F. SMITH AND PAUL GRAY

Introduction: a new beginning for Scottish Parliamentary democracy

After nearly 300 years of full participation in a parliamentary union, Scotland is in the throes of the re-establishment of its own parliamentary democracy. A perceived democratic deficit is being addressed through institutional innovation, and the parliament is expected to become not just the mechanism through which much of Scottish public policy is developed and scrutinised, but also the national forum for civic life. It is perhaps ironic then, that much of the attention of political science over the past 30 years has been upon identifying the complicity of institutional arrangements, such as parliamentary bodies, in a deepening political malaise. If parliaments elsewhere have been unable to reverse an increasing dissatisfaction with the effectiveness of contemporary processes of democracy, why should the establishment of a new forum in Scotland address these same issues for the Scottish polity?

Much of the optimism for the future of Scottish democracy under the new parliamentary arrangements is directly related to the notion that the Parliament represents a fresh break from established British parliamentary tradition and practice. The debates around the establishment of the parliament, especially those which took place within the Scottish Constitutional Convention, have been characterised by an insistence that the new body should be free to adopt what it sees as democratic best practice, free to innovate in the establishment of novel forms of working, rather than aping Westminster precedent.

What has been striking in this, is the extent to which new technologies of information and communication have been envisaged and anticipated as part and parcel of these invigorated democratic relationships within and around the new parliament. The power of information and communications technologies (ICTs) to bring about 'better' ways of working within the parliament, and also to support new forms of participation around it, has been explicitly recognised and addressed in the formulation of initial plans and in the design of the technological infrastructure. In the process, the potential of ICTs to enable and support new democratic arrangements has, for the first time, become a visible stream in Scottish political discourse.

This chapter sets out to analyse why this is the case. It first traces the processes towards the establishment of the Parliament, placing the debate on the role of ICTs in a proper context. The later chapter 'Supporting key relationships around Parliament', for which the factual information was provided substantially by Paul Gray, Chair of the ICT Project Board for the Scottish Parliament, defines some of the key democratic relationships around the Parliament, and explains how ICTs are envisaged as affecting these relationships. This section explores the extent to which the Parliament will exploit capabilities offered by new ICTs, and considers the role of new technologies in supporting and enhancing democratic practice. The chapter then goes on to analyse some of the implicit assumptions concerning technologically-facilitated political change which are contained in many of the plans. In this way, the chapter sets out both to explain and critique the role of new technologies in supporting the democratic functioning of the Parliament.

The background to devolution

The Parliament of Great Britain was created from the Union of the Parliaments of Scotland and England in 1707. While Scotland retained many of the other institutions of nationhood, including a separate legal system, the Union halted the development of a distinctive Scottish Parliamentary tradition. The Scottish institutions which remained after the Union have, since 1939, been bolstered through a large degree of administrative devolution from central government to the Scottish Office, which has been accountable to Westminster through the Secretary of State for Scotland.

The movement for the Scottish Covenant in the 1950s was the first modern manifestation of a public debate about Scotland's role in the Union, the modern Covenanters identifying the postwar Labour Government's policies as posing a threat to the distinctiveness of Scotland. The source of such concern was the government's homogenous approach to policy implementation throughout the UK, which raised concerns over the continuation of distinctly Scottish policy arrangements. The leaders of this campaign sought to place themselves in a long tradition of Scottish resistance to Westminster's desire for conformity throughout the UK, hence their self conscious adoption of the word Covenanters.[1] This rather romantic approach to the assertion of identity was superseded in the 1960's by a wider critique of Scotland's place in the UK, which fed into the emergence of Scottish nationalism as an increasingly credible political movement. This did much to accelerate the topic of Scottish Devolution to the higher reaches of the policy agenda.

The first legislative efforts to establish devolution in Scotland came in the late 1970s, when the then Labour Government brought forward proposals to establish a Scottish Assembly. A Scotland Bill received its

Royal Assent on 31 July 1978, with the Act requiring a referendum before full implementation. While the referendum of 1 March 1979 resulted in a majority of over 77,000 in favour of an Assembly, this figure represented only 32.9% of the electorate, short of the 40% which was required for the Act to be implemented. The Labour Government fell soon after this event, and was replaced by a Conservative administration concerned with pushing back the administrative manifestations of the State, rather than re-casting them in a new form.

The impetus for devolution eventually came to be concentrated in the Scottish Constitutional Convention, a cross-party campaign for constitutional change formed in 1988. This body had a membership drawn from Members of Parliament of the Labour and Liberal Democrat parties, Labour members of the European Parliament, local authorities, the STUC, business, church and civic groups and other political parties. The Constitutional Convention developed detailed proposals for a Scottish Parliament, contained in its final report — Scotland's Parliament.[2]

With the election of the Labour Government on 1 May 1997 the way was clear for Labour, the chief partner in the Constitutional Convention, to implement its recommendations. The Government published its detailed plans for the Scottish Parliament in its White Paper,[3] 'Scotland's Parliament', on 24 July 1997, proposing the establishment of a Parliament with law-making and tax-varying powers. A referendum on these proposals was held on 11 September 1997, endorsing them in their entirety,[4] and the Scotland Bill was introduced in the House of Commons on 17 December 1997 and given Royal Assent the following year. The first elections to the Scottish Parliament are scheduled for 6 May 1999, and the Parliament should be in place by the year 2000.

Creating a 'wired Parliament'

The final report of the Scottish Constitutional Convention echoed that body's sentiment that a devolved parliament should take its cue from democratic 'best practice', either anticipated or already in operation elsewhere, rather than from existing Westminster procedure. The Convention envisaged a Parliament of its time, with sensible working hours, state-of-the-art information resources and sophisticated communications arrangements between Members of the Scottish Parliament (MSPs), the Scottish Executive and the electorate. Central to this vision was that the Scottish Parliament should make extensive use of new technologies of information and communication to create and support a dynamic new democracy.

This was a vision which politicians both promoted and responded to. For example, Jim Wallace MP, leader of the Scottish Liberal Democrats, used a speech at Heriot Watt University to call for the Scottish parliament to be 'the engine of an IT revolution and the blueprint for a new style of computerised democracy, by harnessing digital power and the Internet to put voters and MSPs in permanent instant contact'. Wallace proposed that broadcasters, communications specialists and information technology experts be brought together to devise a scheme which would 'maximise the opportunity for every Scottish resident to participate in the democratic process'. The report by the John Wheatley Centre, 'A Parliament for the Millennium',[5] further developed these themes, which the government broadly endorsed when Scottish Office Minister for Devolution, Henry MacLeish said that he hoped a Scottish parliament would become a 'modern Parliament for a modern Scotland', and a 'laboratory for democracy'. What marks out the debates around the development of the Scottish parliament is the extent to which information and communications technologies were considered as part and parcel of the democratic processes. In a sense, ICTs became part of the rhetoric of democracy in Scotland during this period.

Following on from the positive referendum result, an all-party Consultative Steering Group (CSG) on the Scottish Parliament was established by the Secretary of State for Scotland to take forward consideration of how the Parliament might operate. The CSG was chaired by Henry McLeish MP, but its membership covered the four main political parties and also included members intended to represent a broader range of Scottish society.[6] The remit of the CSG was to consider the operational needs and working methods of the Scottish Parliament, and to develop proposals for the rules of procedure and Standing Orders which the Parliament might be invited to adopt. The CSG delivered a report at the end of 1998 to the Secretary of State, to inform the preparation of draft Standing Orders.[7]

The CSG was supported by Scottish Office officials who were able to draw on advice from a number of expert panels in the relevant fields in preparing proposals for further consideration by the Consultative Steering Group. One of these expert panels was established to assess how the Parliament might make best use of IT and telematics,[8] and the CSG also commissioned research into transferable democratic telematics applications in use in other parliaments.[9] In appointing the expert panel and bringing in specialist knowledge concerning the democratic application of ICTs the CSG continued to respond to the telematics agenda set by the Constitutional Convention, an agenda which found widespread support among party spokespersons. The extent to which parties took up the cause of ICTs, and particularly the Internet (especially its graphical aspect, the world wide web) in 're-inventing' Scottish Democracy was itself symptomatic of the extent to which the transformative potential of new technologies had become common currency. If the capabilities offered by ICTs could revolutionise the worlds of business and commerce, then could the same powerful technologies be applied in the arena of parliamentary democracy; and if so, with what results?

Supporting key relationships around Parliament

The outcome of the planning processes around the parliamentary procedures, and the relationship of ICTs to those procedures, has now been fairly well advanced. This section examines the key relationships within and around the Parliament, and assesses the role of ICTs in developing and supporting these relationships.

The Scottish Parliament is being set up in the face of great expectations. It is to be the central forum of a new, inclusive and participative democracy. But beyond the rhetoric, who will participate in that democracy, in what manner will participation occur, and how will it be facilitated? Will the Parliament operate as busy hub of democratic information exchange, a 'trading floor' through which all important democratic 'transactions' will be routed? Or will the parliament sit as one element (albeit an important one) in a wider polity around which information flows? This is an important question which encapsulates two rather different visions about the parliament, and has consequences for how ICTs are applied around it. Through an analysis of the debates so far, the latter vision, of the parliament as part of a democratic 'network' (in a non-technological sense) seems likely to prevail. In order to arrive at a definitive answer to the question, we must give further attention to determining exactly where the Parliament fits within the polity of Scotland.

The Parliament, by its very nature, cannot be a stand-alone organisation. Introducing the White Paper 'Scotland's Parliament', the Secretary of State for Scotland, Donald Dewar made it clear that the Parliament must set new standards of openness, accessibility and responsiveness to the people of Scotland. He described the people of Scotland as the people the Parliament serves. The degree of responsiveness to public opinion, and the ways in which this might be underpinned, has been identified as a key criteria of the Parliament's effectiveness One of the primary relationships, then, is that which exists between the Parliament and the people, specifically the Scottish electorate.

Yet this key relationship is complemented and made effective because it sits within a web of other relationships; inter alia, there must also be links to the Scottish Executive, to the Scottish Administration, (the names for some of these organisations have not yet been decided), to local government, to the business community, to the education sector, and to the voluntary sector. Linkages must also anchor the Parliament beyond the borders of Scotland; to other legislatures and administrations within the UK, and to Europe and beyond.

ICTs clearly have a vital role to play in establishing, fostering and maintaining these links. The question which is yet to be resolved is in what manner and how effectively this will occur. The Consultative Steering Group has already accepted that the Parliament will definitely need a satisfactory level of ICT provision from the outset, rather than leaving the development of systems completely to the first intake of Members. The issue is further complicated because the first Parliament will sit in temporary accommodation, the Church of Scotland Assembly Building, while a new Parliament building is constructed at Holyrood. Initial provision has had to reflect what was practically possible in the short time available to set up the interim accommodation; and it has also been designed to reflect the fact that there is inevitably some uncertainty about the precise needs of the Parliament and its staff—because the Parliament does not yet exist. There is a clear expectation that once the Parliament has been in operation for a year or two, information and communications technology will have developed further and there will be an opportunity to address medium to long-term needs and planning for ICTs at Holyrood. The basic provision which has been outlined and is being put in place is designed to address the fact that the Parliament must get off to a sound start, if it is to meet the expectations of Scotland.

The Consultative Steering Group has accepted that ICT is essential in assisting democratic participation, and has defined that participation in a wide sense, to incorporate ideas such as community governance as well as individual citizen participation. It also accepted that emerging technologies could make a tangible contribution to greater openness and accessibility and to the increased efficiency of the Parliament itself. This, then, is the second main area of innovation around ICTs; the internal aspect of the 'business' of the parliament. The Parliament has been established against an expectation that it will follow modern and efficient ways of working, and that its accommodation will allow Scottish Parliamentarians and their staff to work efficiently, harnessing the best of modern technology. The Report by the CSG's Telematics Advisory Panel also proposed that the Parliament should establish a general rule of public access to all electronic and printed data, unless a committee voted to the contrary for a specific purpose and under conditions acceptable to the Presiding Officer. The Consultative Steering Group accepted that ICT for the Parliament would be set up on the presumption that Parliamentary information contained on any system will be made publicly available through the Parliamentary web-site unless it is specifically restricted for reasons of security or privacy. The web-site itself is being developed and presented in such a way that it is intended to develop life-long awareness of the Parliament, not simply restricted to those of voting age. It is also intended that the design should accommodate the ability of the public both to make comments, and where possible to take part in open discussions.

Underlying all this is an important realisation that has informed much of the decision making process around systems development. This realisation is a simple one; that making the Parliament open and accessible depends on a great deal more than simple technology. Fundamentally, openness and accessibility depends on how Parliamentary information is managed and presented — and this includes paper as well as electronic information. For example, one important concern is that it is essential to have robust archiving procedures in place to allow long-term access to Parliamentary information. These managerial challenges must be addressed thoroughly from the start, and the Parliament has therefore allocated responsibility for information management to a senior member of its staff.

Against the background that Scotland is moving from a purely representative democracy to a participative democracy, it has been acknowledged that the widest democratic participation will be assisted by ensuring that all the people have access to all the information. This is another significant challenge, but one that must be met. If the information provided is weak, then there is a significant likelihood that this itself will lead to weak participation. From this point of view, an investment in information is an investment in democracy. To a great extent this is a matter which is initially in the hands of the first intake of MSPs, and then to their successors. The onus (and the spotlight) will be on MSPs to ensure that information provision and collection is part of a structured communications' plan and given high priority. It has already been accepted that a great deal of thought and effort will have to go into information content; but once the content is decided an equal amount of thought will have to be given to accessibility and to the infrastructure to deliver and collect the information. Against an acknowledgement that the quality of access to information is a basic right of all citizens, there is a need for access methods which meet the needs of a range of personal abilities and circumstances, and these might include varying levels of reading ability, visual impairments, or the use of English as a second language.

There is some further important background to the notion of democratic participation, and the possible role of ICTs in facilitating that participation. Much of the debate around the democratic application of ICTs has focussed upon the Internet. Yet perhaps only 10% of the population of Scotland have access to the Internet in their homes, with a similar number having access to digital television. So this new, participative democracy must ensure that information is delivered to the citizens of Scotland in ways which are accessible to it. That is likely to mean an important role for familiar media, such as television, radio and papers, rather than an unbalanced concentration on the Internet. It also means that libraries are likely to have a key role to play. Parliament itself will have to consider how it might make use of ICTs to deliver information to the people of Scotland and to seek their views; but it cannot do so on the basic assumption that the citizens of Scotland as a whole use, or want to use, ICTs.

Of course, none of the planning for new democratic mechanisms around the parliament should be set upon the assumption that the majority of the population of Scotland actually knows how the Parliament works. It is the first time since 1707 that the people of Scotland will have its own directly elected Parliament. Collective memory may be long, but it is not that long. So in setting up ICTs, and in designing the information content which will flow through them, it is essential that consideration is given to the level of knowledge which different groupings will require in order to participate meaningfully in the democratic processes associated with the Scottish Parliament.

This relates to the question of political literacy. Is there a role for ICTs in securing and maintaining political literacy among the Scottish public, or is this best achieved in the long-term through the education system? Should the Parliament's investment in ICTs for schools, colleges and universities be centred on seeking to encourage and engage young people in the work of the Parliament? And should the Parliament be using similar, though less formal, initiatives to encourage and sustain interest in the population in life-long learning about the workings of the Parliament? To bring about such a process, the Parliament might consider establishing partnerships with educational organisations in Scotland, such as the Scottish Consultative Committee on the Curriculum and the Scottish Virtual Teachers' Centre, to develop appropriate educational materials and to ensure their inclusion in school curricula.

What is clear from all this is that the use of ICT is not an end in itself. To be worth while, it must help materially and measurably in the achievement of the overall objectives set out in the White Paper. The ICT Expert Panel found that objectives generally fell under two headings — promoting Parliamentary efficiency through supporting modern ways of working with well-defined information technology; and promoting openness, accountability and democratic participation in Scotland by using technology to make information about the Parliament and its work available to everyone. The provision of ICT must therefore be set in the context of the Parliament's businesses, in order that its success can be measured against the degree to which it helps meet the objectives of the organisation.

With that background in mind, ICT for the Parliament has been developed in the light of several principles. It should be innovative, but it should allow the Parliament to develop its use of ICT in a planned and coherent way. It should seize the opportunities which modern well-designed information systems offer for improving openness, accessibility and responsiveness to the people of Scotland. Overall, it should aspire to be an example of best practice in Parliamentary information systems, both in terms of external communications and internal efficiency; and it should lay the basis for delivering the business of the Parliament efficiently and effectively. All in all, the burden of expectation is considerable.

ICTs and democracy: a causal relationship?

The previous sectioned outlined some of the key areas where new technologies are expected to impinge upon the practice of democracy in

Scotland, through the Scottish Parliament. ICTs have been credited with a degree of transformative potential; potential not only to support the operations of the parliament in terms of representative democracy, but to also shift the nexus of political engagement away from pure represent- ative democracy towards actual participative engagement in the political process, possibly through the utilisation of forms of direct democracy.

That technology is such a strong part of the democratic debate in Scotland is a victory for those who have long insisted that the implication of new technologies goes beyond their an efficiency agenda, and that new networks and the informational relationships which they support also contain an important power dimension which should be recognised and analysed. Yet the social science of new technology also suggests that the 'impact' of ICTs on the democratic process is far from clear, and can never be planned with certainty.[10] This is particularly the case when the object of attention is an organisational component of government such as a Parliament, which is both embedded by and serves to embed a set of institutional factors, the longstanding values, norms and conventions which moderate and shape the potential for any change.[11]

The Scottish Parliament may be a new body, but the processes surrounding its creation and initial operations will still be affected by institutional factors. Such factors tend to militate against any aspirations for sudden or radical change in the way the Scottish Parliament goes about its business, in comparison to dominant parliamentary practice in the United Kingdom. It is this realisation which leads us to offer a critique of some of the statements of intent about the role of ICTs in supporting democratic practice around the Scottish Parliament.

The first assumption which must be engaged with is the notion that the Parliament is being drawn upon a blank slate. True, the new parliament will occupy a space long emptied by the previous body, which went under the same name despite the fact that its suspension in 1707 came before the development of full parliamentary democracy. The new Scottish Parliament will bear little relation to that body in terms of its composition, practice or authority. But this does not imply that the Parliament is entirely free from other forces which may intervene to condition the development of its processes, including the uptake of new capabilities offered by ICTs.

This is an important point, especially because much of the potential to create new social and political outcomes with which new technologies are often credited is characteristic of a profound technological determin- ism. This manifests itself where the technology itself is understood to be capable of achieving certain outcomes; the power of the technology, in terms of what it can do, is seen to have its own internal logic which will transform the setting in which it is utilised. Further, such deterministic approaches concentrating on the transformative power of new technolo- gies, are often associated with either very gloomy or unreasonably optimistic scenarios. There is a tendency, then, to see the application of

ICTs in a social or political setting as either helping to strengthen the capabilities of elites and usher in greater social control in an almost Orwellian manner, or creating the conditions for an unprecedented renaissance in political life, along the lines of Athenian democracy. Beyond these limiting approaches, and the extremist scenarios with which they are associated, a number of scholars have attempted to explain why there are such few concrete examples of ICTs ushering in great change in the operation of politics. These analyses place greater emphasis upon the organisational and institutional realities of the social world, and their role in mediating and shaping outcomes facilitated by new technologies. Notably, academics in the United States associated with what has become known as the 'Irvine School' have emphasised the ways in which the capabilities offered by new technologies are often applied in organisational and institutional settings in ways which serve to reinforce existing organisational orders and biases.[12] King and Kraemer,[13] also argue that while ICTs may have serious implications for the establishment and maintenance of political society, those implications are not yet manifest in either the balance between individual rights and government power or the wider relationships between government and the people.[14] However, their research does identify the processes by which governmental officials are elected and appointed, and collective decisions are taken, as being one of the realms where new technologies have had and will continue to have an impact. More specifically, they also suggest there is substantial evidence to show that communications technologies have had a profound effect on the conduct of political campaigns, and in the mobilisation of political action. Such trends are also increasingly apparent in the UK in the arena of party politics.

Other academics have been concerned with the structural effects of ICTs on the bureaucracy of government.[15] In Zuurmond's view, the application of ICTs in organisational settings of public administration assists in the transformation of bureaucracy into 'infocracy'. ICTs may be hailed as having the potential to cut through the bureaucratic structures of government, but in actual fact the technology is used in such a way as to transform bureaucracy from an organisational to a 'virtual' reality. The application of new ICTs is carried out in such a way that while formalisation and standardisation seem to disappear from the organisation, these characteristics of bureaucracy are in fact translated and transformed into the information systems and their architecture. The resultant forms of organisation may appear to be flat, lean, less hierarchical and more open and flexible, but the bureaucratic structure of the organisation is maintained in an 'infocracy'.[16] It is often the case that bureaucratic aspects of organisation are not overcome and certainly do not disappear, but are modernised and standardised through incorporation in the new systems. Theories such as this claim that the interaction between new technologies and their organisational and institutional setting is far more subtle than that anticipated by a deterministic outlook, and that the eventual outcome can only be understood through an appreciation of the choices involved in the development of new systems, and therefore the institutional background against which those choices are made. The crux of the matter, then, is that the technology is essentially neutral; it does not embody any defining characteristics necessarily favouring one set of organisational or political outcomes over another.

Applying this knowledge to the Scottish Parliament, we should consider the nature of the factors which will intrude to shape the uptake of new technologies by that body, the ways in which the technology might actually be used, and the democratic consequences of this. One of the key relationships around the Scottish Parliament, and paradoxically one rarely fully articulated, is that which exists between the Parliament and political parties. Indeed, the electoral system adopted for the parliament (the additional member system) gives greater discretionary power to parties, since they are able to nominate a number of candidates who will be elected through appearing on a list. rather than standing as a candidate in a first-past-the-post constituency contest. Those who gain a seat through this method will then be free of traditional constituency duties, and one can only speculate as to whether their workload will be augmented with party duties. At Westminster, the Whip's Offices are the de facto party offices, with the majority of MPs standing on a party ticket and organised into party groupings in the chamber. Much of the political communication which occurs between the MPs and the public actually occurs through party channels rather than independent or parliamentary channels. Similarly, much of the communication which occurs within Westminster, including those few channels into which ICTs have intruded, depend upon the party. There is a dilemma here, in that parties are an essential part of the existing Westminster parliamentary process, and look certain to continue to be in the new Scottish Parliament, yet the relationship between the two cannot be fully acknowledged because of the dominant doctrine of parliamentary sovereignty. What, then, will be the role of political parties in influencing the direction of ICT use at Holyrood? Will it be neutral, or will parties bring their own agendas, consciously or unconsciously, to bear?

Political parties themselves make good case studies of how the institution of party politics, and the norms and values which the institution encompasses, has acted to moderate any possible new outcomes brought about through the application of ICTs. A great deal of speculation has occurred that new technologies would be used within parties in an explicit attempt to rebuild the mass organisational structures which they once were, and the notion of which they still subscribe to. Evidence suggests that ICTs have actually had a greater effect in strengthening the party's knowledge of the electoral landscape, and in allowing parties to move to take advantage of where majority opinion lies on that landscape, than in widening participation in their organisational structures.[17]

Parties have undergone processes of change which at times seem to border on total re-invention, and the capabilities associated with ICTs have facilitated much of this change, yet the change has not occurred in the way that most people expected it might. The 'effect' on the practice of democracy is difficult to judge, but this outcome is largely in line with other studies suggesting that democracy is now practised to a greater extent at the 'consumption nexus', (the boundary between government and citizen as 'consumers of services') than at the traditional nexus of representative democracy, the Parliament. In other words, the main democratic focus of ICTs has been to promote the ability of government, and parties, to discern and respond to its citizens as 'customers', not to bolster traditional ideas of representative democracy, of which a parliament is such an important part.

Conclusion

That the Scottish Parliament represents an unparalleled democratic innovation in the governance of Scotland is a fact which few would seek to challenge. The new body represents an opportunity for democratic renewal which cannot be underestimated; and the role of new technologies in supporting such a renewal seems to be well articulated by those responsible for identifying the key areas where ICTs may play an important part. Yet at the same time, caution should prevail over the extent to which new technologies can shape the actual end result. The technology itself may be capable of a great deal, but the ways in which it is used will be shaped and conditioned by its users. And, despite overwhelming optimism, the unequal power relationship between elected and electors suggests that the capabilities offered by technology are likely to favour the interests of the former over those of the latter.

1   The original Covenanters resisted moves by the Crown to force Episcopal forms of worship onto Presbyterian Scotland in the Seventeenth Century.
2   *Scotland's Parliament. Scotland's Right*, Scottish Constitutional Convention, November 1995.
3   White Paper, *Scotland's Parliament*, July 1997, HMSO.
4   Of those voting, 74.3% supported the principle of the creation of a Scottish Parliament and 63.5% voted to support the proposal to give the Parliament limited tax varying powers (+/– 3% in the pound). The turnout at the Referendum was 60.4%.
5   *A Parliament for the Millennium*, Advisory Committee on Telematics for the Scottish Parliament, John Wheatley Centre, July 1997.
6   The membership of the CSG was: J. Wallace MP (Orkney and Shetland), A. Salmond MP (Banff and Buchan), P. Cullen QC (representing the Scottish Conservative Party), K. Geddes CBE (Convention of Scottish Local Authorities), Canyon K. Wright (Scottish Constitution Convention), Professor A. Brown (Department of Politics, University of Edinburgh), Dr J. Stringer (Principal of Queen Margaret's College), J. McMillan (writer and journalist who chaired the Constitutional Commission), E. Robertson (Scottish Constitutional Convention), D. Hutton (Scottish Consumer Council), A. Cubie (Lawyer and former chair of the CBI in Scotland) and C. Christie (General Secretary of the STUC).
7   *Final Report to the Consultative Steering Group*, Expert Panel on Information and Communications Technologies for the Scottish Parliament, Scottish Office, Edinburgh, 1998.
8   The membership of the Expert Panel on ICT was: A. Brown (Director of Administrative Services, Scottish Office (Chairman)), A. Baker (Scotland Country Manager, Microsoft Corporation), R. Beattie (Chair of Edinburgh Telematics Partnership and Community Investment Coordinator Edinburgh, IBM UK

Scotland), P. Black (Network Services Director, Scottish Telecom), L. Beddie (Professor of Computing, Napier University), P. Dixon (Regional Director Scotland, Oracle Corporation UK Ltd), P. Grice (Head of Legislation and Implementation Division, Constitution Group, Scottish Office), N. Hopkins (Technical Director, CCTA), A. Mathieson (Keeper, National Library of Scotland), R. McFarlane (General Manager, Office of the Director, BT Scotland), A. Nairn (Secretary, Society of IT Managers (Scotland) and Director of IT, Perth and Kinross Council), M. O'Connor (Director of Business Services, Telewest Communications), J. Wainwright (Director of Information Systems, House of Commons Library), and A. Weatherstone (Head of Architectures and Change Programme, National Australia Group).

9   *Telematics and the Scottish Parliament: Transferable Democratic Innovations*, Centre for the Study of Telematics and Governance (CSTAG), Scottish Office, Edinburgh, 1998.

10 C. Bellamy and J. Taylor, *Governing in the Information Age*, Open University Press, 1998.

11 J.G. March and J.P. Olsen, *Rediscovering Institutions: The Organisational Basis of Politics*, New York, Free Press, 1989.

12 K.L. Kraemer and J.L. King, 'Social Analysis of Information Systems: The Irvine School, 1970–1994', *Informatization and the Public Sector*, 3, IOS Press, 1994, pp. 63–182.

13 J.L. King and K.L. Kraemer, 'Information Technology in the Establishment and Maintenance of Civil Society' in I. Snellen and W. van de Donk, *Public Administration in an Information Age: A Handbook*, IOS Press, 1998.

14 Ibid., p. 522.

15 A. Zuurmond, 'From Bureaucracy to Infocracy: Towards Management through Information Architecture' in J. Taylor, I. Snellen and A. Zuurmond (eds), *Beyond BPR in Public Administration. Institutional Transformation in an Information Age*, Amsterdam, IOS, 1996; and C. Bellamy and J. Taylor, *Governing in the Information Age*, Open University Press, 1998.

16 A. Zuurmond, 'From Bureaucracy to Infocracy: Towards Management through Information Architecture' in J. Taylor, I. Snellen and A. Zuurmond (eds), *Beyond BPR in Public Administration. Institutional Transformation in an Information Age*, Amsterdam, IOS, 1996.

17 C. Smith, 'Political Parties: Continuity and Change in a Consumerist Democracy' in J. Hoff and I. Horrocks (eds), *Democratic Governance and New Technology*, Routledge, 1999.

Challenges Posed by Information and Communication Technologies for Parliamentary Democracy in South Africa

BY CAMPBELL LYONS AND TANYA LYONS

Introduction

Parliaments in developing countries, particularly those in Africa, operate in very challenging circumstances. One of the greatest challenges has been to integrate a highly technical and eurocentric institution with African tradition and experiences of direct involvement in the democratic process. These challenges of integration between parliament as a democratic institution and the indigenous experiences of Africa remain persistent and formidable. The recent history of the failure of democratic regimes in Africa is directly linked to the inability of African parliamentary democracy to generate enduring popular support or assent amongst it's citizens. Parliament is viewed by many citizens as alien, incomprehensible, and distant.

The introduction of new information and communication technologies (ICTs) to African parliaments impacts directly on these existing challenges. Given the past experience of Africa, can the use of ICTs by the South African parliament bring it closer to the people or will it serve to remove and alienate parliament still further? One of the key preconditions for any successful and effective democratic system is participation by citizens in the process. Underlying participation are the twin values of freedom and equality of access to the democratic process.

In South Africa these challenges regarding the increasing use of ICTs by parliament are particularly acute. Firstly, because South Africa has to overcome the legacy of apartheid rule. Under apartheid the majority of South African citizens were actively excluded from participation in the democratic process. Secondly, the current levels of ICT skills amongst South African citizens tend to be both weak and proportionate to levels of income and education. Consequently, the use of ICTs in South Africa presents something of a conundrum. They can be viewed as critical agents for change in overcoming the information gap between the South African parliament and the majority of its citizens. However, the harnessing of ICTs to play such a role is dependent on the presence of a highly literate and technically informed population. Thirdly, access to ICTs is virtually non-existent for the majority of South African citizens. The increased use of ICTs by parliament thus raises the question whether their use will facilitate participatory democracy. Under these circumstances, what is the potential effect of ICTs on democratic participation?

The South African Parliament: context

After the first democratic election in 1994, the South African parliament undertook a number of decisive changes. In embracing a broad, inclusive and transparent approach to the manner in which parliament is run, the doors of parliament were opened to all citizens; not only formally, but substantively, as access was granted to citizens to participate in the legislative process.

This transformation of the South African parliament is most visible in the broad representation of the majority of South African citizens in Parliament, in the functioning of parliamentary portfolio committees, the related provisions that are contained in the Constitution, and in the public awareness campaigns that have been initiated. Apart form the broad representation of the majority of South African citizens, probably the most significant change that has affected parliament has been the manner in which parliamentary portfolio committees function. For the first time, parliamentary portfolio committees have been opened to the general South African public for their commentary and input on proposed items of legislation. In addition, all portfolio committee meetings are open to the press and the general public not only for commentary during public hearings, but also when these committees deliberate on legislation, policy, and matters of public interest.

The South African Constitution also makes it incumbent upon parliament to facilitate public involvement in the legislative process. The public awareness campaign initiated by parliament has sought to educate the broad South African public on the nature and functioning of parliament. Educational activities include: the development and implementation of communication and information strategies for MPs support programmes, networking with private and public sectors about parliament, the coordination of public consultation programmes for parliamentary portfolio committees, the holding of national youth parliaments, community meetings on the workings of parliament, parliamentary tours and 'Members briefing sessions' for visitors to parliament.

Despite these efforts, prior to 1994, the majority of South African citizens were excluded from interacting with parliament as part of standard government policy. This means that many today still do not understand the nature of parliament, its processes or even its raison d'etre. This ignorance of parliament, together with widespread illiteracy, poverty, homelessness and lack of social services such as electricity and transport, impedes participation by the majority of citizens. Thus, the apartheid legacy significantly undermines parliament's efforts to transform into a democratic institution. While access has been relatively easy to achieve at the most basic level of literally opening the doors to citizens, it is harder to achieve equal access in terms of substantive and informed participation in the parliamentary process itself.

Deputy President Mbeki had the following to say regarding the acute challenges facing parliament in upholding these democratic values amidst the socio-economic devastation caused in South African society by apartheid:

During the past four years of Parliament my observation is that, if no effort is exerted towards facilitating the participation of struggling communities like Bitterfontein and Matjiesfontein who are largely uneducated and poor, the opportunity to influence the laws and policies generated by our government will remain the preserve of the enlightened business magnates of Knysna and Wilderness. Our challenge is that with the limited resources that we have, we still take democracy to the poor women working in the farms of Stellenbosch and Paarl, and all over the poverty-stricken areas of this country, where such terms such as illiterate, ignorant, squalor, landless and homeless are still the order of the day.[1]

Avoiding dislocation between this message on the one hand and the socio-economic realities of the majority of South African citizens on the other, poses a significant challenge. This challenge and the context in which the South African parliament finds itself, serves as a reminder that South Africa's parliamentary democracy is still very much in its infancy.

The South African Parliament and ICTs

As part of its communication strategy, Parliament employs a number of technologies as communication media in networking with the South African public.[2] On the whole, these communication technologies can be described as being orientated heavily towards information dissemination to the public, rather than facilitating a free flow of multi-directional information. Currently, the following information and communication technologies are employed by parliament: television, radio and the Internet.

TELEVISION AND RADIO: There is a daily live televised broadcast in real-time of debates in the National Assembly by the South African Broadcasting Corporation (SABC). Complementing this there are also actuality programmes on parliament. For instance, *Parliament Live* is a programme which gives a weekly summary of parliamentary activities. News broadcasts also carry coverage of the day's events in parliament and interviews are frequently held with politicians on issues of national interest. Debates between politicians from the different political parties have also been scheduled with increasing frequency on prime time television. There is also a parliamentary channel on Digital Satellite Television (DSTV), a pay channel, which broadcasts live from the national assembly, as well as the proceedings of parliamentary portfolio committee meetings.

However, according to figures released for 1997 by the South African Institute for Race Relations, 41% of South Africans are without electricity.[3] Radio is the most effective means of communication with the broad South African population. Radio broadcasts of parliamentary events and issues are channelled via SABC Radio. There are also a wide variety of community radio stations which broadcast debates between politicians and which provide commentary on issues of local concern. These broadcasts cover the spectrum of South African languages, enabling people to receive information in their home language. Currently, most debates in both the National Assembly and National Council of Provinces take place in English, as do discussions and deliberations in Committees. Parliament is moving towards improved accommodation of all nine official languages. However, minutes of proceedings, committee reports and announcements are still only available in English and Afrikaans. Legislation is available in English and Afrikaans, although some pieces of legislation have been published in English and Xhosa. If MPs wish to address a debate of either House in their home language translation services are available. The task of accommodating nine official languages is far from complete and radio serves as a crucial source of information for thousands of citizens.

COMPUTER SYSTEMS WITHIN PARLIAMENT: Within Parliament, the use of computers and computer software varies from section to section. Some sections, such as international relations and public participation and information, have relatively current Windows based systems in place. Other sections, such as committees and *Hansard*, operate on computers which run the publications programme Xywrite from an internal network. The Xywrite programme does not make for easy information transfer, except on the internal network, and the use of Internet and e-mail by these sections is severely limited. This is ironic, as these sections are largely responsible for the record keeping of activities of parliament and its committees: yet the recording is mostly disseminated by paper copy upon receipt of a written or verbal request. The committee section in particular receives such requests from the public, media and stakeholder groups on an almost daily basis and this communication is presently not facilitated by the use of new technologies. This is true not only for imparting of information, but also for the receipt of information by committees. Thus, if a member of the public wishes to make a submission on a particular piece of legislation it is not always possible for this submission to be e-mailed to the Committee and one has to rely on the postal system or faxed copies. The Chief Whip of the majority party, Mr Tony Yengeni, has criticised the antiquity of parliament's computers: 'Committees are not even on the Internet. They are not even using windows.'[4]

The problem is not limited to the parliamentary staff. It also affects MPs. A significant proportion of MPs do not themselves make use of e-mail or the Internet, although their party research and administrative support staff do to a large extent. Many MPs do not even have computers in their offices.

INTERNET: Parliament makes use of a Parliamentary web-site for information dissemination. This is, however, not interactive. Political parties also maintain web-sites of similar stature, but with an obvious focus on party propaganda. At present, South Africa makes use of the party list system — this means that in most cases MPs do not have personal links with the communities they are assigned to serve. With longer parliamentary sessions they spend a large part of the year in Cape Town removed from their constituencies. The use of Internet and e-mail could assist in bridging the gap between MPs, their constituency offices and their constituents. Although in some instances the constituency offices are equipped with Internet and e-mail, these tools are currently being under utilised due to lack of skills.

The Parliamentary Monitoring Group (PMG), a number of non-governmental organisations (NGOs) who monitor parliamentary committees, maintains a web-site with information on the activities of these committees. Information on upcoming public hearings and reports of parliamentary committees are posted here. This undoubtedly makes a contribution to public participation in parliament, but there is still the issue of how to reach the majority of South African citizens. In an interview with Zubeida Jaffer, the Speaker of the National Assembly, Dr Frene Ginwala said that:

[h]aving lobbyists and non-governmental organisations here does not mean participatory democracy. We have to consider how we get the population more involved in Parliament between elections.[5]

The statistics (Table 1) on availability of telephones, as published in the South African Institute of Race Relations Survey for 1997–98 underscore the difficulty of reaching ordinary citizens.[6] These figures indicate the large disparity between access to telephone (and therefore conceivably e-mail and the Internet) between Africans and Whites. According to the South African Telecommunications Regulatory Authority (Satra), even if Telkom was to meet its target of 2.8 million telephone lines by 2001–2 this would still leave 3.3 million households without telephones.[7]

1. Access to telephone by race — urban and non-urban, 1995 (%)

	African	Coloured	Indian	White
Cellular phone only				
Urban	0.3	0.3	0.4	1.4
Non-urban	0.1	–	–	0.5
Cellular phone and phone in dwelling				
Urban	0.3	0.5	3.5	7.1
Non-urban	0.0	0.3	0.7	6.0
Telephone in dwelling only				
Urban	24.8	43.7	70.8	76.1
Non-urban	2.8	8.6	62.0	80.9
None (i.e. no access to telephone from neighbour, communal telephone or telephone in shop)				
Urban	24.9	24.4	10.8	8.8
Non-urban	54.6	40.0	12.5	6.3

(1995 was the last year for which figures are available)

It needs to be borne in mind that although there is a great imbalance in the use of telematics in South Africa, especially between the rural and urban populations, in comparison to the rest of Africa, South Africa has a developed infrastructure. National and international telecommunications systems are in place, two cellular telephone networks are available, satellite television stations are in operation and various Internet service providers are available and well utilised by certain sectors of the population. Nevertheless, increasing use of sophisticated ICTs by parliament without an allied social development programme must lead to an increasing alienation of parliament and the undermining of such democratic values.[8]

The potentials and pitfalls of Internet for Parliament

The question regarding the effective management and use of ICTs by the South African parliament is at its sharpest with regards to utilising Internet facilities. From economic, administrative and executive points of view, there is a clear rationale for parliament to optimise its use of Internet facilities. First, increased use of Internet will decrease Parliament's heavy dependency on paper as a means of communication. Second, it will facilitate increased access and more effective communication with government agencies, civil society organisations and the public both nationally and internationally. Thirdly, the internet is a highly effective archival tool enabling vast amounts of information to be stored and accessed with relative ease. Fourthly, it can provide a standardised framework for information procurement, storage, transfer and dissemination. Fifthly, the Internet has the capacity to facilitate spontaneous, informal and formal multi-directional flows of information between parliament and the public. And finally, it brings the South African parliament in line with current global trends with regards to information technology.

This indicates that the increased use of ICTs in parliament may further parliament's capacity to fulfil its functions. The most significant outcome would be parliament's ability to interact at a substantive level with South African citizens. The achievement of this objective will only be successful if it is managed in such a way that the broad South African population is not left out of the process.

If the implementation of an increased internet capacity for parliament is poorly managed, then the quality of the rights of South African citizens, and the prospect of continued democratic governance, may be negatively effected. There is a real danger that parliament may be increasing the gap between rich and poor in South Africa. The benefits of new technologies would only be available to wealthy and educated citizens. Those who are most in need would be most excluded from the democratic process. Clearly, the use of such ICTs by parliament is not wholly an administrative or a technical management issue, but is in particular, a political one. Thus, the management of such technologies should not be left to bureaucrats or technocrats alone, but should be heavily dependent upon careful political management and considerations.

What this also indicates is that ICTs themselves are not inherently good or bad, moral or immoral, limiting or liberating. Parliamentary dependence on the Internet has both significant advantages for the effective running of the business of parliament, as well as significant disadvantages if not managed and used properly. The issue of ICTs and parliaments concerns the manner in which it is used and managed by institutions in conducting their business and whether the manner in which such technology is used to complement the objectives, values, principles and needs of parliament. The challenge for parliament can be said to lie in how it utilises and manages these technologies in support of its democratic values and principles.

Approaches to the challenge of ICTs and parliamentary democracy in South Africa

While it is clear, given the socio-economic context of South Africa, that parliament cannot rely exclusively and solely on ICTs as a means of conducting its business, this does not mean that ICTs cannot be utilised by parliament. Parliament utilises ICTs to some degree in conducting its business. In future, parliament is going to become increasingly reliant upon these technologies, if only for pragmatic reasons. If ICTs are to support democratic participation, a number of steps must be taken.

Those responsible for the development of ICTs the management of parliament's ICT upgrading must take the socio-economic context into account.[9] This would entail that parliament's communication strategy, while allowing for increased dependence on ICTs, would continue to be multidimensional in the sense that many communication media already in use, would continue to be employed. It is inevitable, taking into account the socio-economic status of many South African citizens that parliament will have to continue to duplicate its information dissemination channels and utilise existing channels for multi directional flows of information such as forums, for some time to come.

Legislation must ensure the dissemination of ICT skills throughout the population. For instance, ICT skills could be incorporated into the national school curriculum as a compulsory subject for students. Similarly, the introduction of a nation-wide programme of ICT education and training workshops could be implemented for citizens who have already left school. Such a programme could be run as a partnership between parliament, government, business, non-governmental organisations and community based organisations. Access to ICTs could be provided by situating public access points in community centres, post offices and other agencies.[10]

Constituency offices could play a role by facilitating Internet access and access to video-conferencing technology. However, for this to take effect there would need to be legislation governing the role and function of constituency offices and a change in the electoral system in South Africa. Currently, the establishment and maintenance of constituency offices is optional in South Africa.

While this is by no means exhaustive, we hope it does indicate that there is no need to dismiss the potential advantages of ICTs for the South African parliament given the socio-economic context that parliament finds itself in. What seems to be clearly apparent regarding the effective management of ICT systems by the South African parliament, is that as a developing country, the democratic value of an inclusive parliament will place constraints upon the extent and the manner in which parliament will become reliant upon ICTs. The manner in which ICTs are employed by parliament will be a yardstick by which to assess the extent to which the rights of freedom and equality of access are upheld. The manner in which these information technologies are managed, given the twin pressures of the need for increasing reliance upon such technologies and the exploitation of the advantages thereof, coupled with the socio-economic context of the majority of South African citizens, will be a critical factor amongst others in determining the sustenance or erosion of parliamentary democracy in South Africa.

1   B. Mbeti-Kgositsile, 'Opening Address by the Deputy Speaker of the National Assembly', *Conference Report on Public Participation and Governance in South Africa*, Khululekani Institute for Democracy, 1998, p. 5.
2   J. Percy-Smith, 'Downloading Democracy? Information and Communication Technologies in Local Politics', *Policy and Politics*, 1996, 24/1.
3   *Fast Facts*, South African Institute of Race Relations, February 1999, p. 4.
4   C. Sawyer, 'Budget cuts unite rival MPs', *The Argus*, 17.3.99.
5   Z. Jaffer, '534 laws on: A Speaker too tired for words', *Cape Times*, 23.3.99.
6   E. Sidiropoulos et al, *South Africa Survey 1997–98*, South African Institute of Race Relations, 1998, p. 380.
7   Ibid., p. 381.
8   N. Butcher, *The Possibilities and Pitfalls of Harnessing ICTs to Accelerate Social Development: A South African Perspective*, South African Institute for Distance Education, 1999.

9   M. Muller, 'Managing information technology' in *Managing Sustainable Development in South Africa*, P. Fitzgerald, A. McLennan and B. Munslow (eds), Oxford University Press, 1997.

10   P. Benjamin, 'Multipurpose Community Centres in South Africa', *Conference Proceedings on Information Society and Government Initiatives in Economic Development*, National Information Technology Forum, 1998.

Telematics in the Service of Democracy: The Slovenian Parliament and Other Slovenian Public Institutions on the Internet

BY MIRKO VINTAR, MITJA DECMAN AND MATEJA KUNSTELJ

Introduction

At the time of writing this chapter, NATO bombers are flying over our houses every night heading for Belgrade which until recently was our capital. They do so in the name of democracy and humanity, reminding us that there are indeed different ways and means possible to foster democracy in different countries. During the stormy history of the Balkan peninsula, heavy weaponry has often been used in the name of high principles. What is new in this war is the role of technology. In the past it was clear that wars could be won only by direct fight of man against man. This time there is an impression that technology itself will decide this tragic war and will be the only winner. The common people, regardless of which side of the river they are on, serve only as a food for cannons. They were losers in the past and they are destined to be losers again this time. So, can softer technological means, like telematics and ICT, serve to underpin democratic processes in those new countries of Central Europe which know little of democratic tradition? In particular, can these technologies serve the citizens rather than only those who are claiming to be their representatives and their defenders?

Our brief for this chapter was to report on the Slovenian Parliament and its use of telematic services. Yet after some in-depth analysis we came to the conclusion that in a small county like Slovenia which has less than ten years of independence and democratic history, to focus solely on the Slovenian Parliament would give us only a partial view. Thus, we have chosen to provide a broader perspective into the extent of use of telematic services and ICT in a number of most important institutions of democracy in Slovenia, ranging from Parliament and Presidency to government, state and local administration.

During the time of the former Yugoslavia there were seven parliaments, one federal and six for the republics parliaments which were constituent parts of the state. However, everyone in the country knew that the real centre of power was not inside the mighty buildings of the parliaments or National Assembly but in the Central Committees. In particular, when issues of national importance were at stake, and within

bureaucratic structures of central and local administration it was here
that everyday problems of a common people were questioned. After
nearly ten years of life, in what is now an independent and democratic
country, this bureaucratic structure remains more or less the same and,
if development is to progress to a more democratic society, this is where
change should finally start. This was the rationale that led us to the
decision that we should also include in this survey institutions of public
administration and executive power in order to give a more complete
picture.

Our main concern was the use of telematics, mainly the Internet, as a
means of communication between public institutions and the citizens
and vice versa. There was not enough time available to conduct very
profound research in public opinion or other interest groups which
would give us empirical evidence on the effects of telematics on democratic processes. However, we did survey and visit web-sites through
which these institutions are communicated to the public in Slovenia.
Over the last few years the Internet has become a popular medium with
about 280,000 active Internet users (about 15% of population). Slovenia is one country that has a relatively well-developed Internet use. This
survey mainly focuses on the following questions:

- To what extent are public institutions using the Internet as a
  means of communication with the public?
- What kind of information is offered to the public?
- Is there one-way or two-way communication?
- What is the number of feedback mechanisms established to get
  return information from citizens and other organisations?

For many decades Slovenia was under a communist-dominated political
regime that systematically tried to hide all vital information from the
public. The installation of new communication channels, providing
better access to information of public interest, represents one of the
most important instruments towards a more democratic society. Control over information sources was in the past a main weapon of
manipulation over the citizens. So far we have reasonably good reasons
to regard the Internet as an independent, neutral and powerful medium
for dissemination of information although we know that it can be
misused too. Furthermore, we see the Internet as a rare communication
medium with which we can establish an interactive, two-way communication between public institutions and the citizens and make the
first step towards more 'direct' democracy.

In the following sections, we try to present the extent to which
Internet usage is fulfilling that task in Slovenia. We will also attempt to
analyse and verify the initial hypothesis that telematics can stimulate
and support democratic processes, although our conclusions will be
based more on personal experience and reasoning than empirically
proven evidence.

Country profile

Slovenia is one of the new and small European countries. It has a population of about two million, 95% of whom are Slovenes, the rest being largely from two officially recognised minorities.

Historically and politically, Slovenia belonged to the Austro–Hungarian Empire until 1918. From 1918–91 Slovenia was part of the former Yugoslavia with relatively high-level of autonomy. All federal states and provinces (one of which was province Kosovo, the centre of the Balkan war) had their own parliaments and governments. In 1991 Slovenia declared independence and subsequently became an Associated Member of the European Union. Although ex-Yugoslavia belonged to the club of socialist countries, the Slovenian economy experienced a spell of reasonably rapid economic development in the 1970s and 1980s which brought Slovenia to the top of the most developed Central European economies at a time when the Eastern European block started to fall apart. After an initial post-independence fall in economic fortune, solid growth rates since 1993 of between three to four per cent are reassuring and should bring the 1999 GNP per capita close to $12,000 per capita.

Slovenia has parliamentary democracy in two Houses, comprising the National Assembly with 90 seats and the National Council with 45 seats. Members of both bodies are directly elected. The country is divided into 58 administrative districts performing territorial function of the State with 192 municipalities performing functions of local self-government. The government, including all ministries and other governmental agencies, employs approximately 29,000 servants with an additional 3,000 employees in municipality administration.

Public institutions and the Internet

As elsewhere, in Slovenia the Internet has become an everyday word. Because of the rapidly expanding market and promising profits, private companies are profoundly aware of it. But the public institutions look at it from a different point of view. There is no profit for them, but they still have a sense of requirement to be present in the new cyberspace and so most of them are. However when we surf on the web, we find out that the representation completely depends on individual institutions.

The first pages of different public institutions are much alike, but the content is very different. In particular, the usage of foreign languages varies. Awareness that the Internet is a global medium and that the English language is its most powerful tool is still in the background, hence the percentage of web-pages in foreign languages is still rather small. The second problem lies in understanding that the Internet is much more than a mere 'announcement board' and that information on display should not be seen as something static as in a book. All too often the content of the pages is old, invalid, simply empty or gone.

Public institutions still have to learn the advantages and importance of this electronic medium in the new cyberspace.

In terms of content, there prevails basic information about activities, people, telephone numbers, addresses and e-mail addresses. Pages for one public institution or even different departments of the same institution are not standard, so one must always adapt to different structures and navigation arrangements. The contents of pages differ, from simple basics to ones that include Java programs, multimedia and other interactive additions. Most of the pages have hyperlinks to other sites with similar information. There is still a widespread belief that the basic information itself is enough and much too little attention is paid to updating, design and development of user-friendly sites.

ONE-WAY OR A TWO-WAY COMMUNICATION IN UNDERPINNING DEMOCRATIC PROCESSES: Despite the fact that generally the Internet is more and more seen and used as a two-way communication medium, Slovenian public institutions use it largely as a one-way communication channel. They use it more or less as a 'shop window' displaying information which they regard as important for their public appearance. It still remains to be seen when it will be realised that with two-way communication the necessary contact with citizens must be established, and through this resultant exchange of information, suggestions, opinions, comments and ideas enabled. In terms of underpinning democratic processes, two-way communication is required, since this would enable communication between both sides on a partner-like basis. However, this is probably the weakest point of the present state of democratic developments in Slovenia and the key point of this discussion. Citizens are not seen as partners in shaping decisions that are of common interest. Instead the key personnel in public administration and other public institutions, including Parliament still see their role as superior to citizens. The way in which telematics has been used thus far confirms this observation well.

Use of ICT and telematics at National Assembly of Slovenia

There are 90 deputies of the National Assembly directly elected every four years. Their main duties, as in other countries, relate to legislative, voting and controlling functions. The first includes passing law, changes to the constitution, national budget, etc. Voting functions include the election of the Prime Minister, Cabinet ministers, Constitutional Court and Supreme Court judges, etc. The last deals with questions from National Assembly deputies to ministers and the government. In the Slovenian case, the first function had demanded most of the available National Assembly session time since, over the last few years, the country has changed the wholly legal system and harmonised it with the 'acquis communautaire'.

The main occupation of the deputies is to be actively involved in the legislative procedure. The procedure is defined through the Standing Orders of the National Assembly and must be considered by deputies, expert co-workers and other people involved in legislative procedure. The arrival of new technologies like computers, local area networks (LAN) and the Internet has enabled the informatisation of this procedure as well as a major part of the other work of deputies. Years of planning, many pilot projects, testing and training were required before the whole project succeeded. Development of the whole information system commenced after Independence. Several generations of technology changed in the meantime, starting with the DOS environment with DW5 word processor and LAN, until the last phase, when transition to a document handling, Lotus-Notes, environment took place.

The main task of the information system (IS) of the National Assembly is to assure an efficient and up-to-date follow-up of National Assembly events. The whole concept of IS in the National Assembly is document oriented. Databases hold information on sessions, reports, laws, key documents and other documents. Because of the decentralisation of the whole system, the database is also synchronising government, ministries, the President of the Republic, and other public institutional databases.

The concept of a document-oriented system is based on the folders in which logically related text documents are inserted. For example, one folder contains documents related to one law, from first draft to final vote. In this folder, sub-folders with different documents such as reports, announcements and proceedings are included. One of the most important capabilities of the IS is a full-text search. Any word, in any law, act or report can be found. Tape-recordings can also be searched for any word uttered during the sessions.

The beginning of the process is normally triggered when a document arrives at the main office. These documents should be in a certain format but are often received in various forms being generated from different word processing formats. Although IS can handle diverse packages, i.e. attached documents, all files are converted to a standard format. Scanning paper documents is still not supported due to impractical graphical format (inability to text search) and poor accuracy of optical character recognition (OCR) technologies. Although OCR can be more than 90% accurate, it is still not feasible in the parliamentary context as every single letter is important. Telematic services based on the information system described here are available to deputies, journalists, citizens and other governmental institutions.

TELEMATICS IN THE SERVICE OF THE DEPUTIES OF THE NATIONAL ASSEMBLY IN SLOVENIA: Today each deputy has their own personal and/or portable computer with a network interface card or modem, for connection to a LAN and the Internet. Each deputy has an e-mail address and all deputies of the National Assembly are presented to the public through their web-pages. Basic information about each deputy as well as their contact e-mail address can be found on the web-pages. In order to obtain an overview of how keen as frequent users of telematic services are Slovenian MPs we sent to all of them a short questionnaire. The results of this survey are shown in Figures 1–3.

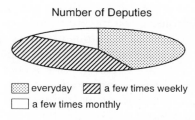

Figure 1. The use of the Internet by the Deputies

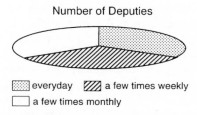

Figure 2. The use by the Slovenian Deputies of National Assembly IS

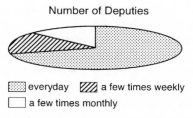

Figure 3. The use of E-mail by the Slovenian Deputies of National Assembly

In addition to the usual computer-based office solutions and access to all documents stored in a database of the National Assembly's information system, deputies have at their disposal the following specific telematic services:

— Preparation and convocation of sessions including the changes of agenda, reservations of the assembly rooms where sessions will be held.
— Creating letters, session invitations, timetable changes, and cancellations.
— Verbatim records of the sessions. All the sessions are recorded on

tape. On the basis of the tape, written records are processed and placed on the National Assembly database within 20 minutes of them being spoken. The records are thus accessible to deputies, government and media representatives. One can, therefore, follow a session over the computer network whilst it is happening. Literal notes are made from the written records. Each deputy can have their words amended. Spelling and grammar are also corrected. The literal notes are accessible to the public but due to the literal note correction time these are not accessible until three to four days later. The written records can also be inserted in folders, allowing the documents to be clearly presented.

— 'Questions and suggestions' from deputies and groups of deputies to ministers and government is a form of electronic discussion available to the MPs.

NATIONAL ASSEMBLY IN RELATION TO PUBLIC MEDIA AND THE CITIZENS: The IS department of the National Assembly provides information to the public about the work of the National Assembly and its working bodies. It provides the conditions for media representatives to carry out their work within the Assembly premises, monitors media reporting on the work of the National Assembly, and issues the *Gazette of the Assembly* and other publications. In cooperation with individual departments, and in accordance with the regulations on the provision of information to the public, it also prepares the necessary explanations and reports to public inquiries.

Reporters: National Assembly sessions are normally covered by numerous reporters (over one hundred) from different areas of the public media. In the past, two levels of information access have been available; the press room in the National Assembly connected through computers to the LAN and BBS system that could be accessible from newsrooms of individual newspapers. There is also an updating service that constantly inserts new data, documents and written records in the National Assembly's database. This provides a 24-hour access of up-to-date information to the press. Usually, there is not more than a 20-minute delay in updating information whilst the session is running.

Citizens: Most information about the National Assembly, deputies, their work, laws in progress, etc. is accessible to citizens on the web-pages and Internet. Information can be found about the President and Vice-president of the National Assembly, a list of all MPs with their personal information and e-mails, a list of groups of deputies and working parties, and their members. Detailed history including the most recent developments of the National Assembly can also be found. Descriptions of publications written by deputies (some in Internet text files) are also available. Issues of the National Assembly's newspaper are also presented together with a photo-history. Additional hyperlinks are available to international National Assemblies.

From the IS of the National Assembly the following materials are available to citizens via the Internet:[1]

— The Constitution of the Republic of Slovenia.
— Adopted laws (the database is renewed daily on the basis of announcements in the Official Paper of Republic of Slovenia).
— Adopted Acts (The database contains all Acts adopted from the second mandate period and published in the Official Paper of Republic of Slovenia, national budget, national projects, resolutions, explanations of laws, decrees, etc.).
— Suggestions of laws (from the current mandate period that is in procedure).
— Suggestion of Acts (from the current mandate period that is in procedure).
— Standing Orders of the National Assembly.
— Sessions of working bodies.
— Literal notes from sessions (the database has literal notes from the current mandate period).
— Data can be found through an alphabetical index or a full-text search.

Web-pages are well-linked, well-designed and user-friendly. The public, however, do not have access to Constitutional court cases, deputies' questions, input documents, etc.

This brief description of the National Assembly's telematic services show that they are organised mainly in one direction, i.e. from the National Assembly to the outside world. There are practically no in-built feedback channels through which the outside world in the form of citizens, can influence the work and decision-making process of the National Assembly.

The use of telematic service within general Public Administration

Contemporary Public Administration could be treated as a complex and cooperative information system which maintains an information underpinning for decision-making and for carrying out public services. The Internet, as a modern communication network, offers possibilities for more effective performance of some public services not only inside Public Administration but also in relation to the users of these services.[2]

A precondition for implementation of these services is suitable information infrastructure (hardware and software). Thus, the Government Centre for Informatics (GCI) is responsible for the development of a Slovenian Public Administration information infrastructure. With the construction of their own data communication network, the installation of a central computer and servers, the GCI in effect gave most state institutions an opportunity to offer their information services to internal and external users. The information infrastructure enables faster, more effective and thus reasonable execution of administrative processes between state institutions. At the same time it provides easy and fast access to administrative information, enabling citizens to be incorporated into the governmental decision-making process.

A 'bottleneck' of fast development tele-services in Public Administration often arises from legislation which has not yet adapted to the capabilities of modern information technology. For example, because of juridical invalidity of electronic documents (they do not have an original signature and seal) they are used only for information and assistance at work, and they cannot serve as evidence. Furthermore, some statutes and laws still require a paper-based record so that transfer of data to electronic media is not yet allowed or possible. Although the government is aware of these weaknesses, a lot of time will elapse before the legal system will be adapted to the use of new technologies.

TELEMATIC SERVICES AVAILABLE TO PUBLIC SERVANTS: Almost all state institutions have local networks installed which are connected to the data communication systems over which they have access to central computers and servers located at the GCI. There is an existing standard communication infrastructure for standard services which is offered over GCI on the government communication network.[3] The standard telematics services are:

E-mail: Enables public servants to communicate and to interchange official information and documents. Official communication with other institutions and citizens is also possible.

Internet: Public servants can with use of Internet browsers (e.g. Netscape Navigator, MS Internet explorer, etc.), approach Slovenian and other world web-sites. For example, they can use Judiciary Information Server (IUS-INFO) which contains legal Acts valid in Slovenia, court provisions, experts articles, etc.

Intranet: Users of the data communication network can access local servers, i.e. other state institutions servers such as: Parliament (legislative procedures database); Ministry of Finance server; Central Statistical Office (statistical indicators); Surveying and Mapping Authority (register of spatial units), and common application servers such as ISPO (Information System for Supporting Decision-Making) or INFOKLIP (Information System for Reviewing the Press) are also available.

SLOVENIAN PUBLIC ADMINISTRATION AND THE WEB: Whilst the State takes care of the development of information infrastructure, the most important State institutions themselves decide the content of their web-pages. For this reason web-pages from individual state institutions are differentiated from each other, though they also have some common points. All 15 ministries are present on the web. In addition there are the government (in the narrow sense of word); the Slovenian President; the majority of government agencies and directorates in the structure of ministries; and 58 administrative districts also have their own web-pages. Our research mainly focussed on what information citizens can obtain across the web and how they can respond with requests and suggestions. At present we do not have any information as to the extent to which available telematic services are actually used by citizens.

Web-pages of the ministries and institutions within their organisational structure: Ministries provide mainly basic information about themselves (e.g. telephone numbers and addresses), their organisational structure and information about their activities (Figure 4).

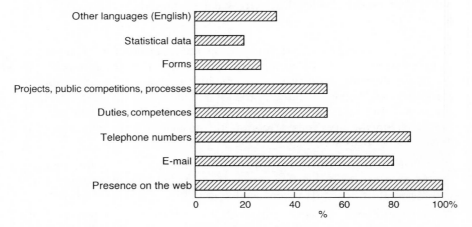

Figure 4. Type of Internet information available from ministries

In most cases (80%) citizens can send e-mail messages (applications, requests, entries for public procurements, annotations and other questions) to public institutions. In some cases (27%) ministries offers at least one form; they also use standard forms which can be printed or downloaded to disk. Interactive forms were not detected. All web-pages are in the Slovene language, only 33% of ministries also have web-pages in other languages, usually English. In some cases we found other information such as calendars of events and conferences, news, notices, work reports, directions about concrete questions, information on actual problems, publications, articles, legislation in the field of competencies of the ministries.

Government and the President of the Republic: The Slovenian Government is poorly presented on the web. Only basic information exists about its function, with a list of members (with their telephone numbers and some e-mail addresses) published.

On the President's web-pages, which are also in English, are some speech extracts and interviews, and interestingly, some videos. We did not find any e-mail addresses which would enable citizens to turn to the President of the State with their problems or proposals.

Administrative districts: The web-pages of administrative districts are very similar. Here again is basic information including telephone numbers, office hours, e-mail addresses, organisation structure and description of their duties and competencies.

As is shown in Figure 5, only in some cases are there also descriptions of administrative processes together with legal framework and a list of necessary documents which must be provided by a client. In some cases forms can be downloaded by the public (10% of all administrative districts include at least one). Use of foreign languages is an exception. Only one administrative district has web-pages in English. In some cases there were work reports and statistical data.

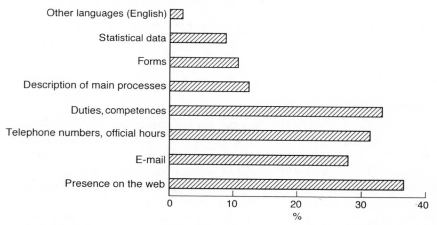

Figure 5. Type of Internet information available from administrative districts

Telematics and Slovenian municipalities: Local administration reform started in 1994 and as a result, instead of 65 municipalities there are now 192. The majority are, however, small and economically weak. The development level of municipalities differs to a great extent, as do the services provided to the citizens, including information services.

Municipalities are part of the local self-government system in Slovenia and are very independent in carrying out local functions and services. This independence can also be seen through their appearance on the web, which varies to a great extent. Out of 192 municipalities in Slovenia, only 31 or 16% of them have their own web-pages. There are several reasons for this small percentage. It appears that some municipalities do not have an appropriate information infrastructure, some do not have adequate financing, and others simply do not bother with the Internet. Present on the web are only those municipalities which existed prior to local administration reform and those who are tourism oriented. Only 11% of all municipalities (68% of those on the web) give the public an opportunity to send questions, proposals, requests, etc. (Figure 6), and surprisingly, only two municipalities describe their functions and competencies.

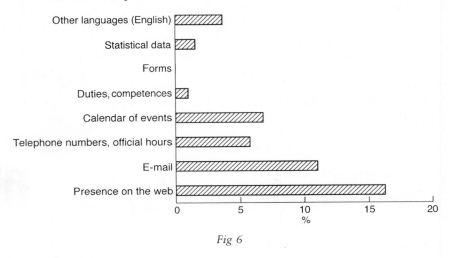

Fig 6

Conclusion

What can we conclude? On the one hand, it can be seen that in Slovenia the Internet definitely has made a 'breakthrough' as a new and important communication channel between parliament, governmental organisations and local authorities and between groups, citizens or voters on the other hand. In this sense we are making first steps towards so-called 'tele-democracy'.[3] However, when we try to evaluate the quality of this information exchange and the motives which lie behind this development and relate it to the capabilities of new communication technologies, then we have less ground to be satisfied. The most important reason why many past regimes have failed is that they were ignorant of the basic information needs and interests of the public. All public media information was strictly state controlled. With the rapid growth of new communication technologies, and the Internet in particular, new hopes were raised — maybe so far in vain? As can be concluded from this chapter, institutions are interested in being present on the Internet and in disseminating a 'good image' about themselves to the public. However, they are much less, if at all, interested in receiving opinion feedback, or even critical remarks, about their work from their customers, although there are the technical means available for so doing.

We cannot avoid the impression that this rush amongst public organisations to use the Internet as a new 'announcement medium' is mainly technology-driven instead of being driven by an honest desire of public organisations that something should be changed in how they communicate with the public in order to stimulate the development of democracy. To summarise, telematics is definitely providing citizens with more in-depth information about the work and actions of public institutions than was the case in the past. Yet the citizens' opportunities to play a more direct and active role in the decision-making process in important common public affairs has so far has changed little.

1   Hyperlink: http://www.sigov.si.
2   M. Jarkovic and R. Krasevec, *Informacijska Infrastrukturai n Internet v Slovenski Javni Upravi* in scientific papers, INDO '97, Portoroz, October 1997, pp. 99–106.
3   M. Ambroz, *Daljinski Dostop v Komunikacij Skem Omorezju Drzavnih Organov* in scientific papers, INDO '97, Portoro, October 1997, pp. 85–6.
4   J.A. Taylor, B. Bardzki and C. Wilson, 'Laying Down the Infrastructure for Innovation in Teledemocracy: The Case of Scotland' in *Orwell in Athens*, W.B.H.J. van de Donk et al. (eds), IOS Press, Amsterdam, 1995, pp. 61–77.

Speaking Up in the Internet Age: Use and Value of Constituent E-mail and Congressional Web-sites

BY MATT CARTER

Introduction

It is often claimed that the Internet has the potential to strengthen the democratic principles upon which our nation is based. One test of that claim is the extent to which offices in the US Congress are using the opportunities provided by the Internet to make their policy positions known to the public and to communicate with their constituents.

As part of its Non-profits' Policy and Technology Project, OMB Watch sent surveys to all Congressional offices asking how they respond to e-mail from constituents. The survey sought to determine whether members take e-mail communication as seriously as other forms of communication and how an e-mail correspondent might most effectively communicate with her or his member. In addition, OMB Watch conducted a review of 70 web-sites operated by House and Senate offices (50 House, 20 Senate). At the time of the review, there were 227 Republicans, 207 Democrats and one Independent in the House of Representatives. In the Senate there were 55 Republicans and 45 Democrats. The review of the web-sites sought to determine how consistently the sites are maintained, how often members use the sites to publicise their policy positions, and how accessible their sites are for constituent interaction.

Despite our attempts to increase the survey response rate through follow-up telephone calls to randomly selected offices, only 37 Congressional offices participated in the survey. Sixty-eight offices stated that they do not respond to surveys at all. As a result, all findings from the survey are not necessarily representative of Congress as a whole. One possible reason for the lack of participation by Congressional offices is survey fatigue. Two other surveys on Congress and use of technology were conducted prior to the OMB Watch survey, one from the *New York Times* and one from Bonner & Associates and American University (both discussed below), that reached offices within a few months of the OMB Watch survey.

Overall, the web-site review and the survey found that Congress has a substantial and growing presence on the Internet but that there has been inadequate response to the possibilities the Internet provides for members to reach and to be responsive to the needs of their constituents. More specific findings include:

Nothing is as effective as personal communications with Congressional offices regarding viewpoints on policy matters. According to the survey, the form of communication that Congressional offices take most seriously when considering a policy position remains the personal letter sent through the mail, followed by personal visits and telephone calls. Communication via fax and e-mail also ranked highly, but considerably below personal visits. This suggests that, as long as fax and e-mail communication have an 'impersonal' feel, they may have difficulty gaining general acceptance from members of Congress.

For e-mail or any other form of communication to be taken seriously, it should be both personalised (as opposed to a form letter) and from a constituent. For all forms of communication, the individual letter or call ranked significantly above the form letter or coordinated call. In addition, many Congressional offices, as well as the House Information Resources office, have indicated that they are creating a means to filter out e-mail that is not from constituents. Most of these filters require using e-mail through the world wide web. This may mean changing the e-mail addresses for all House offices, thereby limiting the ability to e-mail those offices to constituents with web access and those to whom the office chooses to give its address. Many offices that currently use filters (whether automated or by hand) stated that they do not respond to e-mails from non-constituents. This limits the accessibility of members, as citizens outside their districts cannot communicate with them via the Internet, even though they may have valid concerns (such as a question or comment about a member's committee work).

Members are not using e-mail to communicate with their constituents, even when they receive e-mail from constituents. According to a February 1998 survey by Bonner & Associates and the Center for Congressional and Presidential Studies at American University (B&A/ AU), most Congressional offices that receive e-mail do not respond to the letter via e-mail, instead responding via postal mail. The OMB Watch survey further found that most offices that did respond via e-mail only stated that they had received the correspondence and would be responding via postal mail if an address were included. The B&A/ AU study also found that only 15% of Congressional offices used e-mail to 'keep [constituents] up-to-date on issues that may be important to them' (p. 2).

Although e-mail on policy matters does not rank high today in terms of how seriously members take it, it is likely to have a powerful role in the near future. In a 1992 survey by Burson-Marsteller, Congressional offices ranked communication via facsimile very low, claiming that the fax should only be used in emergencies. Today, faxes are quite common and highly regarded in Congress. Although e-mail is newer than faxes, it already ranks as highly as faxes do as a means of communication. Additionally, the general use of e-mail has grown significantly over the past year. Thus, it is not unlikely that e-mail will become a highly accepted form of communication. This change will require Congressional offices to operate in new ways, such as linking e-mail queries to policy position statements on office web-sites and responding to constituents via e-mail.

Although almost all members of Congress have web-sites, these sites vary greatly in quality and accessibility of information. Because there is no standard for what or how information is presented on the web-sites, some members provide detailed, accurate, and timely informa-tion, while other sites are outdated, difficult to navigate, and uninformative. This makes it difficult for a citizen to use the web to find information about their members' stances, as the site may not be updated, or may not contain the information that they are looking for. Even if the site is later updated, the user may not return.

These findings have significant implications for non-profit organisations, which are increasingly working to encourage their members and the public to engage in public policy matters. For example, OMB Watch's web-site contains a service called Activist Central that allows visitors to the site to send e-mail to members of Congress on selected issues. Similar services are offered through the National Education Association, the AFL-CIO, several environmental organisations, such as Defenders of Wildlife, and others.

This research raises many questions about the value of such services in attempting to reach members of Congress other than one's own, or indeed in communicating with one's own members. To the extent that Congressional offices implement filters or keep e-mail addresses private to limit receipt of e-mail to that from constituents, it raises concerns about access in a democratic society. Citizen participation is vital to the health of a democracy, and if a means of participation as direct and accessible as the Internet is not utilised, a great chance for increased participation will be missed.

Background

In its December 1997 issue, *Wired* Magazine published the results of a survey that indicated that people who are most connected to the Internet are also more civically engaged in general, including commenting on public policy issues and voting ('The Digital Citizen', *Wired*, December 1997). According to this model, if we are able to get more people connected to the Internet, we may also be able to reverse the downward trend in political participation that social critics have been examining for more than a decade. In addition, the Internet itself may become a tool for increased citizen participation in public policy matters, along the lines of the 'Electronic Town Hall' that Ross Perot mentioned during his 1992 presidential campaign. In fact, Cokie Roberts and Steven Roberts note this possibility with great trepidation in an 5 April 1997 column in the *Salt Lake Tribune*: 'No more pandering to the big contributors, no more deals between members, just the voice of the people will be heard! . . . We hear that and shudder.'[1]

The Internet makes it possible for citizens to become much more directly involved in the public policy process than ever before. At the same time, it runs the risk of overwhelming Congress with the immediate demands and opinions of the citizenry: direct democracy at its worst. No matter what one's opinions are on the merits of direct democracy, however, the Internet is here and will likely significantly change the way Congress does its job. The primary question left unanswered is how members of Congress will prepare for these changes.

Before this year, virtually no research existed on the use of e-mail to communicate with members of Congress. For example, a 1992 Burson-Marsteller survey did not include e-mail as an option for communicating with Congress. In fact, the survey indicated that such (then) new technologies as fax machines were not useful mechanisms for communicating with Congress because they created frustration among Congressional staffers.[2] The report quotes one staffer as saying: 'It [faxed material] does not get our attention. It's rather offensive.' Another staffer added: '[T]he fax was meant for urgent materials. I find myself, unless we've requested [a fax], almost just throwing the stuff away out of spite.' We wanted to test whether the perceived value of faxes has changed and whether e-mail may go through the same cycle.

The only known survey about e-mail was a *New York Times* survey sent via e-mail in October 1997 to all of the Congressional offices with addresses listed on their web-sites (a total of 261 offices), asking the offices to respond. Seventy per cent of offices did not respond.[3] A second survey, conducted by Bonner & Associates and American University's Centre for Congressional and Presidential Studies (B&A/AU), was released after we conducted our survey. The B&A/AU survey was far more detailed than either the OMB Watch survey or the *New York Times* survey, interviewing 270 Congressional offices on a broad range of issues related to Congressional use of the Internet.[4] The OMB Watch survey focused specifically on how members of Congress use the Internet and e-mail to communicate with constituents.

Additionally, we were concerned about the utility of Congressional web-sites in conveying policy positions. Despite the fact that most Congressional offices have web-sites, there has been no research on the quality of these sites. We focused on how effective the sites are in conveying the member's views on policy and legislative matters.

Web-site review

SUMMARY: OMB Watch chose 50 House members and 20 senators at random and reviewed their web-sites, if they had them. At the time of the review (July 1998), all 100 senators had web-sites, as well as almost 400 House members. The focus of the review was how timely the policy content on the sites was, how easily a visitor could contact the member via the web-site, and how easily a visitor to the site could find information on a member's policy positions. Web-sites were graded on these three criteria, and the results are reported in the appendix.

Not surprisingly, the sites varied widely in all three areas of review, owing at least in part to a lack of a coordinated structure for designing and maintaining web-sites in Congress. Although more than a third (25) of the web-sites were current to within a month, eight appeared to be at least a year out-of-date, and one, Rep. Norman Dicks (D-WA), did not have a web-site at all.

As a note of caution regarding the timeliness of the sites: senators in contested elections are restricted from updating their sites near primary and general elections, and are required to post a notice about this on their sites. This rule exists because the official Senate web-sites are financed at taxpayer expense, and the Senate does not want to risk any campaigning on these sites. Senators in contested elections are not allowed to post any new information, to avoid any argument about what is and is not campaign material. Therefore, it is possible that some of these sites would have been more timely if this were not an election year. The House does not have a similar rule. As the 3 November 1998 election drew near, we revisited the Senate sites to see whether they were following the Senate rule. We found that all of the affected senators were in compliance.

Many sites in both the House and Senate made use of the Library of Congress' search engine, THOMAS, to allow visitors to their sites to find bills sponsored by the member. These sites generally provided a link to THOMAS, and often provided the language for a search for bills sponsored by the member. Some sites instead chose to place bills directly on their sites.

In addition, while many sites contained press releases about the member, often including policy positions, only a few sites contained direct links to voting records. In no case did an office identify upcoming votes and specify his or her views on the bills. Nor was there an opportunity for constituents to express their views on the upcoming bills.

On the other hand, many offices provided policy viewpoints on certain specific issues that may or may not have upcoming votes. Some offices have added search engines to make it easier to find things on their site. Others have explored use of audio and video. A few have received certification of compliance with standards for accessibility to those with disabilities. In general, though, without standards and procedures in place for providing information to visitors to web-sites, it seems unlikely that there will be consistent and comprehensive information available.

Most of the sites offered an opportunity to e-mail the member through the site. Some representatives use a service called Write Your Representative, designed by the House Information Resources office (see below for fuller discussion of this system). The Senate does not have a similar system, although many senators have their own form directly on their site that allows constituents to contact them. Most of these sites either required that the writer input her or his address before sending the e-mail (through Write Your Representative) or requested that the writer include her or his postal address in the e-mail so that the member could respond to the e-mail using postal mail.

Another aspect common to many of the sites was constituent services. Almost all sites included information about the district the member represented and ways for constituents to request services from the member. Two sites, by Rep. Gil Gutknecht (R-MN) and Sen. Harry Reid (D-NV), offered constituents a form on which they could set up meetings with the member. A few sites, such as Sen. Edward Kennedy's (D-MA), also offered such services as an e-mail listserv for constituents.

RESULTS OF WEB REVIEW

Timeliness: Table 1 summarises the timeliness of policy materials that were found on congressional web-sites. In general, the Senate web-sites were much better in being kept up-to-date than the House sites. Ninety per cent of the Senate web-sites had added policy information (e.g. press releases, speeches, position papers) within the last six months B and 45% had added materials that were less than a month old. In comparison, only 69% of the House web-sites had added policy information within the last six months — and only 35% had materials that were less than a month old. Several of the House web-sites had materials on their sites that were not dated, but the content raised questions about how current they were.

There seems to be little difference between the parties with regard to timeliness of materials on the web-site. Thirty-eight per cent of Republican offices and 40% of Democratic offices had the most up-to-date sites B sites where materials have been added within the last month. Roughly one-fifth of Republicans (20.6%) and Democrats (17.1%) do not keep their sites up-to-date, with policy information that is more than six-months-old.

E-mail and interactivity: Some offices make a significant effort to interact with constituents. For example, in addition to e-mail communication, Sen. Judd Gregg (R-NH) has an on-line survey to obtain constituent opinions about the tax code and the efficiency of the IRS. Rep. Sander Levin (D-MI) has an even broader survey to solicit viewpoints of constituents on a broad range of issues from campaign finance reform to tax cuts and balancing the budget to drug abuse to trade issues.

1. Timeliness of Material on Congressional Web-sites (%)			
	Total	GOP	Dems
Congress			
Under 1 month-old	37.7	38.2	40.0
1–5 months-old	37.7	38.2	37.1
6 months or older	18.8	20.6	17.1
No dated material	5.8	2.9	5.7
Total	100.0	100.0	100.0
House			
Under 1 month-old	34.7	40.0	33.3
1–5 months-old	34.7	36.0	33.3
6 months or older	22.4	20.0	25.0
No dated material	8.2	4.0	8.3
Total	100.0	100.0	100.0
Senate			
Under 1 month-old	45.0	33.3	54.5
1–5 months-old	45.0	44.4	45.5
6 months or older	10.0	22.2	0.0
No dated material	0.0	0.0	0.0
Total	100.0	100.0	100.0

The Levin survey also asks constituents to identify high priority legislative issues and to comment on them. While these surveys appear to be innovative and not often used, it is unclear from this research whether these surveys get updated with any regularity. The Gregg survey remained on his web-site even after IRS reform legislation was enacted.

Some are attempting to build on their e-mail communication to strengthen interactivity and dialogue with constituents. For example, Rep. Gil Gutknecht (R-MN) gives constituents an opportunity to register to receive e-mails from the Congressman.

Sen. Patrick Leahy (D-VT) has a robust e-mail form for constituents to use. The user can use a pull-down menu to select whether the senator need not respond or whether the response should be by e-mail or postal mail. The e-mail form also allows the user to indicate through another pull-down menu the general topic of the e-mail, thereby making it easier to sort e-mail to the appropriate staff. A few other Senate offices also use the pull-down menu to identify the general topic.

Not everyone is eager to use e-mail as a means for increasing interactivity. Rep. Barney Frank (D-MA) does not provide an option to e-mail him through his web-site. Instead he posts the following message: 'I do not maintain an E-mail address. The significant increase in mail volume that would result would place too great a strain on my resources and my staff's ability to keep up with their already heavy work load. However, I will, as always, gladly respond to any question, comment or inquiry received by letter or phone call. Thank you.'

Rep. George Gekas (R-PA) also has no option to send him e-mail through his web-site. He lists the address and phone number for his three district offices and his Washington office. He also has an on-line guest book that allows 'visitors' to sign in. The sign-in also requests the visitor's e-mail address, although it does not allow for comments to be sent electronically. Eleven other House members—6 Republicans and 5 Democrats—join Frank and Gekas in not offering e-mail interactivity. Only one Senate member, Dan Coats (R-IN), did not have e-mail services.

Table 2 shows that overall, roughly one-fifth of the Congressional sample sites did not have e-mail, a few more Republicans (20.6%) than

2. E-mail Interactivity from Congressional Web-sites (%)

E-Mail	Total	GOP	Dems
Congress			
With instructions/easy to find	58.0	64.7	51.4
Without instructions/hard to find	18.8	8.8	28.6
Without any instructions	4.3	5.9	2.9
No e-mail	18.8	20.6	17.1
Total	100.0	100.0	100.0
House			
With instructions/easy to find	59.2	64.0	54.2
Without instructions/hard to find	10.2	4.0	16.7
Without any instructions	4.1	4.0	4.2
No e-mail	26.5	28.0	25.0
Total	100.0	100.0	100.0
Senate			
With instructions/easy to find	50.0	55.6	45.5
Without instructions/hard to find	40.0	22.2	54.5
Without any instructions	5.0	11.1	0.0
No e-mail	5.0	11.1	0.0
Total	100.0	100.0	100.0

Democrats (17.1%). Table 2 also provides information about the quality of the e-mail services that are provided. House web-sites had significantly easier to use e-mail services, both in terms of the instructions that were provided and in location on the web-page. Forty per cent of the Senate web-sites had hard-to-find e-mail links; whereas only 10.2% of the House sites were hard to find.

Type of e-mail: Within our sample, there are three ways for constituents to send mail to members. The most basic is the 'Mail To' command, which is a piece of HTML code that acts like a link, but sends an e-mail from the user's web-browser. This can be problematic because not all web-browsers support this feature, and there is no filter to check whether the sender lives in the member's district, which could cause some mail to be ignored without the sender's knowledge, as not all sites ask for the sender's address. The 'Mail To' command is the most popular way for members to receive e-mail from their web-sites, used by most of the senators in the sample (68.4%) and more than a third (38.9%) of representatives.

The second most popular way for members to receive e-mail from their web-sites is through the use of an independent service. The two found in our sample are Write Your Representative, which is run by the House and discussed later in this paper, and Citizen Direct, which is run by an independent organisation. Both of these systems serve as filtering tools, in that a user must enter a postal code within the member's district in order to send mail. Citizen Direct also allows users to set up an electronic 'Communication Center' where they can receive replies from members. This allows those without e-mail accounts to communicate with their member. While no senators in our sample use an independent service, nearly half (47.2%) of the sampled representatives use either Citizen Direct or Write Your Representative.

The third type of device used is a form directly on the member's site. These are similar to those used by Write Your Representative and Citizen Direct in that they generally require the user to enter an address, although the private forms usually do not automatically reject mail from out of the member's district. Some of the forms in the sample also have a feature where the user can select the general issue area they are writing about, possibly speeding up the process of delivery to the correct staff member. Nearly a third (31.6%) of the Senate sites in the sample have their own e-mail form, while few (13.9%) of the sampled House sites use a private form.

Access to policy materials: Most policy materials on Congressional web-sites are press releases, although several offices have begun posting position papers and speeches. For example, Sen. Bob Kerrey (D-NE) posted his New Economic Agenda speech from 17 September 1997 in both text and video formats. The user can click on the video format to see the senator speak before the National Press Club. Kerrey's use of video is quite unusual among web-sites reviewed. Only one other site in the sample — that of Rep. Ernest Istook (R-OK) — used video for explaining policy positions. Audio is also used, mostly in the form of homepage greetings, although Sen. Harry Reid (D-NV) does explain several of his policy positions in audio format.

A few offices, such as Rep. Jim Nussle's (R-IA), provide a link to information about their voting record or statements made in the Congressional Record. However, in virtually every instance the link goes to either the Congressional Quarterly or THOMAS web-site, thereby allowing the user to conduct a search for the voting record. The user must learn the search instructions in order to find the record. Almost all of the sampled sites have a link to bills sponsored and co-sponsored by the member. Most of these are in the form of customised links that query THOMAS and return the bills automatically, however, some sites do not have a customised link, and the user must manually find the bills. Other sites, such as Rep. Terry Everett's (R-AL), list bills that the member sponsored or co-sponsored directly on the site.

In general, it is not easy to find a member's position on a particular policy. Only a few sites, such as Sen. Edward Kennedy (D-MA), have search engines on their sites. Some members, such as Gil Gutknecht (R-MN), do group their press releases by issue area, although many members organise their releases by date.

Some sites in the sample did contain issue papers, most notably Sen.

Patrick Leahy's (D-VT), which has several statements in over 15 issue areas.

Table 3 provides information about the accessibility of policy materials on Congressional web-sites. Most offices (50.7%) had few or hard

3. Access to Policy Materials through Congressional Web-sites (%)

Access to:	Total	GOP	Dems
Congress			
Many substantial press releases with much legislative info.	11.6	11.8	11.4
Many substantial press releases with some legislative info.	31.9	17.6	45.7
Few of buried press releases of substance	40.6	55.9	25.7
Few of buried press releases of little substance	10.1	8.8	11.4
No policy materials	5.8	5.9	5.7
Total	100.0	100.0	100.0
House			
Many substantial press releases with much legislative info.	12.2	16.0	8.3
Many substantial press releases with some legislative info.	30.6	12.0	50.0
Few of buried press releases of substance	36.7	56.0	16.7
Few of buried press releases of little substance	14.3	12.0	16.7
No policy materials	6.1	4.0	8.3
Total	100.0	100.0	100.0
Senate			
Many substantial press releases with much legislative info.	10.0	0.0	18.2
Many substantial press releases with some legislative info.	35.0	33.3	36.4
Few of buried press releases of substance	50.0	55.6	45.5
Few of buried press releases of little substance	0.0	0.0	0.0
No policy materials	5.0	11.1	0.0
Total	100.0	100.0	100.0

to find policy materials; 5.8% had no policy materials available. There seemed to be little difference between House and Senate offices, but large differences between Republicans and Democrats, particularly in the House, where 68% of Republican sites and 33.4% of Democratic sites had few or hard to find policy materials. Of Congressional offices 43.5% had policy materials that were easy to find, with 11.6% of them having very robust access opportunities.

CASE STUDIES OF GOOD SITES: REP. ERNEST ISTOOK AND SEN. BOB KERREY:

Rep. Ernest Istook (R-OK): Rep. Istook's home page is an example of what can be done when a page uses the potential of the web. Visitors are greeted with a short news section containing summaries of new press releases and links to the full story. There is also a weekly column near the top of the page. The rest of the front page is a directory of the remainder of the site, with a short description of each part. This site, unlike most Congressional sites, allows one to go to a specific section in one click, instead of guessing what section information is in.

One particularly interesting section of the page is 'In Congress', which is a central collection of links to the activities of Congress. Real time images from C-SPAN (the cable network that televises congressional proceedings) of both the House and Senate floor are available (although they are only refreshed when the page is reloaded) as well as live streaming audio of both C-SPAN and C-SPAN2. There are links to the day's floor schedule and current proceedings (from the Majority Whip's Office), as well as a link to the day's House Committee meetings (through the Library of Congress). A section labelled 'This Week' contains links to the Majority Whip's weekly notice, a link of all House Chamber action for the past three days, a link to all of the bills up for consideration in both the House and Senate for the week (through the Library of Congress), and a link to House Committee Actions for the past three days. The site also contains a section with links to all bills introduced in the 105th Congress (through the Library of Congress), with the full text of each bill. There is a similar section for the 104th Congress, including all the bills signed into law during the 104th Congress, as well as those vetoed.

Other notable features of the site include a searchable archive of past press releases (which number in the hundreds). There is also a section where one can sign up to receive a periodic e-mail newsletter from Istook. The site also includes a link that searches the Congressional Record for all references to the Congressman.

This site is exemplary not because of any one feature, since many of the components exist on other sites, but because it offers a comprehensive set of services. This site could serve as a model for Congressional offices interested in providing a great amount of information with little staff time being invested. Because the Istook site borrows from a variety of sources, it requires minimal staff time to keep it up-to-date.

Sen. Bob Kerrey (D-NE): Sen. Kerrey's is another example of a good site. It has much information without being cluttered, and is easy to navigate. The most impressive thing about Sen. Kerrey's site is the wealth of information. The press release section has more than a hundred press releases. There is also a section that contains Kerrey's floor statements, dating back to 1989. There are several hundred statements in all. One problem with all this information is the lack of any index. Only one section, 'Kerrey Initiatives' sorts information by subject. The press releases and floor statements are arranged by date, which makes it difficult to find releases on a specific issue, although the site does have a search engine on the front page. There are also several speeches in audio format on the site.

The site contains its own e-mail form, which requires the user's address and asks for an e-mail address, if the user would like an e-mail reply. The innovative feature on this form is a pull-down menu that allows the user to choose from almost 30 general issue areas as the topic for the message. This feature presumably streamlines the communication process by allowing delivery to the proper staff member without reading the message. Another innovation is the 'Ask Bob' column. Constituents can write or e-mail a question and specify that they want it to be part of the 'Ask Bob' column. Kerrey then posts the question and his answer for all to see. As the web-site indicates, the column 'provide[s] Senator Kerrey with yet another opportunity to open a dialogue with Nebraskans and answer questions in a public forum on concerns or questions that other Nebraskans may share'.

One area where the site is lacking is in access to legislative information. There is a link to THOMAS, although it is not customised, and the user must know how to search the system. The link for the senator's voting record takes the user to the Congressional Quarterly VoteWatch site, where the votes must be found manually. This site also contains many Nebraska links, which are not uncommon. Almost every member has a set of links for things such as universities, cities, and sports teams within their district or state. Kerrey also has a 'constituent services' section which details how Nebraskans can order a flag, how to contact his office for internship opportunities, and how to handle problems with the federal government through his office.

Survey on constituent e-mail

OMB Watch sent the survey to each office in the House and Senate and then made follow-up calls to randomly selected offices. The final number of respondents to the survey was 37. The 37 responses to this survey offer an insight into the role of e-mail in legislative offices of Congress today. Thirty-two of the offices reported the ability to receive e-mail, and twenty reported that the volume of e-mail has increased significantly since last year, with most of that increase due to the growing popularity of e-mail around the country.

VALUE OF E-MAIL: Respondents were asked to rank the importance of various forms of communication from constituents when considering a policy position. Letters ranked highest, with personal visits and telephone calls following. Faxes and e-mails ranked highly, but below these more traditional forms of communication. Scoring poorly in the survey were petitions, sign-on letters, and post card campaigns, with form letters via e-mail receiving the lowest marks of all.

In addition, the survey compared the amount of attention that members give to various forms of communication in considering a policy position. The results were quite similar to the questions on importance of the forms, with letters receiving a great deal of attention from almost two-thirds of respondents. The only form of communication which any respondent reported giving no attention to is e-mail, with one respondent reporting this.

RESPONDING TO CONSTITUENT E-MAIL: The majority of offices that receive e-mail reported that they send an automated reply via e-mail promising a fuller reply via postal mail. Almost all offices print their e-mail before responding, reflecting a lack of an efficient means of identifying constituent e-mail and responding to it. The B&A/AU survey found that about a quarter of offices respond to e-mail by both e-mail and postal mail, while more than 70% respond by postal mail only.

DESIRABILITY OF E-MAIL: Respondents noted that e-mail is both easier and more timely than other modes of communication with members, allowing constituents to share their views directly with their members. Others noted that e-mail is also very inexpensive and provides greater access to the member.

PROBLEMS WITH E-MAIL: The OMB Watch survey and the B&A/AU survey clearly indicate that members of Congress are very concerned about being overwhelmed by e-mail. Precisely because it is so easy and quick to use, it is far more likely that someone will e-mail her or his member rather than taking the time to write a letter, put it into an envelope, put a stamp on it, and mail it. Many respondents indicated that this is why they rank e-mail lower than other forms of communication.

Another significant problem respondents identified is the possibility of spamming, or writing to every member at the same time with little or no effort. Because it is often less easy to tell who is sending an e-mail than who is sending a letter, respondents expressed concern about being overwhelmed by coordinated efforts by interest groups to reach them, at the expense of constituents.

A final major concern about e-mail raised in the OMB Watch survey relates to its immediacy. Because constituents can send e-mail so quickly, they often expect to get a response just as quickly. In addition, e-mail encourages what one respondent called 'chatters', or constituents who e-mail whenever some idea hits them, sometimes as often as several times a day. Some of these 'chatters' also make requests that are very time consuming, such as asking for detailed policy positions from the member on a different issue each day, making it much more difficult for staff to respond to all of the letters they receive.

WRITE YOUR REPRESENTATIVE: In response to these concerns, the House Information Resources office has created a web-based e-mail system that all House offices can use, called Write Your Representative. Through the member's web-site, or through the Write Your Representative site itself, a visitor can type in her or his postal code and then send an e-mail to the member who represents that area. In this way, a person can send an e-mail without even knowing the name of her or his representative.

According to Reynold Schweickhardt, a former staffer in the House Information Resources office and one of the founders of Write Your Representative, the House will soon be replacing its current e-mail addresses <*name@mail.house.gov*> with new addresses that will not be made publicly available unless the individual offices choose to publicise them. This will likely significantly reduce the amount of spam and also make it far easier to reduce out-of-district e-mails.

The Senate does not currently have a system similar to Write Your Representative, but many Senate offices, as well as some House offices, use a similar private system called Citizen Direct. At this point, there does not seem to be a plan to coordinate efforts across the chambers.

Unanswered questions and areas for further research

This study has raised several questions that require further investigation. First, the web review indicated substantial unevenness in both quantity and quality of Congressional web-sites. Should Congress set standards for the type of information, layout of sites, and accessibility of the member via the site, and if so, how should this be done? What would the implications of such standards be?

Second, since members reported in the survey that they often do not respond to e-mail from non-constituents, how can a citizen or non-profit public interest group contact a member of a congressional committee if they are not a constituent of that member? Particularly if Congressional offices move toward limiting electronic access to their offices, will committee staff be more available?

Third, it may be useful to test Congressional responses to e-mail sent from a variety of sources. This study included sending e-mail to several Congressional offices as sample tests, but virtually no response was received. A more comprehensive test would be quite revealing in terms of actual versus reported interest by Congressional offices in receiving e-mail comments from constituents.

Also, several recent legislative battles have included an e-mail component. Examining the effect of e-mail on these campaigns B both in terms of whether it increased citizen participation in the efforts and in terms of how members responded would be instructive to groups considering making e-mail part of their campaign repertoire.

Finally, to what extent do the results of this research extend to state legislatures? Anecdotal evidence indicates that faxes are unpopular in some state legislatures because offices often share a fax machine. Therefore, e-mail may be preferable to faxes in reaching a state legislator.

Technological advances such as the Internet and e-mail present members of Congress with great opportunities to increase their ability to communicate with and to effectively represent their constituents, but members of Congress are very nervous about how to take advantage of these tools without being overwhelmed by them. Congress must begin thinking about how to deal with advances in communications technology in ways that promote effective democracy.

One possible way to address some of the overload would be for

Congress to recommend policies and procedures for web-sites and to offer training on web design as part of training for new members. Recommendations might include maintaining a broad range of policy statements and voting records on members' web-sites, along with a search engine that would allow visitors to find information. In addition, e-mail responding to constituent questions could then point the constituent to the site. It might even be possible to create an auto-responder for this process, although that would require significant development.

The message for non-profit organisations and for citizens is that, although e-mail is not now as well regarded as personal letters, its popularity and regard are likely to increase significantly. At the same time, the advent of e-mail requires even greater attention to traditional advice about communicating with a member of Congress: be clear, be brief, and be a constituent.

Appendix: Web-site Review Scorecard
House

Member name	How timely*	Ease/quality of information**	Ease of contacting†	Type of e-mail‡
Thomas Barrett (D-WI)	4	3	2	A
Roscoe Bartlett (R-MD)	3	2	0	n/a
Howard Berman (D-CA)	3	4	4	B
Kevin Brady (R-TX)	4	3	2	O (own form)
Donna Christian-Green (D-VI)	0	1	2	A, B
Bob Clement (D-TN)	4	3	3	A
Diana DeGette (D-CO)	3	2	4	C
Jay Dickey (R-AR)	3	2	3	A
Norman Dicks (D-WA)	no site	no site	no site	no site
Terry Everett (R-AL)	4	2	3	A
Thomas Ewing (R-IL)	2	2	3	B
Jon Fox (R-PA)	4	2	1	A
Barney Frank (D-MA)	2	3	0	n/a
George Gekas (R-PA)	1	2	0	n/a
Paul Gillmor (R-OH)	1	1	0	n/a
Ben Gilman (R-NY)	4	2	4	C
Bart Gordon (D-TN)	0	0	3	A
Gil Gutknecht (R-MN)	4	4	3	B
Darlene Hooley (D-OR)	4	2	2	A
Henry Hyde (R-IL)	n/a	0	0	n/a
Ernest Istook (R-OK)	3	3	4	O (own form)
Barbara Kennelly (D-CT)	4	3	3	A
Ron Klink (D-PA)	3	2	0	n/a
John LaFalce (D-NY)	4	3	4	B
Steven LaTourette (R-OH)	4	3	4	B
Jim Leach (R-IA)	4	2	3	A, B
Sander Levin (D-MI)	1	4	4	B
Jerry Lewis (R-CA)	3	2	0	n/a
Thomas Manton (D-NY)	n/a	1	3	A
Ed Markey (D-MA)	3	3	4	B
Matthew Martinez (D-CA)	2	3	4	B
Robert Menendez (D-NJ)	0	0	0	n/a
Jim Nussle (R-IA)	4	4	4	B
Solomon Ortiz (D-TX)	0	1	0	n/a
Richard Pombo (R-CA)	0	2	3	A
Deborah Pryce (R-OH)	3	2	3	A

Jack Quinn (R-NY)	4	2	0	n/a
Frank Riggs (R-CA)	1	1	3	A, B
Bob Riley (R-AL)	2	4	3	A, C
Tim Roemer (D-IN)	4	3	1	A
Edward Royce (R-CA)	2	2	4	B
Charles Schumer (D-NY)	3	2	0	
Pete Sessions (R-TX)	4	4	4	O (own form)
David Skaggs (D-CO)	4	3	3	A
Louise Slaughter (D-NY)	3	3	4	O (own form)
Gerald Solomon (R-NY)	0	1	0	n/a
John Tanner (D-TN)	0	3	2	O (own form)
Gene Taylor (D-MS)	n/a	1	0	n/a
John Tierney (D-MA)	4	3	4	B
Fred Upton (R-MI)	3	2	3	A

Senate

Joseph Biden (D-DE)	4	2	2	A
Richard Bryan (D-NV)	3	2	2	A
Robert Byrd (D-WV)	4	3	2	A
John Chafee (R-RI)	4	3	3	A
Dan Coats (R-IN)	1	2	0	n/a
Susan Collins (R-ME)	4	2	2	A
Pete Domenici (R-NM)	0	0	2	A
Wendell Ford (D-KY)	3	2	2	A
Robert Graham (D-FL)	4	2	3	A
Judd Gregg (R-NH)	3	3	3	A, O (own form)
Edward Kennedy (D-MA)	4	2	2	A
Robert Kerrey (D-NE)	4	3	4	O (own form)
Patrick Leahy (D-VT)	3	4	4	A, O (own form)
Mitch McConnell (R-KY)	3	2	1	A
Carol Moseley-Braun (D-IL)	4	4	4	O (own form)
Jack Reed (D-RI)	3	3	4	A, O (own form)
Harry Reid (D-NV)	3	3	2	A
Jeff Sessions (R-AL)	4	3	3	A
Robert Smith (R-NH)	3	2	4	O (own form)
Ted Stevens (R-AK)	3	2	3	A

* 0, more than 1 year-old; 1, 6–12 months-old; 2, 3–5 months-old; 3, 1–2 months-old; 4, under 1 month-old; n/a, could not find any dated information.

** 0, no press releases/issue statements; 1, few/buried press releases of little substance; 2, few/buried press releases of substance; 3, many substantial press releases with some information on sponsored bills; 4, many substantial press releases with interface to sponsored bills/voting record, (note: this is a subjective ranking, and situations not covered, such as a site with few Press Releases or Issue Statements but with links to Voting Records and Floor Statements would be given a higher rank).

† 0, no e-mail; 1, e-mail in 'mailto' format without any instructions (i.e. 'please include address'); 2, e-mail in 'mailto' format with instructions/form interface but hard to find; 3, e-mail in 'mailto' format with instructions and easy to find; 4, form interface that is easy to find, (note: form interface includes 'Write Your Representative', Citizen Direct or the office's own form).

‡ A, 'mailto' format (HTML code that sends simple e-mail through the user's browser); B, 'Write Your Representative'; C, Citizen Direct, O, other.

1   'Internet Could Become a Threat to Representative Government', *Salt Lake Tribune*, 5.4.97, p. A–11.
2   'Communicating with Congress 1992: A Survey of Congressional Offices', Burson-Marsteller, *World-wide*, June 1992.
3   'More Members Are Plugged In, But Few Are Making Connections', *New York Times*, 5.1.98.
4   For more information, visit American University's Center for Congressional and Presidential Studies web-site: *http://www.american.edu/academic.depts/spa/ccps/Research.htm*

Bridging the Gap between Parliament and Citizen — the Internet Services of the German Bundestag

BY PETER MAMBREY, HANS-PETER NEUMANN AND KERSTIN SIEVERDINGBECK

Introduction

The German Bundestag is the supreme legislative authority in German constitutional law. Since 15 January 1996 the Bundestag has had its own homepage (http://www.bundestag.de) on the world wide web. On that day the web-site was presented to the press by the President of the German Bundestag concurrent with the setting up of an Inquiry Commission on 'New Media: Germany's way into the information society'. The introduction of Internet Technology was aimed in two directions: internally, to aid the immediate work of MPs and externally to make information available to the public as part of public relations. This chapter reports on the external function. Apart from informing citizens, the new digital media were introduced as a means to make parliament more responsive to citizens than before. This was a qualitative step towards a new relationship with the public beyond offering information.

In this chapter we shall consider the history, content, and experiences of the last three years. It will be shown that the Internet Services, as powerful and well-accepted communication channels, managed to close the gap between parliament and citizens. We are at an early stage of the introduction and use of these technologies. The potential of the digital media as tools for new ways of public relations are obvious. Their development has to be shaped, with the public in mind, as an evolutionary long-term project.

The potential of information and communication technologies (ICTs) for political use

Networked digital media offer numerous windows of opportunity to enhance communication between individuals, groups, and organisations. We are at an early stage of adopting and shaping information and communication technologies (ICTs) for social and political use. However, radical shifts happen in the manner in which individuals work, conduct their business, learn, and are entertained. New guiding visions are coming forth, like 'e-commerce', 'cyber-democracy', 'digital government', etc.[1] On the other hand, new concerns emerge about jeopardising privacy, identity, and inclusion. In recent sociotechnical and -economic developments, politics and parliaments are involved twofold: as part of the governance of ICTs, and as application fields in their own right. Digital media provide the following potential:

— Possibility of multi-directional interaction: ICTs support mass communication as well as communication between individuals. Everybody can 'send and receive', no hierarchy dominates;
— Time and space are losing importance: The combination of text, video, sound, and the enormous, steadily growing amount of accessible data enhance the individuals' capacity for action and perception;
— Digital storage, reproduction and distribution capabilities open up chances never seen with paper as a medium;
— Networking via computers and shared protocols are only limited by infrastructure, no longer by national borders.

These four points illustrate the *technical* potentials. The *social* and *political* goals and perspectives are still to be developed and applied. Although this has been happening for some time now, it will need constant attention.

ICTs in the German Bundestag

In the 1960s, the German Bundestag started to use ICTs for administrative purposes. In 1968 its Executive Committee decided to develop a documentation and information system for parliamentary materials based on ICTs. This marked the beginning of activities which aimed at using new digital media as strategic tools for parliamentary work. Three stages were planned. Firstly, the development of a computerised documentation and information system for the Bundestag's parliamentary materials; secondly, the obtaining of information from external data bases; and thirdly, a simulation of the consequences of laws based on econometric models. The latter succeed neither in the Bundestag nor in federal ministries, probably because the expectations of the quality of the predictions were too high. All these activities were the responsibility of the administration supporting MPs in their daily work. According to the dominant computing philosophy of that time, the technical foundation consisted of centralised mainframes. The service concept followed the idea that staff personnel provide services to the MPs with the assistance of computers. The guiding vision was that men served men using computers as tools.

This changed in the mid-1980s when MPs asked for decentralised, local and personal support by ICTs. In 1985 an initiative was undertaken by MPs to have direct and personal access to ICTs provided by the German Bundestag. A commission of the Executive Committee was founded, 'Assisting MPs by information and communication technologies and media in the German Bundestag and the constituencies'. An in-depth study was carried out about the aims and consequences of the use of computers for parliamentarians which showed the options and risks of their introduction and application. The results were then discussed under different perspectives.[2] Based on this study and by the agreement of all parliamentary groups, the Executive Committee decided to introduce ICTs to assist the work of MPs in their offices, both in the Bundestag and in their constituencies. Within five years computers became everyday tools for parliamentary work. Whilst in 1985 only two MPs used word processors for their work, based on their own initiatives at the beginning of 1990 most of the offices (400) in Bonn and in the constituencies were equipped with and used the new facilities. Administrative staffing support training for and maintenance of the applications grew during this time from zero to nearly one hundred officers. This rapid development and spread of ICTs within the organisation coincided with paradigm shifts in the perception of how ICTs might be best utilised.

From the beginning, ICTs were a tool of the administration to assist MPs indirectly. Later, MPs used ICTs as a direct personal tool for themselves. This led to a new role for the legislator, as he became a direct and autonomous user of ICTs, although most MPs relied on their personal staff. Thus ICTs started as technology for experts and became technology for everybody. At the early stages, i.e. the phase of office automation, computers were mainly used for word-processing, layout and copying.

A second phase saw ICTs increasingly used as communication channels, i.e. to send or disseminate and receive information and to integrate MPs into his or her information network independent of his or her physical location. MPs came into immediate reach whenever they wished to be on-line. This was the phase of 'tele-cooperation'.

The phase we are now entering sees ICTs as a means to reach audiences directly, without being dependent on intermediaries like mass media. ICTs link people and groups, and establish communities. Perhaps we may call this the phase of ICT-omni-presence.

This development took place in three parallel organisational groups of parliament: There is the administration of the Bundestag, the staff of the groups (factions) of the Bundestag, and the MPs themselves. In the mid-1980s the factions' staff developed 'faction management systems' for their members, and in the beginning of the 1990s they started to provide services for them. The Internet services as they exist now derived from experiments with an interactive videotext service to provide information both to parliamentarians and citizens. Being part of the central data processing staff, these activities using Teletext and now T-On-line, gave birth to the services. These experiments started in 1978 but the concepts suffered from a limited number of users caused by the limited acceptance and possibilities of this technology at that time. The Internet offered the technological breakthrough for these ideas and was used as the new technical foundation for the public relations activities.

Internal and external aims of Internet applications of the German Bundestag

New uses of ICTs and their applications are constantly emerging. The Internet opens up new opportunities by immediately linking people to documents and people to people. Computers using the same protocols (TCP/IP) can interconnect and exchange information regardless of time and distance. In March 1999, a survey[3] reported that nearly 20% of the German population 'surf' the Internet. Over nine million citizens have Internet access in their offices and 5.4 million in their homes. The numbers are steadily increasing. From the perspective of parliament's administration the Internet can be used for internal and external purposes. The German Bundestag established explicit aims for the internal and external use of the Internet.

INTERNAL AIMS — ASSISTING THE IMMEDIATE WORK OF MPS: Specific sub-goals are:

Providing easier access to outside resources for MPs;

Providing easier access to internal information services such as Bundestag Materials Documentation and Information System (DIP), legislation in progress (GESTA) materials, press agency announcements, daily press-documentation files (via the Intranet-Services);

Providing message transmission via Internet mail.

EXTERNAL AIMS — ENHANCING THE RELATIONSHIP BETWEEN PARLIAMENT AND CITIZENS: For public relations four main goals were established:

Increasing accessibility to the Bundestag by the public: i.e. developing the means whereby the public can contact the Bundestag directly through an easy-to-manage address, an e-mail function and other dialogue applications such as brochure ordering, and the mailing list;

New and different presentation of the Bundestag using new media: actually presenting Bundestag information in live multimedia form with pictures and networked information (optionally including sound and video);

Broadening participation of citizens by providing actual and authentic information on the Bundestag to stimulate interest in further parliamentary work;

Bolstering transparency of events in parliament to make them less time-dependent: e.g. transcripts of plenary debates can be downloaded the following day.

The Internet services being part of the administration and under parliamentary control of the Executive committee of the House, has made them a real challenge: they require high standards in trust, authenticity, and balance of information. Privacy concerns of the public have to be taken seriously.

Contents of the Internet services: The German Bundestag home page comprises an 'information section' (right column on web-page) and an 'interactive section' (left-side column on web-page):

The 'information section'

Focus — im blick

New material is provided from the public-relations field. Announcements of on-line conferences, telephone campaigns, dates of public-relations events in the constituencies, e.g. mobile exhibitions are displayed. *Focus* provides details of non-routine events in the plenary chamber and covers topics such as 'politics and the arts'. The special section 'Go to vote in '98', focussing on the recent elections with much information and many events, has found a home in *Focus*.

Topical matters — aktuelles

Parliament-related information is presented in a variety of ways: the House's own press service 'hib' (*heute im bundestag* (Today in Parliament)) and 'wib' (*woche im bundestag* (The week in Parliament)) are currently being replaced by 'Focus on the Bundestag', which will also be available on-line. The agenda of the plenary chamber with all matters for discussion in their most up-to-date form and transcripts of plenary debates for downloading are posted here. The facility for downloading transcripts of plenary debates and the Official Transactions in full-text give everyone the means of being fully up-to-date on events in parliament only one day after the debate.

Members — abgeordnete

All information about the people's representatives: there is a 'Who is my MP?', interactive search by federal states, constituencies and local lists; there are biographies of all MPs from A to Z; information subject to statutory public disclosure; results in constituency or State lists, committee membership; statistics (e.g. women in parliament). Since February 1998, MPs can set up their own home page here (within the German Bundestag service) or establish a link to their home page with another service-provider. At the moment 120 MPs make use of this facility.

Organs — gremien

This page provides a tour through the entire Bundestag: the 'Presidium' and Council of Elders with their functions, listing of all standing committees, committees of investigation, commissions of inquiry and their composition; information about parliamentary commissioners for the armed forces etc. The idea behind this site is to inform the public about the activities, groups, and organisations, which form the parliament.

Europe — Europa

This section provides information on Europe, international affairs, interparliamentary relations, and election dates in the EU. Details and application forms for the German Bundestag exchange programme for young people can be ordered.

Information library — infothek

This section provides primary data from the public relations site and regular events. Also available are calendars of parliamentary meetings, electoral procedures, election dates and results, a history of parliament, the Constitution, information on legislative procedure and details of vacancies in the administration. Even job announcements can be found here. Also available are links to national and international organisations.

Databases — datenbanken

This is a gateway to the Documentation and Information system for parliamentary events (DIP) which contains the index of subjects and speakers, the full text of publications and plenary transcripts and the progress of legislation (GESTA). The 'World Directory of Parliamentary Libraries', which is a catalogue covering all the parliamentary libraries in the world, can also be accessed. In addition, wide-ranging data on party finance; an A to Z of parliamentary terms; and the public list of registered organisations and their representatives (lobby list), are available.

Berlin — Berlin

This contains information about the *Reichstag* building, and other information about the German Bundestag buildings in Berlin and the new 'Parliament in the Capital'. The section also gives details about events in the Berlin visitor service and the exhibition 'Questions addressed to German History'. The current 'relocation dates' describe the German Bundestag's move from Bonn to Berlin.

English version

The service also provides an English version. Via a Union Jack icon on the home page one can access general information on the functioning and working of the German Bundestag in English, and also a list of MPs with references to German biographies. Visitors to the English home page can also put their names down on-line to visit the Bundestag and order the English publications from the public-relations department directly. A French version is at planning stage. Finally, there is a gateway to the services of the parliamentary groups and factions.

The 'interactive section'

The interactive services can be found on the left-hand-side of the Bundestag homepage and they are represented by special icons to make them intuitively understandable.

Web-TV — web-TV live

Since October 1998, the German Bundestag has been offering its plenary sessions live via web-TV in cooperation with the Multimedia Centre of German Telekom. Using RealNetworks' video streaming technology and a powerful video-server-architecture through German Telekom, the television signal from the Bundestag is transmitted live onto the Internet throughout the session. Depending on the type of access available (analogue modem or ISDN), Internet users can choose from two video qualities (20 kbit/s and 45 kbit/s). There have been times that up to 500 made use of this service simultaneously, during the constituent meeting of the Bundestag. The videotext service of the German Bundestag will also be integrated in the Internet transmission in future, and an on-line archive will be set up to retrieve speeches through a keyword search. In June 1998 a peak of 1232 users 'clicked into' the debate on 'German unity', all within two hours. The high line costs for such live transmissions paid by the users is an obstacle which still has to be faced. The majority of users do in principle welcome web-TV.

On-line conferences — diskussionsforen

For the last three years, the Divisions On-line Services and Public Relations have been offering on-line conferences as a service for parliamentary bodies (usually committees). These conferences do not take the form of a normal Internet chat running under IRC software, but are based on a software module which was programmed specifically for this purpose and requires nothing more than an Internet browser in order to participate. In this way, between two and five MPs can answer the questions asked by Internet users on a current topic for one to two hours at regular intervals. This new public relations medium proved to be particularly successful in the run-up to the Bundestag elections, when the chairmen of the parliamentary groups of the parties represented in the Bundestag each made use of the services of the on-line debate with the public on several occasions. Often, far more questions are received than an MP can answer in the time available. In that case, the remaining questions are printed out and delivered to the MP's office.

Mailing list — mailingliste

A mailing list was created in order to provide information on new developments for those members of the Internet community who are particularly interested in politics. It has been in use for over two years now and currently includes some 16,000 subscribers. This mailing list keeps the reader posted on exhibitions and meetings that are open to the public, as well as new publications from the Public Relations Division. On-line conferences are also announced via this channel.

On-line registration for visits to the Bundestag — Besuchen sie uns

The possibility of booking a real visit to the German Bundestag is available as a special service for virtual Bundestag visitors. One to three visitors can reserve a one-hour visit to a plenary debate on the available dates offered in a list box. This presupposes that all the personal details of the visitors are given, so that they can be checked by the security service beforehand. This facility is well appreciated by Internet users.

Mail box: e-mail and delivery service — briefkasten

The least spectacular, but most frequently used element in the field of the interactive services is the electronic mailbox. An average of 25–30 messages per day are received here, although the figure can be as high as 100 on peak days. The special feature is that all e-mail is handled via predefined e-mail forms. These have to be sent singly, in order to reduce, or virtually eliminate, the problem of so-called 'mail bombs'. Another advantage of this method is that every citizen can send an e-mail to the Bundestag from any computer, without the necessity to have their own e-mail address. To avoid the Internet users having to wait too long for a reply, a reply mail is sent automatically as soon as a message is received, indicating to the originator of the message that it may take several days for their mail to be forwarded and processed.

Ordering information materials — infomaterial

All material available in printed form or all CD-ROMs can be ordered on-line through this function.

FTP download files — download (FTP)

This sector of the Internet services gives a day-by-day review of everything that happens in the plenary session of the Bundestag. The stenographic minutes can be downloaded individually onto a PC either in the form of Winword documents or as PDF files, arranged according to date, or searches can be conducted in them on the basis of individual items of the agenda. There are plans to introduce a separate search engine for this sector in the future. Publication of the official record one day after the parliamentary debate rounds off the information on the proceedings in parliament. Special occasions, such as Nelson Mandela's speech before parliament during the last electoral term, or the final reports of study commissions, are also available to interested users via this function.

Full-text search — suche

The entire Internet content of the German Bundestag is accessible via its own search engine. Apart from full-text search, one may use a thesaurus.

Use and users: some statistics

One evaluation criterion to assess the offers of an Internet service is the use by its clients. In the following we distinguish between a 'hit' and a 'session'. A hit is a download of a page and a session is the temporary presence of a user in the domain. During a session, a user typically downloads (hits) several pages. The duration of a session and the time and date can be measured.

HITS: In the first year users accessed Bundestag pages about 3.5 million times altogether (hits). In the second year hits almost tripled to 10.1 million, and in the third year a total of 28.6 million hits were counted. In the 'hot phase', preceding and following the Bundestag elections (September, October and November 1998) more than 11.4 million hits were measured within these three months.

The first figures of hits from 1999 show a steadily growing amount based on the figures of the average development (between 2.5 and 2.7 million hits per month). The peak during the election time shows how useful citizens regarded the services as an up-to-date and authentic source. Although the mass media reported continuously during this time, the hits rose dramatically. This may imply that citizens prefer using the Internet to inform themselves. However, there doesn't seem to be a competition between existing mass media and the new services. They don't substitute existing media channels but add the authentic voice of parliament.

SESSIONS: The number of sessions (users) relates to the number of hits. In January 1998 more than 76,000 sessions took place. In December 1998 over 118,000 users were counted. During the election month of September 165,000 users visited the pages. The average duration of a session was 13.5 minutes. This leads us to assume that people tend to explore and are willing to spend time on it.

It is surprising that there is hardly any difference in time spent on-line between weekdays and weekend, or between working hours and leisure time. This emphasises the necessity for services being constantly accessible around the whole week and for 24-hours-a-day. Approximately 56% users visited the pages during working hours and 44% during leisure time. It shows that the users expect up-to-date information.

THE USERS: In spring 1997 a user survey was conducted with the object of matching the technical presentation and content of the Internet services even more closely to the wishes and requirements of the public. Over 2,400 users completed a questionnaire. At the beginning of 1999 a second survey was undertaken to learn more from the users. More than 2,600 users replied. Although the amount of answers was surprisingly high compared to other surveys[4] done via the Internet they are *not representative* but simply show the most active users who are willing to comment on existing services and to participate in shaping future applications.

GENDER: The average user is male (86.2%). Only 13.2% of those who responded were women although approximately 31% of Internet users in Germany are female. The astonishing fact is that within two years there was nearly no change towards a more equal use of technology and resources. The percentage of female users grew only about 1.2%. The educational level of men and women is both high and similar. Surveys of the information behaviour of the German population do not report on such great differences in using media such as TV, newspapers, or radio. If the gender-specific information behaviour is not media dependant, other factors come into consideration. An explanation could lie in the differences between the genders in availability, access, and attitudes towards new digital media. This gap between genders is still open to interpretation and solutions are needed to make the services more attractive and accessible for female users.

AGE: The survey from 1997 showed two big groups of users: those up to 25 years and those from 25 to 35 years each represented more than one third of the total. But in the 1999 survey a decrease of nearly 13% can be analysed. The percentage of those aged under 20 years stayed the same. The highest users are the groups of those older than 35 years. The average user grew older. Actually 20% of the users are aged 35–45 years. 12 % are between 45–55 and approximately 5% are older than 56 years. Despite the frequent assumption that it is 'computer kids' who make up the majority of Internet surfers we see a more balanced curve and a greater acceptance of the Internet services by older users.

EDUCATION: In 1997 more than half of all users had a university degree (technical university: 36.7%, university 15.8%) and almost 30% had A-levels. In 1999 the percentage of those with technical university diploma grew by 2.4% but the other groups with higher education fell by 6%. Almost 20% of the users now have education levels below A.

The percentage is growing. This is a hopeful sign that Internet use is becoming more popular within broader parts of the population.

FREQUENCY OF USE: In 1997 the number of first-time users was slightly greater than that of frequent users. Over 40% of users returned quite frequently (40.9%) and 15.2% regarded themselves as regular users. These numbers changed very much. In 1999 almost 43% described themselves as regular users, almost the same percentage regarded themselves as frequent users and the percentage of the first-time users dropped to 13.2%. This shows that the services did not only attract attention because they are new. Citizens regard them as helpful resources and visit them frequently.

REASONS FOR USE: The biggest group (36.3%) was looking for overall information about the parliament, 30% searched for specific information and 13% were looking for actual up-to-date information. Besides these main reasons there are other aspects which attract the public to visit the pages: educational aspects (11.2%), taking part in discussions, arguing, and having contacts (5%). 3.6% hit the pages because of their professional work, as many as those motivated by fun and curiosity.

Conclusion

The access figures and user comments are evidence that the Internet Service has succeeded in becoming a valuable medium for citizens within a short time. New forms of interaction broadened existing public relations of the parliament for citizens. The ease of access to information of the Bundestag, the immediacy, and download facilities are well used as new forms which mitigate or even bridge the gap between a parliamentary institution and the citizen. The aims defined by the German Bundestag are challenges to shape and constantly reshape the Internet Service according to the wishes and needs of the Internet users if the public is to be offered an optimal parliamentary service. We want to comment briefly on the guiding visions mentioned before as criteria for successful public relations.

ENHANCING THE ACCESSIBILITY OF THE BUNDESTAG BY THE PUBLIC: Public relations via the traditional media was used by two groups: pupils and teachers as well as the elderly. Using digital media, another group became active which hitherto had not been particularly represented, i.e. well educated persons between 25–40 years of age who are busy in their daily work. This group used to be unable, due to lack of time, to visit meetings or study information materials. The Internet offers them new ways of access. Distance is no barrier any more. This group shows a great interest especially in the interactive section. Another group benefits from the services as well, the physically impaired. The results of the surveys show the great level of contentment with the services.

Nevertheless, there is always the demand for new and more documents, applying new interface designs to enhance navigation and use, and there is always the demand for quicker downloads and greater server capacity. The high expectations of users with respect to future design and technical expansion are evident.

NEW AND DIFFERENT PRESENTATION OF THE BUNDESTAG USING NEW MEDIA: A mailing list was created and steadily grows. Web-TV sessions were shown and are rated positively by the citizens despite high transmission costs. On-line conferences were introduced as a new public relations medium. Debates of these on-line conferences were often disseminated by several other mailing in addition to the services' lists and by news groups so that success is even greater than measured by the number of participants.

BROADENING THE PARTICIPATION OF CITIZENS BY PROVIDING ACTUAL AND AUTHENTIC INFORMATION AND STIMULATING INTEREST IN FURTHER WORK: The more information presented on the Internet the more problems will arise to identify authentic and up-to-date information, regardless of whether we are dealing with a parliamentary web-site or that of any other organisation. Fakes make it unclear for the citizen on which information they can rely. Only the Bundestag can speak for itself, while other information providers select and control in respect to their perspectives and goals. Control and ownership of the media will become a major aspect for a democratic society. In establishing its own channels, the Bundestag guarantees a voice of its own to the public which is exempt from the influences of private groups. Furthermore, the Bundestag can guarantee privacy and anonymity for those who participate in the services.

BOLSTERING THE TRANSPARENCY OF EVENTS: This service relates to the new forms of providing information and easier access. It lowers the hurdles of time-dependent access and therefore offers an additional way to information.

A lot of goals have been achieved, as shown in this chapter. Overall, in their short time of existence, the German parliamentary Internet Services have become a reliable medium for a growing percentage of citizens. They have used the Internet as an inclusive medium which addresses all citizens. That is why efforts have to be undertaken to enhance the participation of female users, citizens with lower educational levels, and groups which are stimulated in their interests by 'infotainment' and the like. Is the digital, interactive parliament the future for the citizen? Whether one agrees or not, the principles of visibility, interaction, and responsiveness as guiding visions of a democratic parliament can be enhanced by Internet technologies if this is desired by politics. Of course, it will not create the hyperactive political citizen but it enhances the mutual awareness of Parliament and citizens. Public relations for parliaments should be developed as a forum for public dialogue and not as a hi-tech poll for measuring the shifting currents of popular opinion.

1   H. Schorr and S.S. Stolfo, 'A Digital Government for the 21st Century', *Communications of the ACM 1998*, 41/11, 1999, pp. 15–19.
2   Abschlußberichte 1–5, Studien der GMD, St Augustin, PARLAKOM, 1986.
3   'Studie der Gesellschaft für Konsumforschung', *Computer Zeitung*, Nr. 19/4, 1999.
4   *Electronic Democracy — A Literature Survey*, paper prepared for the Kettering Foundation. London, Scott, March 1994.

The Danish Parliament Going Virtual

BY KARL LÖFGREN, KIM V. ANDERSEN AND METTE FRITHIOF SØRENSEN

Introduction

On 10 October 1997 the Danish Parliamentary web-site was posted on the world wide web. Democratic ambitions deriving from a web presence have, in Denmark as elsewhere, resided in rhetoric surrounding the introduction of the parliamentary web-site. This rhetoric has stressed new forms of communication and information so as to invigorate and enlarge popular participation. What has been missing is both a definition of what me mean by the term 'democracy', and how specifically, the parliamentary web-site will contribute to it.

Based on March and Olsen's work on democratic governance,[1] four ways are proposed for understanding the contribution to democracy of the parliamentary web-sites: access and participation; adaptation to the political system; the development of democratic identities and political capabilities; the development of public debates.

The Danish political system

The Danish political system differs greatly from that of Westminster. As an ideal, the 'Westminster model' is characterised by single-party governments, a largely two-party system, a majoritarian electoral system, a unitary system of government, an unwritten constitution, and sovereignty of parliament. In sharp contrast, the postwar period of Danish political life has been characterised by a multi-party system; shifting minority governments, most often formed by coalitions, and a high integration of societal interest groups and associations in the policy-making processes. As a consequence of this, the attainment of consensus and unanimity is deeply embedded in Danish political culture. This consensual approach is clearly exemplified in the resolutions on the annual Budget Act, in which the involved parties agree not to break the settled agreements within an agreed period of time. As a consequence, the government in office always strives to create broad coalitions, well aware that an electoral defeat will not necessarily change already settled acts.

The Danish political system approximates to, an ideal-type of 'governance'; a contemporary democratic context where 'government' is replaced by an imperative of self-organising modes of governing.

This concept of governance is expressed through the development of the Danish parliamentary web-site in two main ways. Firstly, one of the explicit objectives for setting up the web-site was to make it more easy for 'organised interests' to obtain information about the parliamentary process. Thus parliament is just one out of several 'arenas' for policy-making, but one in which coordination of the different arenas, together with the exchange of information and data between the actors, is substantial. Secondly, this consensual political culture was sustained by the lengthy planning and implementation process (three years) which took place internally prior to the public introduction of the parliamentary web-site.

An important aspect for understanding the background to the intro-duction of the parliamentary web-site in Denmark is the central political drive to place public authorities on the Internet. Since the first national 'IT-strategy' in 1994[2] there has been a call to all public bodies to establish a presence on the Internet, so as to 'to contribute to simpler, faster and more flexible government administration'.[3] This, in conjunc-tion with a high penetration of Internet access among the public (see Table 1), has resulted in a high number of governmental web-sites, each with 'democratic ambitions'. The parliamentary web-site must naturally be conceived in the light of this trend.

1. Danish Households with Access to the Internet by Age Group 1998

Age group	PC and Internet access at home	Total number of households
16–29	87,707	428,258
30–39	85,367	455,598
40–49	82,244	470,794
50–59	54,516	418,210
60+	16,088	450,611
Total	325,921	2,233,471

Source: Statistics Denmark (1998), special run: PC and Internet access

The Parliamentary web-site

The launch of the parliamentary web-site on the Internet in 1997 was seen as a way of accomplishing several democratic objectives. The purpose of the parliamentary web-site is to make a large number of the documents from the legislation process available to interested citizens, to the industrial sector, and to the press. The web-site should also be seen as an opportunity to obtain information about debates in the Chamber, MPs and finances.

Undoubtedly, setting up the web-site is seen as a step towards greater integration of both organised interests and citizens in parlia-mentary activities. By implementing multi-directional communication through the Internet, parliament has expressed a wish to promote the use of democratic rights by interest associations and citizens through direct access to the political discourse. However, Erling Olsen, former Speaker of the Danish Parliament, and chief initiator of the web-site, states:

The public 'onset', in particular journalists requesting material released from the parliament, was the initial trigger that created the idea [of establishing a parliamentary web-site]. The parliament wished to service these groups in a far more efficient manner and to ease the workload for the parliamentary administration. Another objective with the web-site was to provide solicitors and civil servants the possibility to follow the legal processes down through 'the hierarchical line'. A third objective was the wish 'to play with open cards' in relation to the public.

Hence, the preparation of the web-site did not primarily emphasise the democratic objectives of enlarging popular participation and creating avenues for direct influence into policy-making. Rather, more functional aspects have been the driving forces for the implementation and maintenance of the web-site, primarily undertaken by members of the 'Parliamentary Administration'.

Partly as a result of this approach, the web-site has been largely designed for 'traditional' users (i.e. politicians and journalists), for the final product requires the user to have specialist software. Moreover, the user is assumed to have a comprehensive knowledge of the legislative process, as the material consists largely of unedited abstracts.

Participation and access through the web-site

Participation, and equal and fair access to participation, is a universal democratic norm as well as one of the cornerstones for understanding democracy. Within much of the visionary discourse on electronic democracy enlarging public participation through electronic forums is considered to be the main problem. Indeed, it is often considered to be the *only* problem for reinventing democracy in an electronic context. Thus, if the general population could be provided with universal access to the new technology, institutional changes and universal suffrage would (automatically) ensue.

The key criteria for success concern whether the parliamentary web-site has: (a) increased political participation and (b) generated a measurable positive effect on other forms of participation. We examine this further by looking at three different aspects of the debate about participation.

POSSIBILITIES FOR ACCESS: Although a high number of households and workplaces in Denmark are connected to the global world wide web (Table 1), the majority of the Danish population remains disengaged from the parliamentary web-site. This does not imply that those people without easy access to the Internet are altogether cut off from obtaining parliamentary information, for traditional channels, such as public libraries, have for a long time been supplying the public with parliamentary information at no cost. Nonetheless, the majority is cut off from the easy and user-friendly mode of obtaining parliamentary material. One comment about this comes from the Minister of Trade and Industry, Pia Gjellerup:

In the internal parliamentary system, all committee proceedings are available for the public. You can [as a citizen] subscribe to these documents, but they are not very cheap. However, this material can be provided on the net. So I definitely anticipate there is reason to have ambitions on behalf of the net, as it ensures access to topics of interest [for citizens]. Naturally there isn't anyone who is able to know about everything that is going on, but just the availability to follow those topics in which you hold an interest, or to pursue something you have read in the press is progress. This demands that vital resources are spent on systematisation of the material. The web-site is not interesting in a work situation unless you can work with it. It must be logically designed in order to get a return. This is the real challenge.

We can conclude that there is still some way to go before the majority of the population has achieved access to the parliamentary web-site, though the importance of this is questionable as the information published on the web-site has not developed from that which has been available through traditional channels.

DIRECT PARTICIPATION: Even though it is almost impossible to capture accurate data on the actual use of the parliamentary web-site, some figures are revealed in the number of visitors to the web-site, as well as from the number of electronic inquiries to the web-master. From our figures on the number of 'hits' on the web-site we can reveal that a high number of Internet users have actually made use of the system and that they are usually external users. Of course, this does not disclose who the users are, though a plausible guess, judging from the impressions of those responsible for the maintenance for the web-site, is that the active user group is a small circle of people using it for professional reasons.

As the web-site first and foremost is designated for one-way communication (i.e. dissemination of parliamentary information) it accommodates very few possibilities for actual participation and as such it does not enhance the participatory side of democracy in a strong way.

INDIRECT PARTICIPATION: Users interviewed conceived the web-site as having had few measurable effects on other forms of political participation. As a predominantly practical tool (for professionals) which basically supplements other sources of information from the parliament rather than nourishing popular participation, the effects of the web-site on indirect participation are said to have been inconsequential. Although the initial discussions did emphasise the web-site as a tool for enlarging democratic participation and to bolster general interest in parliamentary politics, the final 'product' became mainly directed to the traditional users. As far as more interactive use of the site is concerned the outcome is still uncertain.

As one Danish MP, Christine Antorini, from the Socialist People's Party, states: 'In reality, it might be that it is e-mail, rather than the web-site as such, that suddenly allows you to become accessible to people.'

Adaptiveness to the political system through the web-site

Parliament's utilisation of new ICTs should clearly be such as to enable adaptation to its democratic commitments to professional users and to citizens in general. Here different interpretations of how the web-site does and should match the democratic process, plays a crucial role in defining the adaptiveness facilitated by the web-site. By asking the different groups involved (politicians, civil servants and journalists) how they perceive the system, and how they feel the system operates with respect to political processes, we have been able to identify opinions on political adaptiveness.

What we have learned from the interviews is that the web-site by and large adheres to a traditional and idealistic (not to say, obsolete) picture of the daily work of the parliament. The image visualised by the web-site is the image of an institution wherein different opinions confront each other in the Chamber and where consensus is reached by means of discussion and deliberation. Moreover, the focus is on the 'results' rather than the processes themselves. This image of 'the most intelligent argument wins', as the core practice of parliament is rejected by those we have interviewed. Rather, as the representative from the journalists (Lars Rugaard, of Radio Denmark) stated:

From my point of view, the main limitation is that the web-site does not sufficiently focus on the 'real' parliamentary processes, that is, the work within the standing committees. The web-site is too fragmentary, and does not cover the real law-making processes, which take place in the parliamentary committees. All else equal, the web-site gives a distorted image which only focuses on the confirmation of decisions that have already been discussed and settled in advance in the committees.

A similar, though more positive train of thought can be detected in the statements of the Minister of Trade and Industry:

The web-site does not reflect the lawmaking processes within the parliament. The committee meetings are [still] closed events. The net won't change this situation, as it can't make it more transparent. However, the net is much better to inform about the committees' work, since what is classified are the meetings themselves, which usually are not as interesting as you might otherwise believe. What you can find are the appendices, which are covered in the press only to a limited extent. This means that you have far more resources to follow the standing committees' work. So far, this fact has not been reflected [in mass media]. Rather, the focus is on the sessions.

As a supplement to other available information for politicians and others involved in politics on a professional basis, the web-site does enable some adaptation to democratic processes, therefore, though it is considered to be inadequate, Clea Bach, Head of Section at the Danish Ministry of Research and Information Technology, states:

The Internet channel will not increase accessibility of information for civil servants, for whom the present supply of material and dissemination of information for their work is relatively satisfying and prompt. So it [the web-site] will still merely function as a supplement.

To sum up, the parliamentary web-site does not correspond to actual democratic decision-making processes. Rather, we are tempted to say that the web-site corresponds to an ideal of a parliamentary system based on a constitution which no longer exists. As such, the web-site presents users with a deceptive image of the parliament and democratic processes.

The development of democratic identities and political capabilities

One way of identifying actors' democratic identities, is to study their explicit and implicit approaches to democracy in relation to the parliamentary web-site. We have identified three different approaches which operate as a common basic standard for understanding the democratic identities which key actors hold:

(1) Those who have been in charge of the development and implementation of the web-site primarily employ the functional approach. This approach involves strategic and practical perspectives on functionality, end-users, design and criteria for success. As such, a rather instrumental perception of democracy predominates, wherein a well-designed infrastructure for communication enables democracy.

(2) The *professional approach* is mainly employed by those who are making use of the web-site as part of their daily work (e.g. solicitors, journalists, civil servants etc.). For this group democracy entails a number of procedures and rules which set the framework for the group's every-day practice. The web-site can here enhance their possibilities to unburden their work situation.

(3) The *citizen-oriented approach* addresses the possibility for citizens actively to use the web-site to become more included in the policy-processes, and to affect political decisions. This approach is a less functional and procedural way of perceiving democracy. Rather, it stresses the web-site as a new arena for the active citizen to come through with his/her opinion, and to have an influence.

The group of people that carried out the implementation of the web-site had no intentions whatsoever to revolutionise the political system. The design 'point of departure' for the web-site lay in the experiences of professional users and their needs, rather than with a larger group of politically interested citizens. In this way, the *functional approach* came to predominate, and both the design and content selection became targeted to a rather narrow 'inner circle'. Thus the main considerations came to be improvements in parliament's service obligations for these people. Thus the parliamentary administration group succeeded in accomplishing what they had set out to do. And even though there existed in this group some rather different citizen-oriented ideas around the establishing of a parliamentary web-site, these fall away in design and implementation.

None of the professional users of the web-site who responded to the interviews felt that the web-site had changed their positions substantially, for example, by giving them more information about the parliament, or changing their relationships to elected politicians.

In relation to political capabilities, the question is two-fold. Firstly, the *political competence*, i.e. knowledge about politics, and learning about using new media in politics, on the involved actors. Secondly, the *political resources*, in particular the possibility, and the will to participate, within the same group. In order to address the question about changing political capabilities we asked both users, and organisers, if they perceived that they had learned something from the use of the web-site, and if they felt that the web-site had enhanced their political resources.

Many of the groups involved had been at the core of politics for a very long time, and it is questionable whether that they have learned anything new about politics. As the use of the web-site is still limited to one-way communication, the contacts with the users have been few and have therefore not come to increase the knowledge of political communication for the organisers. For the other professional groups this is the case too. As one of the journalist interviewees stated: 'It would be appalling if it turned out that we actually learned something new about politics from the web-site.'

We can only speculate about the consequences in terms of changing political resources and capabilities for the normal citizens. All things being equal, there is a strong possibility that politically interested citizens have been provided with a new resource for acting in a political context. The new modes of achieving political information will inevitably strengthen their capabilities of becoming involved in the political discourse. Moreover, the pedagogic elements of the web-site including 'dictionaries' and 'help-functions' will enable less educated citizens to gain access to parliamentary material.

The development of public debates

In most democratic theories, no matter what tradition they derive from, the possibility for deliberative debates based on civilised argument prior to the decision processes is stressed as an important part of democratic governance. This is also something put forward by March and Olsen themselves: 'Democracies make decisions by means of discussion and deliberation, and a key democratic objective is to form a community of reasoned debate for such collective democratic decision-making.'[4]

As a part of the celebration of the 150th anniversary of the first Danish Parliamentary Constitution, the parliamentary web-site in February 1999 invited the whole population to assert their opinions on the current constitution and to express their desires for changes in the constitution via specially designated conferences on the web-site. The idea is that the Members of Parliament can encounter the population in a more direct and egalitarian way on an issue that is of importance for the whole polity. There are currently (April 1999) 20 different topics covering the major elements included in the constitution, e.g. the role of Monarchy, the freedom of speech, the issue of sovereignty in relation to Europe, etc. The conferences have so far been well visited and six weeks after the introduction the number of 'postings' exceed more than 600. The general impression is that the more general and 'open' issues have attracted more attention than those concerning specific institutions. For example, whilst nobody has wished to discuss the institution of impeachment, a discussion that the regulation of genetically modified organisms should somehow be included in the constitution has generated so many postings that a new conference group was established.

These electronic conferences are by no means novel in a Danish context. Both the main political parties, as well as a number of commercial web-sites, have for quite some time now provided space on their web-sites for public debating.

Parliament has said that these conferences are meant as an experiment with the objective of yielding experiences in relation to future, more widespread, use of communication technologies. However, there is still some uncertainty about what the outcome of this conference is to be. From what we have learned, the postings will be compiled and presented for the members of parliament after the conferences have concluded, but what happens thereafter is still not clear. This fact has also been addressed by some of the participants in the conferences in their postings to the editors (or the 'web-master'), where the answer has been that this is still an open question.

It is possible at this stage to identify some patterns in these debates:

— The participation of parliamentary politicians on the web-site has up until now been quite limited. Some politicians have started off the debates by writing longer discussion papers to the conferences. These have resulted in comments and questions from the public. In a few cases the politicians have tried to follow up these replies, but the discussion has died away. The reason for the lack of politicians participating can be found in one statement we obtained from a politician (Christine Antorini): 'My working day is not adjusted for me to go and check all different electronic conferences and newsgroups that are up and running. As an example, there is currently electronic discussions going on both within my own party's debate-fora, as well as on the debate-fora on the Constitution [. . .] I cannot follow everything.'

— The often-anarchistic debate-style derived from other forms of electronic debating has also spread to these conferences. That means that some of the participants have not taken account of the precise topic of the conference, nor tried to contribute to a more deliberative discussion. As an example, in the conference regarding the relationship between Church and State several of the postings are actually about legalisation of drugs. This is clearly misplaced.

— There is here, as in so many other electronic conferences, a tendency that politically alienated issues become predominant. The issues raised are not in line with 'mainstream' politics, and, as found in earlier studies[5] the new media have a tendency to become overtaken by those single-issues that elsewhere are not fully discussed in the mass media.

— The uncertainty of whether a posting to a specific conference will have any impact on 'concrete politics' is reflected in many of the messages. Some of postings also reveal that citizens have posted questions and comments to the politicians involved directly without receiving any response whatsoever.

— The level of interactivity is very low. Many of the postings are 'statements' written in a 'to-the-editor' style, with little or no response from other participants. Although the majority of postings receive some sort of feed-back from others, many of these replies are not 'listening' to the initial posting, thus leaving an impression of persons debating at cross purposes. This also means that the level of development is very low in the debate, and that the deliberative element is absent.

Given these facts, it is hard to say that public conferences on the Internet are a success for democracy, let alone an invigoration of parliamentary life. There is reason to suspect that these conferences have been set up by parliament to test new technical features and to build knowledge in the light of the web-site, rather than actually to trigger the debate about (altering) the constitution. Having said that, the organisers seem to have learned a lot from other similar experiments with electronic debating. The editors are much more active in responding to the participants in terms of both technical and organisational questions. They are also helpful in directing questions regarding formal procedures to the staff of the parliamentary library.

Conclusion

What we can conclude, on the basis of our material, is that the parliamentary web-site has had very little effect on representative democracy in terms of increasing popular participation and granting politically interested citizens new channels of influence. Rather, the web-site is a new consumer-service for professional users, whose preferences and needs have been taken into account in the design-process. As such, the web-site will hardly revolutionise Danish democracy as we know it, but will perpetuate already existing power structures since it still is embedded in what some authors earlier have coined a 'consumerist' framework of democracy in the information age.[6] However, the one way that the web-site is actually securing popular participation is in terms of providing new political resources for the politically interested. In this instance, the new possibilities of obtaining information more easily and of learning more about parliamentary life are strengthening citizen capacity to enter the political discourse.

1   J.G. March and J.P. Olsen, *Democratic Governance*, NY, Free Press, 1995.
2   L. Dybkjær and S. Christensen, 'Info-Society Year 2000', *Ministry of Research and Information Technology*, Copenhagen, 1994.
3   'Action for Change: IT Policy Plan 1997–98', *Ministry of Research and Information Technology*, Copenhagen, 1997.
4   J.G. March and J.P. Olsen, *Democratic Governance*, NY, Free Press, 1995, p. 84.
5   H. Sachs, 'Computer Networks and the Formation of Public Opinion: An Ethnographic Study', *Media, Culture and Society*, 17, pp. 81–99.
6   C. Bellamy and J.A. Taylor, *Governing in the Information Age*, Milton Keynes, Open University Press, 1998.

Parliaments on the Web:
Learning through Innovation

BY J.A. TAYLOR AND ELEANOR BURT

Introduction

This chapter is based upon work commissioned by The Scottish Office in July 1998, on behalf of the All-Party Consultative Steering Group (CSG) on the Scottish Parliament.[1] The primary objective of the work was to bring forward examples from many different countries of the way in which the implementation of a parliamentary web-site might support public participation in the democratic process. The extent to which any telematics application supports democratic participation depends on a number of factors, including, most profoundly, the democratic philosophy of the initiators themselves.[2] With this in mind, a number of web-sites both parliamentary and governance-related were examined through two sets of lenses. The first of these, that of *web-site content and design*, sought to provide examples of the types of capabilities and innovations which are possible. The second lens, that of 'democratic impulse',[3] sought to examine web-site capabilities and innovations in relation to three broad types of democracy, namely representative/parliamentary democracy, associational/pluralist democracy, and direct democracy.

Democratic impulses and electronically enhanced democratic innovation

The role of information and communications technologies (ICTs) both as energising and modernising democratic processes has long been promoted. Much of the early work on simple forms of 'push-button democracy', or tele-democracy, written in the 1960s and 1970s, made large-scale assumptions about the potential of computing and telecommunications technologies to transform democratic practice. Its contemporary equivalent is the 'cyber democratic' potential of electronic networks, not least amongst them the Internet where, again, the assumptions about its potential to transform and improve are grand in scale. The Internet provides for vast riches in the form of available information, riches that can be plundered at will rather than simply administered. Moreover, through e-mail, bulletin boards, discussion groups and electronic forums, the Internet establishes the prospect of high levels of interactivity between citizens, parliaments and governments. Whereas the democratic impulse of those earlier experiments and innovations in tele-democracy was essentially emerging from a direct democracy model, new networks such as the Internet, together with the applications that sit upon them, now promise democratic enhancements across the range of democratic models. Thus, a new and more broadly based 'cyber-democracy' is emerging, one that enables democratic dialogue, discourse and active participation supported by computer networking in general and by globalisation processes associated with the Internet, in particular. The Internet is thereby thought capable of facilitating challenge to the monopoly of existing political hierarchies and revitalising citizen-based democracy through amplifying the power of grassroots groups to gather critical information, organise political action, sway public opinion and guide policy making. It promises, too, the provision of opportunities for direct citizen expressions of policy preferences and for significantly closer and more direct communication between elected members and citizens. Viewed in the context of the three democratic impulses informing this present study, the Internet provides for a synthesis. Potentially, it fosters and augments each of them.

Web-sites: the framework for analysis

In undertaking the research that forms the basis of this chapter, we visited 30 web-sites worldwide. While the web-sites were predominantly those of national parliaments, other governance related sites were included as these might offer transferable applications. The related sites included regional, provincial, and state assemblies, government sites including regional and local authority sites, and a small number of independent sites. The research covered web-sites in Northern and Southern Europe, North America, Australasia and South Africa. British Commonwealth countries were a core focus for the research, the ones selected being Canada, Australia, New Zealand and South Africa. We also visited and analysed the sites of some of the Provinces and States of Canada and Australia.

A series of analytical categories facilitated systematic evaluation of the web-sites. These categories were derived both from academic writing on the nature and meaning of democracy and from our first stage scrutiny of a number of parliamentary web-sites. Also influencing our thinking in constructing this analytical framework is our own sense of the information requirements of the citizen who is engaging in the democratic process.

The analytical categories derived in this way and applied to each of the country studies reported here are five in number, with each of them revealing forms of democratic innovation. They cover information and educational support for citizens; the service providing aspects of democratic activity by parliaments, parliamentary innovations supporting 'active citizenship', and the sensitivity embedded in web-site design to questions of accessibility. The final aspect of our analysis covers miscellaneous innovations. Analysis of each of these categories, though in particular *parliamentary innovations supporting active citizenship*, was enhanced by sensitivity to the extent to which aspects of the sites supported characteristics of representative/parliamentary democracy, associational/pluralist democracy, or direct democracy. Thus, within the five generic categories we looked for *prima facie* signs that sites supported characteristics of these democratic impulses — however weak or embryonic. Pivotal here was some degree of interactive capability within the site, for example publicly available e-mail links to parliamentarians, hot-links to independent discussion groups, organisations and other associations able to represent citizens views to parliaments, or opportunities to vote or, perhaps, to give evidence electronically. The nature of the interaction would indicate the democratic impulses in play. Thus the examples here, signal the existence of representative/ parliamentary democracy, associational/pluralist democracy, and direct democracy, respectively. [It was not our remit to judge the efficacy or impact of web-site applications within the democratic process, nor was our objective to evaluate the degree to which sites supported specific forms of democracy. With regard to the first point, other studies have shown that the web is not the panacea of fundamental democratic ills. With regard to the second point, this would have required more substantive research than was possible within the time-scale of the project.]

The democratic impulses that we drew on for our work, are intentionally pure, conceptually distinctive types of democracy useful as a basis for analysis. Actual practices and processes of democracy are necessarily more confused and complex, so that in any particular polity a unique blend of democratic practice will be found, combining elements and aspects of each of these main types.

Democratic impulses

REPRESENTATIVE/PARLIAMENTARY DEMOCRACY: The British democratic tradition rests heavily upon the traditions of the representative form of democracy. This form of democracy places the member of parliament at its core, taking forward the view, associated with Edmund Burke, of the member as the supreme agent of democracy in the polity, someone to whom the citizen cedes authority for the period between elections. The member of parliament proceeds on the basis of their independent moral authority to which the people have endowed political legitimacy.

Modern parliamentary democracy also attaches high significance to the central role of politicians in constructing and sustaining political debate and in the making and prosecuting of political decisions. However, whereas the pure model of representative democracy places emphasis on the moral independence of the member of parliament, this form of democracy admits the notion of parliamentary groupings. Parliamentary democracy is clear in allowing that the member of parliament is part of the collective decision processes associated with party-led democratic behaviour. Equally, parliamentary democracy stresses forms of legitimate connectedness between parliaments and external actors and groups. Central to this conception of democracy is the forming of legitimate channels through which politics can flow. Establishing the formal rules of lobbying, making available contact points for ordinary citizens and proffering opportunities for individuals and groups to engage in the parliamentary process are all part of this perspective.

ASSOCIATIVE/PLURALIST DEMOCRACY: This democratic impulse places emphasis upon the role of extra-parliamentary political behaviour by interest groupings and intermediary bodies of a variety of kinds. It is a form of democracy that brings forward three views of parliament. From the first viewpoint parliament is seen as necessarily and advantageously influenced and enriched by the discourse generated through the interplay of these groupings and bodies. Indeed the core role of the parliament in this form of democracy lies in establishing the ground rules within which these forms of political discourse take place. The second perspective sees parliament as situated in a dialectical (and potentially inertial) relationship between opposing interest groups each vying to influence the policy process in their favour. Thirdly, in its most extreme form the parliamentary institution is interpreted through this particular democratic lens as an irrelevance, ratifying the policies of more powerful associational interests.

DIRECT DEMOCRACY: This democratic impulse derives from a view that sees the relationship of the citizen to parliament and government as essentially *direct*. Thus direct democracy assumes that the citizen relationship to parliament is not strongly intermediated either by the Member of Parliament, as in representative or parliamentary democracy, or by interest groupings, as in pluralist or associative democracy. It is from this democratic impulse that much of the early enthusiasm for the application of ICTs came. Lying at the heart of this view of democracy is the provision to citizens of opportunities to vote on the issues of the day, enabling them to bind their parliament or Council, and allowing them in effect to govern themselves.

Some direct democracy projects appear radical, particularly those setting out to replace rather than complement established forms of political interaction. This might initially suggest that they are of little value in helping to select systems suitable for enhancing the operation of a Parliament. In practice, however, much of the public feedback facilitated through operational systems is advisory, and respects both the responsibility of elected parliamentary leadership to make decisions and the responsibility of citizens to communicate with those who govern.

Sensitivity, then, to these democratic impulses and particularly to the capacity of web-sites to support them through forms of 'electronic interaction'—between citizen and parliament—enhanced our evaluation of the sites.

Parliamentary web-sites: the findings

In this section we turn to presenting the findings from the research. Drawing mainly from the parliamentary sites, we include other sites where these provide examples of potentially relevant capabilities not identified within the parliamentary sites themselves.

EDUCATING AND INFORMING FOR CITIZENSHIP THROUGH THE WORLD WIDE WEB: Providing basic information about parliament and government in the most general terms is a ubiquitous feature of parliamentary web-sites. Many offer 'educational' descriptions of parliament, its history and procedures, including contemporary issues such as parliamentary oversight of public spending. Linkage arrangements to other sites vary enormously as the examples below demonstrate.

All web-sites that we looked at contained some personal and other details about members of parliament—curricula vitae of MPs; their diary engagements; their voting records; recording of their pecuniary and other personal interests.

The main findings of the research were:

— The provision of general, 'educational' information represents the largest single component of most web-sites. Some sites—Australia, British Columbia and South Africa are very good examples—provide fact sheets on their parliament that can be downloaded. Moreover, there is generally information on the site about how to visit parliament physically. The New Zealand site provides an on-line booking facility for schools wishing to visit parliament. There, a schools booking form can be completed on screen and transmitted over e-mail.

— Many sites provide historical material about parliament. The US Senate site, for example, provides extensive historical virtual tours including an opportunity to look at the art and statuary of the Senate building. The Danish site is unique amongst those examined in providing a modern history of the party political structure of Danish parliaments. A table is included on the site that gives details of the party political composition of the Danish Parliament from 1960–95. Some sites contain very strong histories and tours of aspects of the parliament building itself. British Columbia is the most striking example, offering a 360 degree 'movie' of the debating chamber in the legislative assembly, written in Quicktime software that can be downloaded from the Internet. The Austrian site also permits a room by room exploration of the parliament with simple 'click on' facilities.

— Fulsome information about parliamentary committees is to be found on almost all sites. The home page of Parliamentary Committees is usually accessible from the main site. Often the e-mail address of parliamentary committees is provided.

— In the case of the US House of Representatives, the House Rules and the House Ethics Manual are both accessible from the site. Similar documents are available on the Australia, Queensland and Quebec sites also.

— Budgetary information is carried on some sites. The Austria site has a section on how parliament uses checks and balances to control the budget. The full text of the budget appears on the British Columbia site.

— Many parliamentary sites provide hyperlinks to government sites, the Australian and UK sites provide good examples. The Australian site provides access on its front page to Commonwealth Government sites.

— Most sites provide some CV and biographical material about members of parliament. Parliamentary sites in general offered access to the 'home pages' of Members as part of the main site, though the quality of these home pages varied considerably. Most home pages provide an e-mail address of the member, ubiquitously so on the US sites. Whereas some aspects of sites are available in different languages, members' home pages were only ever available in the host language.

— The only instance of a 'web-available' diary that we found was that of the Irish President, though this appears on the government rather than the parliamentary site. It appeared to be up to date and gave details of 'today's' meetings and visits as well as those planned.

— One interesting innovation on the UK parliamentary site is an easily used facility that allows the user to determine who is their local MP. The user inputs their postcode and the system responds with the name of the MP.

— The strongest recording of members' voting records appears on both US sites, though records are organised by reference to a specific debate rather than by reference to the member as such.

— The strongest site for the declaration of members' interests was the South African site. There, all registered interests are available including property ownership. The Register of Interests for the UK House of Lords is available on the site. On the Finnish site the pay-rates of Members are included as are details of pay increases according to length of service. Also on this site are details of allowable expenses, including the extent of free travel available to Members.

— Some parliamentary sites offer hot-links to political party sites. The Austrian site has direct links to each of the Party web-sites of those five parties represented in Parliament. Others, Belgium is a case in point, offers only notes about the political parties rather than hot links to the party site. In Belgium, the contact name and address for the party is included on the site. No such links to Political Parties are provided on the US or UK sites.

PARLIAMENTARY PROVISION OF SERVICES TO SUPPORT DEMOCRACY: Parliaments are not, of course, service providers and, whilst we found some small evidence of 'service provision', broadly defined, our research findings show that this is the least developed aspect of parliamentary support for democratic activity. Services to the citizen were being offered from a number of parliamentary web-sites, however, and here we focus upon identifying specifically which services were being offered from the parliamentary site. The most advanced form of this activity that we noted was where direct ordering from the site by the citizen was being made possible.

The main findings are:

— The ordering of parliamentary and government publications is enabled on some sites either directly, Austria, or indirectly by providing hot links to Crown Printers, Office of Official Publications etc. as in the British Columbia and the UK sites. In Austria the citizen can e-mail the services department of the parliament for information about parliamentary publications and a telephone helpline is also available. There is access to on-line catalogues of parliamentary materials.
— The Canadian and British Columbia sites provide details of student placement opportunities in Parliament, and the UK site includes details of job opportunities and vacancies in parliament. The European Parliament site provides details of how recruitment to posts within the parliament is undertaken, including the application procedure.

PARLIAMENTARY ENHANCEMENT OF ACTIVE CITIZENSHIP THROUGH THE WORLD WIDE WEB: The active polity is one that supports active citizenship, and a core aspect of our research into the content of parliamentary web-sites was the extent to which the site appeared to support forms of active citizenship. We looked for specific features that might arguably support such active citizenship. These included:

— Evidence of the extent to which public participation in policy formation and feedback was being encouraged on the site.

— The provision on the site of timetables for current parliamentary debates and opportunities within them for citizen involvement.
— The development on the site of discussion forums on selected parliamentary topics and the identification on the site of current issues upon which citizen views were elicited.
— The ease with which public policy and legislative documents can be accessed from the site was also noted, as was the extensiveness of their provision.
— The availability on the site of any form of voting facility whereby the direct expression of preference or judgement was being elicited.

The main findings from the research are:

— Several sites explained how the citizen might best contribute to the development and formation of public policy. The South African site, for example, explains how views might be expressed, although it provides no electronic means for so-doing. The New Zealand site explains how to make both written and oral submissions during the legislative process if the citizen is called upon to do so. Additional to this facilitation of citizen involvement during the passage of legislation, some sites, including those for British Columbia and Quebec, encourage e-mail submissions to their working committees. Other features of sites that support policy interventions include the provision on the US Senate site of a 'lobby registration form' that can be submitted electronically; the downloading of Member contact lists allowed for on the Australian site, designed to encourage feedback to members; and the downloading facility on the US House of Representatives site of Member and Committee lists in an address label format.
— The majority of sites contain some information on the parliamentary timetable. The French and Spanish sites are good examples of ones where the timetable of the programme of the parliament's work is clearly set out. The Spanish site, for example, has a 'news' section that gives information on the 'order of the day' and a further section that sets out business for the following week in Congress.
— The Portuguese site contains summaries of parliamentary sessions and search facilities that allow the user to access topics of interest, where they have been the subject of parliamentary debate. Records of plenary meetings are available on screen with the option of accessing the summary or full version of each meeting. The Irish site affords access to parliamentary debates back to 1997 and accompanies it with a key word search facility. Providing electronic access to official documents, parliamentary proceedings and legislation is commonplace. Canada and Australia provide good examples of sites where this is accompanied by strong search

facilities. Sites vary in the extent to which documents are 'read only' or are available for downloading.

— Some sites, the Australian site is a good example, offer further stimulation to policy interested citizens through the provision of hyperlinks to extra-parliamentary news and discussion groups.

DESIGNING PARLIAMENTARY WEB-SITES FOR CITIZEN ACCESSIBILITY: The previous three sections were concerned to offer analysis and illustration of how web-sites are being used to offer substantive improvements in the democratic process. We will return to the matter of substantive innovation in the final section of this analysis in which we examine a miscellany of innovation on these sites. At this point, however, we look somewhat differently, not at substantive innovation but at aspects of design innovation where that innovation is seeking to facilitate access to these sites. Thus, this part of the research was concerned to evaluate the sites themselves in terms of largely technical and design features. We looked, for example, at the provision of search engine facilities, at whether there was a 'site map' and at whether there was a user help service. We looked too for the provision of instruction and advice on how the citizen might link electronically to the parliamentary web-site and at whether citizen users were able to identify where their nearest public access terminal is located. Our research into these sites also included whether they are supported in one or more languages, whether there are touch-screen or voice-activated facilities and whether there are additional facilities to support disabled access. We noted too the ease with which sites could be located and worked through, their general layout and the time taken to download material from them. Finally, we attempted to ascertain the frequency with which they are updated. Whilst, as with the previous sections we were keen to log specific features in this instance we explicitly made qualitative judgements about the usefulness or adequacy of the features that we saw.

Our main findings are:

Help sections are often very supportive of users, though the nature of that support varies considerably from site to site. Some of the most interesting examples are:

— Information provided on the Internet browser that is needed to gain full access to the site, as well as the provision of links that enable the downloading of the necessary Internet browser. The Ireland site is the best example here.

— Provision of links to specific software required for downloading parts of the site e.g. Adobe Acrobat Reader — Queensland, South Africa, Quebec and British Columbia (QuickTime software).

— Information provided on how to set up a web-page, as in Australia.

— The web-master's e-mail address is included on some sites, for example Queensland and British Columbia.
— Excellent site maps are provided on the French and Australian sites.
— There is provision of a 'Guest Book' facility on some sites that enables the recording of comments about the site. Lower Saxony goes furthest in this respect by including previous comments of site visitors as well as their e-mail addresses.
— Most sites are presented in more than one language. The Belgian site is the most multi-lingual site that we found, being available in four languages. English is usually one of the languages used though often, in non-English speaking countries, the English language section is a reduced version of the site. On the Quebec site all material which has a permanent quality is in both English and French though all news items are in French only. The Italian site was an exception to the rule of at least bilinguality, being available only in the indigenous language and whilst the Dutch site offered an English language option it was very difficult to access.
— A key feature of sites where accessibility is of prime concern, is the provision of text only versions of parliamentary proceedings and reports that intentionally make access speedier because of the omission of images. The US House of Representatives and the Assembly of British Columbia are good examples of this practice.
— Many sites offered a disclaimer on the content of documents on the site. Throughout the Canadian sites that we examined and on the Queensland site it was made clear that the definitive version of documents was the printed version.
— The updating of sites is patchy both amongst sites and within them. The rate of updating often varied from page to page. Some parts of site might be updated both frequently and at regular intervals whilst other parts might scarcely be updated at all.

A MISCELLANY OF INNOVATION: In this final section of our analysis of parliamentary web-sites we draw attention to a miscellaneous range of innovations that are relevant to the general theme here of enhancing representative/parliamentary democracy yet do not fall readily into the other categories.

These miscellaneous features are:

— Many sites, France, Spain and Portugal are good examples, have an access to other systems section part of which facilitates access to 'Parliamentary sites of the world'. On the Portuguese site each country with which links are possible is listed alphabetically and once a country is selected from the list the hot-link to that other country parliamentary web-site becomes available.

— The Irish Government site supported live 'chat' with the President of the Republic and included transcripts of the conversations that took place. Two 'chats' were recorded at the time that this site was visited. Members of the public had either e-mailed their questions in advance or were able to ask questions direct on-line. The President gave immediate responses on screen during the live chat period.

— The German site provided a facility for logging on to the 'World Directory of Parliamentary Libraries'. This section contains a country list of all parliamentary libraries. An on-line question-naire is provided for staff from these various libraries to complete whenever a significant change occurs in their library, thus ensuring updating.

— The Belgian site contains a currency conversion table for all European currencies converting into Euros.

— The Cyprus Government page has a 'mirrored facility', i.e. a replica site available if the main site is inaccessible.

— Many sites had a European section including lists of Members of the European Parliament.

— On the New Zealand and Canada sites there is a screen that advises when parliament is not sitting

— The Queensland and Quebec sites explicitly count the number of visitors they receive.

Transferable applications: ideas and innovations

While there is, obviously, much to be learned from the Parliamentary sites, valuable innovations and potentially transferable applications lie outwith the parliamentary arena. We turn now to examine a selection of high-profile sites providing additional ideas to enhance citizen participation within the democratic process. Project Vote Smart offers a range of capabilities designed to enhance citizen participation within representative/parliamentary democracy, as well as supporting associational or pluralist impulses. Amsterdam's Digital City and The Santa Monica PEN provide further examples of the way in which web technology might support associative or pluralist forms of democracy. Stimulating and sustaining direct democracy is clearly at the heart of Network Pericles, a telematics initiative that permits electronic voting by citizens.

Amsterdam's 'Digital City'

The 'Digital City' project in Amsterdam provides a good illustration of the democratic potential of 'wired cities', based upon the democratic impulse of associative/pluralist democracy. The project has been designed to provide easy access to government information at a local and national level, as well as information on community organisations and citizens groups, and has been interpreted as an answer to the perceived failure of established political institutions, otherwise the 'democratic deficit'. Digital City aims to provide a platform upon which citizens and groups can exchange ideas and challenge established politics.

Digital City is an advanced web-site allowing users very high levels of interaction both within the site itself and between themselves. The site was designed on the principle of theme-based 'town squares' that serve as virtual meeting places on particular issues, with each square containing eight buildings which can be rented by 'information providers', whether businesses, voluntary sector organisations, community groups or government and municipal departments.[4]

Public electronic network (PEN), Santa Monica

The PEN in Santa Monica, California is a public electronic network accessible via home computers and public terminals to provide access to information and services, electronic mail and networked conferencing on a variety of topics. Launched in 1989, it was the first free-to-the-user, public sponsored interactive local communication network in the USA. The network places great emphasis on interactive communications among citizens as well as between citizens and public officials. PEN can be used at no cost via home computers or terminals in 13 public places around the city. Citizens can access information about city services, send e-mail to city staff, elected officials or other PEN users, and participate in numerous computer conferences on topics of local concern. PEN demonstrated that it was possible to design a public access network in such a way that it would actively involve people who had no access to PCs either at home or at work, and who came from social groups whose take-up of new technologies and whose influence on public policy has been historically low.

Whilst the PEN has not radically transformed collective political action in Santa Monica, action, it has nonetheless supported group political activities and has led on several occasions to the formation of citizen groups. For example, within six months of the establishment of PEN, an on-line discussion group was formed both to support discourse and to initiate political action that would enhance services for the homeless. Moreover, the homeless were well represented among the active participants in the debate.[5]

Project vote smart

Project vote smart (PVS) is to be interpreted as a project designed to facilitate the citizen's ability to influence their public representative. PVS is an information service for citizens enabling them to identify their public representative through a 'zip code' identifier. It then allows the citizen to identify the issue positions of their representatives or those standing for office, their campaign funding and their voting records. It also explains how to participate in the electoral process.

Thus PVS aims to provide a powerful tool for the achievement of public accountability by allowing users to examine the records of their elected representatives, enabling them in effect to monitor and supervise them, as well as to compare their campaign promises with their actual performance once in office.

A measure of the system's success came during the US Presidential election in 1992 when the project received over 200,000 calls, 34,000 on election day alone. These callers talked with volunteers and student researchers on the hotline, and received answers to their questions about where candidates stood on significant issues, their voting records, the sources of their campaign donations and their biographical backgrounds.

In 1995 PVS established a web-site which became one of the most comprehensive national political sites during the 1996 elections. Despite its focus upon elections, PVS is a year-round system and, during non-election years, its focus changes to offering citizens a way to monitor those they elected by using the hotline and on-line computer access to track voting records, performance evaluations, campaign finances and key legislation. Moreover, a facility called 'Congress Track' allows citizens to track the status of major legislation through the committee process on a daily basis over the hotline and on the web-site.

Network Pericles

Network Pericles was established in Greece in 1992 as an experimental project whose chief aim was to enhance citizen participation in the Athenian political process. Pericles springs from the impulse to direct democracy as is manifest in the way it provides political information, encourages communication, facilitates discussion and enables electronic voting.

Network Pericles supports direct democracy in three main ways. First, it allows citizens to submit issues for debate and for vote. If the number of citizens seconding a motion is sufficient according to the rules then the motion is listed as one to be decided by public vote. Importantly, Government cannot veto citizen initiatives once the required level of support has been achieved. Secondly, the system also enables the conduct of referenda whose votes may be either consultative or binding. Thirdly, citizens are enabled to correct, amend or annul decisions that have been taken previously by them, either in respect of motions voted upon or politicians elected.

Finally, Pericles is accessed from public kiosk facilities. Access from homes or offices, rather from these public facilities, has been restricted so as to reinforce the community aspects of democratic processes.[6]

Electronic innovations and democracy: conclusion

We have shown in this chapter how ICTs in a number of forms, though not least the Internet and the world wide web, are becoming incorporated into democratic life. For Parliaments seeking to stimulate democracy, in an era when their status is judged to have been ebbing away, there are numerous ways in which they might seek to support democratic activity. We have referred to opportunities for parliaments to stimulate deliberation and discourse in the polity through the provision of networks that support wide citizen and group access. We have referred, too, to innovations that are aimed both at providing the citizen with a stronger voice, through direct voting, for example, and with supporting the strength of that voice, by providing information about public representatives, to take a further example. We have suggested that whilst the core democratic impulse of such systems is either towards associative/pluralist democracy or direct democracy, nonetheless parliaments may gain greater legitimacy through the opportunities that such innovations present for parliaments themselves. As parliaments come nearer to the centre of political life through the awareness that derives from closer understanding of wider, more socially inclusive discourse, so parliaments will [re]gain political credibility.

The majority of this chapter has looked at the growing incorporation into representative/parliamentary democracy of Internet technology and the presence of parliaments on the web. Here is a more parliament-centric view of the information age than that referred to immediately above. For, as we have seen, these web-sites are often providing extensive facilities that can enable citizens to visit and exit at will, using the (virtual) parliament more completely than has ever been possible in the days when parliaments existed only at the physical level. Yet, as we have seen there are many qualifications that must be borne in mind. Web-sites vary enormously both between themselves and, often too, within themselves. The quality of information provided varies significantly; the design of sites varies hugely too in terms of the imaginativeness of design — the incorporation into sites of features that enable ease of access and navigation; the 'parliamentary paradigm' that holds back from encouraging strong and active citizenship is more in evidence than a more holistic, view of democracy that seeks to support and listen to a powerful citizen voice; and, whilst access to the Internet is currently expanding rapidly, far more citizens in most countries do not have assured, regular access than those that do.

Nonetheless we have offered a view of technological invasion of the democratic sphere, with the new forms of information provision and communication that come along with this wave of technological change. Some have argued that the Internet gives rise to democracy in cyber form, a form as yet little understood but one which threatens profoundly what has preceded it. The citizen in the cyber-democracy can fetch information rather than be provided with it. The citizen can challenge the authority of experts, professionals and politicians as never before. If the strong visions of cyber-democracy are to emerge in practice then what we have brought forward here as evidence of current activity can only be the blandest hors d'oeuvre to the feast of electronic democracy that is yet to come.

1   *Telematics and the Scottish Parliament*, Report by Glasgow Caledonian University. The Scottish Office, Edinburgh, HMSO, 1998.
2   F.C. Arterton, *Can Technology Protect Democracy?* Roosevelt Study for American Policy Studies. Washington, DC, Sage, 1987.
3   *A Parliament for the Millennium*, Edinburgh, John Wheatley Centre, 1998.
4   L. Francissen and K. Brants, 'Virtually Going Places: Square-hopping in Amsterdam's Digital City' in R. Tsagarousianou, D. Tambini and C. Bryan (eds), *Cyberdemocracy: Technology, Cities and Civic Networks, Routledge*, London, 1998.
5   S. Docter and W.H. Dutton, 'The First Amendment Online: Santa Monica's Public Electronic Network' in R. Tsagarousianou, D. Tambini and C. Bryan (eds), *Cyberdemocracy: Technology, Cities and Civic Networks*, Routledge, London, 1998.
6   R. Tsagarousianou, 'Back to the Future of Democracy? New Technologies, Civic Networks and Direct Democracy in Greece' in R. Tsagarousianou, D. Tambini and C. Bryan (eds), *Cyberdemocracy: Technology, Cities and Civic Networks*, Routledge, London, 1998.

Wiring-up the Deck-Chairs?

BY CHRISTINE BELLAMY AND CHARLES D. RAAB

Introduction

The notion that there is a strong link between technological change and the nature and quality of democracy is well-established in debates on the political significance of information and communications technologies (ICTs). Some writers have claimed that the direct connectivity and instantaneous communications associated with ICTs have played a major role in the irreversible decline of democracy based on parliamentary institutions: 'We have outlived the historical usefulness of representative democracy and we all sense intuitively that it is obsolete.'[1] They are far from agreed, however, about what might replace parliamentary democracy.

Some commentators believe, for example, that the technologies of the *second* media age, the age of electronic networks and cyber-communications, will strengthen trends that became apparent in the *first* media age, the age of mass communications. The increasing deployment of network technologies will reinforce the politics of mass society, divorcing individuals from active participation whilst yielding evermore precise knowledge of their preferences and behaviour through the devices of computer-aided marketing techniques. Other commentators believe, in contrast, that the interactive technologies of the second media age will turn out to be 'citizen technologies', facilitating rich, authentic, self-referencing communication that the state will decreasingly be able to control. The ever-changing, rapidly proliferating, multi-centric networks of the cyber revolution will inevitably promote new democratic forms, whether they be the virtual, Athenian-type republic of 'active citizens', the communitarian revival of civil society, or the emancipatory politics of cyberspace.

For other writers still, however, the assumption that new forms of technology-supported democracy will inexorably emerge from the ashes of parliamentary democracy is one that is dangerously misplaced. For them, the one unarguable fact about electronic democracy is that it will not be inscribed onto a blank political slate, but must be developed within a framework formed by existing institutions. If a new, more vigorous democracy is to emerge, a democracy founded on the rich information-handling and communications capabilities of ICTs, it can be nurtured only within the institutions of representative democracy and responsible government as they operate at the end of the twentieth century. The paradox is that new democratic practices must emerge from a political system that, by common agreement, has become deeply flawed.

The purpose of this volume is to see if ICTs could provide a catalyst for reinventing parliamentary democracy: that the new capabilities associated with ICTs, especially those associated with interactive networks and Internet technologies, could help to reinvigorate our present institutions, for example by opening up government to public scrutiny, widening interest and participation in electoral politics, revitalising communications between electors and their representatives, and strengthening the efficiency and influence of Parliament itself. Whilst not rejecting such scenarios out of hand, we offer a note of scepticism. ICTs could probably play a significant role in enhancing the information and communication infrastructures of contemporary politics, but this role has yet to be convincingly established in its day-to-day life. However, the democracy that ICTs may help to re-invent is not likely to take a *parliamentary* form: indeed, the wider political and social system is developing in ways that may continue to marginalise parliaments. It will become ever more clear that parliaments are 'dignified' constitutional organs, unable to restore their 'efficient' functions of representing and combining interests and holding the Executive to account.

The most convincing democratic uses for ICTs arise from the vastly increased opportunities for individuals to acquire the means for direct, unmediated political communication, and to do so, moreover, on the basis of access to a more plural, less easily manipulated range of information resources. ICTs appear to offer significantly enriched opportunities for the formation and articulation of interests and opinions, whether this be done through on-line bulletin boards, the virtual public squares of civic networks, distributing electronic petitions, e-mail messages to MPs or electronic citizen juries. It is much less clear, however, that ICTs can contribute significantly to strengthening traditional techniques for *aggregating* interests and opinion, particularly beyond the micro-political level. Yet it is the concentration of the deliberative process in Parliament itself, in the forum of the 'political nation', that constitutes the main traditional justification for a *parliamentary* form of democracy. The function of Parliament is not only to register opinions, but to interpret their significance, in order 'to keep [government] responsive to the underlying currents and more important drifts of public opinion'.[2] The parliamentary form of democracy implies that Parliament represents the public to the government, whilst — as we shall see — helping to shape the stories by which government is held to public account. Parliament is the 'linchpin' of this system of government,[3] the 'essential intermediary' between government and people. The aggregation and reconciliation of interests or views, and accountability, are therefore the two crucial functions of representative and responsible government. However much the reinvention of democracy, with or without ICTs, may constitute an exciting departure, it is neither stuffy nor old-fashioned to think that the loss of these functions would be at least worrisome, and possibly even dangerous, especially if the development of new extra-parliamentary processes to perform these functions was more difficult to achieve, or was accorded low priority.

ICTs *and the reinvigoration of parliamentary democracy*

A burgeoning literature on ICTs suggests that technology *could* be used to enhance parliamentary democracy. One way of categorising the applications of ICT resembles Arnstein's well-known 'ladder of participation', which was brought forward to demonstrate the crucial difference between the appearance and reality of democratic involvement, between 'going through the empty ritual of participation' and establishing 'the real power needed to affect the outcome of the process'.[4] Successively higher rungs defined eight levels of 'participation' ranging from manipulative attempts to 'educate' the public into accepting planners' own preferences, up through the one-way dissemination of information, though token attempts at consultation, towards processes that could offer increasingly rich possibilities for genuine partnership, citizen empowerment and control.

Arnstein's ladder demonstrates the complex interrelationship between information and power strategies. By analogy, we have arranged proposals for exploiting ICTs in the context of parliamentary democracy in a somewhat shorter and more crudely constructed 'ladder of informatisation'. Although we do not propose here to examine all its rungs, this ladder is brought forward to illustrate the broad, but equally significant, distinction between the use of ICTs to strengthen the efficiency and effectiveness of the state in controlling and serving citizens, and the use of ICTs as 'citizen technologies'.

The most widely-canvassed ICT proposals seem to fall into four main categories (Figure 1). On the lowest rung, we place proposals for strengthening parliamentary democracy by enhancing the efficiency,

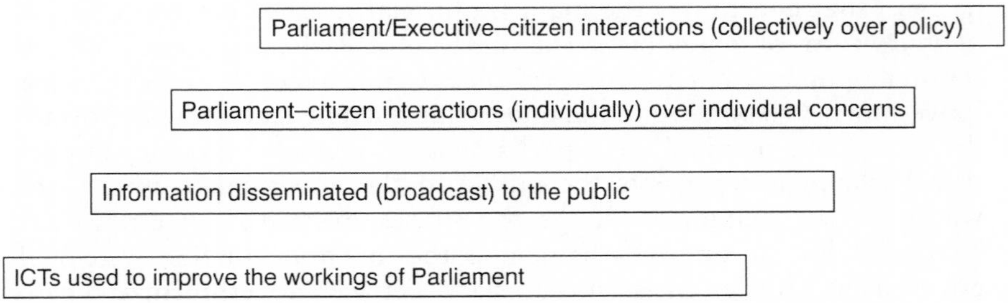

> Parliament/Executive–citizen interactions (collectively over policy)

> Parliament–citizen interactions (individually) over individual concerns

> Information disseminated (broadcast) to the public

> ICTs used to improve the workings of Parliament

Figure 1. A 'Ladder of Informatisation' from the Standpoint of Parliamentary Democracy

effectiveness, influence and prestige of Parliament itself. These are important innovations that improve the way in which MPs work, but they do not necessarily provide greater opportunities for citizen participation. Many of them may be seen as a response to the long-standing claim that a major source of parliament's failure to deliberate wisely and to scrutinise government effectively lies in the low quality and independent information possessed by MPs. ICTs could help address this problem, for example by providing on-line access to significantly enhanced library and research services.

On the second rung, better *public* provision of information is available through networked technologies, such as the Internet or cable TV. These technologies offer swift, cheap and effective ways of disseminating information about parliament, including records of its debates; copies of bills and parliamentary papers; information about MPs, including their availability to constituents, voting records or position statements; information from Ministers, such as answers to parliamentary questions; and information about elections, including party manifestos and campaigning materials. A search of the web-sites maintained by British political parties and the British Parliament will yield manifold examples of all these categories of information — with the exception of systematic information about the performance of individual MPs — as would similar searches of comparable sites in most OECD countries.

These two categories of technology-mediated innovation are focused primarily on the use of network technologies as accessible sources of richer, more comprehensive, more flexibly-organised information resources. They make relatively few demands on the capabilities of ICTs for supporting interactive communication. Nevertheless, as other articles in this Issue illustrate, ICTs could also be used to support qualitatively different kinds of interaction and participation in the democratic process. Our third category of innovation is therefore intended to capture a range of proposals for exploiting the interactive capabilities of technologies, such as telephone helplines or e-mail, to build new kinds of relationships between representatives and those they represent. For example, ICTs might offer direct e-mail communication between MPs and their constituents or between candidates and their electors.

The third rung, however, remains more or less within the orbit of communications involving citizens as *individual* participants in the democratic process, largely interacting with representatives over their individual concerns. The fourth rung, on the other hand, involves proposals for using ICTs to offer members of the public opportunities to participate more directly, and more collectively, in the policy 'input' processes of parliamentary democracy; as we shall see, it may also enable more direct and collective approaches to holding representatives and governments to account. The history of electronic democracy is littered with experiments — often presented under such evocative names as 'electronic town meetings' or 'city forums' — to use cable TV as a means of involving voters actively in election hustings, in discussions with elected representatives or in confrontations with public officials. The Internet can offer further opportunities for conducting on-line citizen juries or other kinds of deliberative panels, all designed to offer MPs, parties and government strategic guidance on the issues of the day, particularly in the formative stages of making policy or creating legislation. It is also possible to conceive of arrangements that could permit members of the public or representatives of pressure groups to give on-line evidence to parliamentary committees.

There is no particular shortage of practical examples of innovations on all four rungs of this ladder, but most of the examples that have found their way into the growing literature on electronic democracy are demonstration or experimental projects established by high-tech commercial companies, social researchers or advocacy groups. These are important experiments, if lessons can be learnt from them. But systematic study of indigenous, institutionalised reforms in the fabric of parliamentary democracy shows a less promising picture. It would also show an almost exclusive concentration of innovations in the lower rungs of our ladder. Great strides have been made in recent years in enhancing the availability of information over electronic media, such as the Internet. Indeed, Westminster is active as well. *Hansard* is now on-line and is updated daily; despite earlier worries over cost and copyright implications, the Parliamentary web-site provides a free, easy-to-use way to keep abreast of Command Papers, legislative stages, parliamentary debates and Select Committee reports. The UK government's web-site offers profuse information from Whitehall departments and agencies, including press releases, background briefings, White and Green Papers and public service information. But from a democratic perspective, the use of electronic media has been disappointingly restricted. Much of this plethora of information consists of material that was already available in printed form. Neither as academics nor as citizens can we dismiss this as a negligible advance. Yet the increasing use of ICTs has failed, in the main, to stimulate the generation of new kinds of information resources — for example, data about individual MPs' voting patterns or their positions on the issues of the day — that would make a genuinely fresh contribution to either the processes of representation or to the substance of accountability.

Contemporary uses of the web are also better seen as attempts to create more flexible, more efficient, forms of broadcasting than as efforts to establish interactive, two-way public communications that might encourage the gathering of public opinions or allow the taking of popular initiatives. By early 1999, only 37 British MPs had established a web presence, and fewer than 190 possessed an e-mail address.[5] MPs appear, moreover, to use e-mail more often to contact each other than to communicate with constituents.[6] Furthermore, this restricted, unenthusiastic use of electronic media is not unusual in British public life. Successive surveys of the web-sites developed by English and Scottish elected local authorities all show, for example, that there is a clear bias towards the one-way dissemination of standard information, such as basic public-service data or information about economic development.[7] A recent analysis of the use of ICTs by British political parties similarly found a heavy emphasis on using technology for internal housekeeping and membership processing, alongside a growing focus on political marketing and campaigning.[8] There was, in contrast, little interest in establishing direct interaction between candidates and voters. Overall, then, few sites offer members of the public opportunities to interact directly with the democratic process, for example by e-mailing elected representatives (with the expectation of an equivalent reply), participating in electronic hustings, or conducting on-line discussions of policy issues. Such useful opportunities as do exist, including UK Citizens Online and occasional discussions on the Number 10 web-site, stand apart from mainstream politics and do not seem, as yet, to have impacted substantially on their processes.

At first sight, this picture may be contrasted with the apparently richer use of electronic communications by members of the US Senate and House of Representatives.[9] with the growing involvement of American political parties in interactive communications with electors and with the explosion of interest in electronic democracy in the community networks movement and the public tele-computing lobbies. E-mail has become a popular way for citizens to communicate with Capitol Hill, while the public squares and bulletin boards of the civic nets buzz with electronic conversation. Even here, however, the impact on Congressional procedures is patchy and limited. E-mail has not supplanted letter-writing and the telephone as the medium of Congressional business. Most e-mail messages to Congress go through a cumbrous process that produces written replies, and representatives fear being swamped by more traffic than they can sensibly handle. Most disturbingly for the implications of electronic communication for representative democracy, representatives are tending to filter out or ignore messages from non-constituents, making it difficult for not-for-profit groups — including those spawned by cyber-politics — to establish alternative routes of access to those that are used by powerful insider interests. This last problem illustrates a more general issue: that amidst the hyperbole associated with the cyber revolution, there is little hard thought and little practical concern being devoted to working out how the political networks generated in cyberspace should and could map onto the real-world politics of representative democracy, except perhaps in the case of the establishment of new parliaments, as in Scotland.

All this seems to illustrate one of the leading positions in the debate about the political significance of ICTs: the 'reinforcement' thesis that existing institutions tend to tame new technologies and shape them to their own purposes. Technology becomes a tool in the processes by which power structures are reinforced.[10] However, support for this thesis is less clear than might first appear, and the future might hold surprises. For example, long-term decisions about the use of technology in the Scottish Parliament will be for the latter to take, and it must remain an open question whether its members will tailor the technology to suit their own, or the public's, priorities and convenience.

It could rightly be objected that the picture we have described above is simply a reflection of the first, hesitant steps along the relatively long trajectory towards the apogee of the second media age: after all, the Internet only came into popular use in the mid-1990s. The passage of a few years is hardly sufficient to assess the full democratic significance of ICTs. For this reason, we propose at this point to move the argument on, and turn from the empirical question — the question concerned with assessing progress, or the lack of it, up the ladder of informatisation — to a more fundamental 'in principle' question. Even if all elected representatives were to be wired up to their constituents and were to communicate openly and interactively with the cross-cutting networks of cyberspace — even if the processes of parliamentary democracy were to be fully informatised with ICTs — how far would these changes address its malaise?

The problems of contemporary parliamentary democracy

In order to address this question, we need first to explain how this malaise has been brought about. Several well-established, mutually-reinforcing phenomena are usually associated with the steady decline of parliamentary democracy:

— the growth of the mass political party as a response the creation of the mass electorate, leading to the development of oligarchic party machines;
— the accompanying development of party discipline both in Parliament and outside, leading to the control of the elected house by the political Executive;
— the development and commercialisation of the media of mass communications, leading to the erosion of the public sphere by highly managed forms of sound-bite politics;
— the increasing complexity of social and economic problems, and the growing interdependence between the institutions of civil society and government organisations in developing and implementing policy, leading to the transfer of policy-making outwards to the twilight world of policy networks;
— the shift of power and authority upwards to the European Union and downward to regions and nations, exacerbating the 'hollowing-out' of the British state.

These phenomena are not of ephemeral or transitional interest, but denote long-range structural changes in and around the British political system. They are deeply implicated in the 'elective dictatorship' of majority governments and in a growing loss of political competence on the part of both representatives and voters. The result appears to be a growing democratic deficit, as confidence in parliamentary institutions has become eroded. There has been a turning-away from mainstream political activity into new social movements and single-issue politics, while the most significant influences on, and accountabilities for, public policy are now brought to bear through the complex and diffused networks of contemporary governance. British politics and government is, in short, no longer so clearly centred on the core processes of parliamentary democracy: we may be moving towards the 'post-parliamentary state'. The question, then, is whether there are good reasons to suppose that advances in technology could help to restore the centrality of parliamentary institutions to democracy. Could the rich information resources and the proliferating communications networks of the second media age make possible the reinvention of a parliamentary democracy?

Despite our earlier scepticism about the 'reinforcement' thesis, history suggests that the deeply conservative strain in the existing parliamentary system is more than capable of fighting back against reforms, including those facilitated by technological change. Members will not give way to megabytes; neither will cables or electronic channels supplant the corridors of power within which MPs seek to influence policy or remedy their constituents' grievances. Profound challenges to parliamentary democracy as it now operates are hardly likely to be mounted by such simple, bolted-on expedients as multiplying channels for transmitting information, increasing the volume of its flow, or even creating new opportunities for political interactivity and communication. If informatising Parliament means little more than technologising government's ability to broadcast information to Parliament, or Parliament's ability to broadcast or to send individual messages to members of the public, then it will come nowhere near to confronting the wilful inertia of a system in which information and communication are much better seen as power resources than as ones to be shared.

Parliamentary innovations of a democracy-enhancing kind have always been cautiously and experimentally undertaken, and modest in their ambitions. The struggle to establish Select Committees shadowing government departments—perhaps the shining hope of attempts to improve accountability—is an object lesson. The glacial pace of Freedom of Information enactment and the reform of the Official Secrets Act are others. It is hardly a new discovery to say that wider constitutional changes, including reform of the Lords, devolution, and changes to prerogative powers, have been undertaken with all deliberate procrastination because it has suited Executive power-holders to perpetuate existing and historical settlements. Nor has Westminster itself been particularly seized of the necessity of change in many of its internal procedures, such as division arrangements, working hours, and the expiry of Bills at the close of a session; all are measures that would have significant consequences for the distribution of power.

Experience with 'old technology' appears, too, to offer little cause for optimism either that Parliament will grasp the opportunities of opening up its business to the public at large, or that it would engage the public if it did. The newspaper press no longer routinely and extensively conveys the deliberations of Parliament, whether on the Floor or upstairs. The televising of parliamentary debates, Ministerial Questions and committee hearings had a long gestation and was introduced with much misgiving. Many would say that the bright lights have added little lustre to the reputation of Parliament; the prevailing public image is more that of a bear-pit than of a nation's representatives handling the great affairs of state. The viewing audience for clips of Select Committee sessions, in which accounts of stewardship are often dragged out of civil servants and ministers to telling effect, is minuscule. Broadcasting Parliamentary business has signally failed to shift the parameters or locus of power.

It may be objected, however, that the technologies of the second media age constitute new kinds of ICTs, capable of offering communications and information facilities that are qualitatively different from the simple extensions of broadcasting on which these examples are based. For the visionaries of the cyber-age, the ever-expanding networks of cyberspace constitute a new kind of medium through which control over human communication and connectivity is passing inexorably from producers to users. Their radical, anti-institutional promise goes far beyond the limits of broadcasting to embrace truly interactive communications that could facilitate the making of political demands and the expression of opinions outside the set-piece rituals of elections and the channels controlled by established policy networks and parties. Just as the history of communications provides rich examples of successful and unsuccessful threats to existing patterns of control, such as pirate radio stations and citizens'-band broadcasting, so the proliferation of digital channels and cyber networks poses a clear potential challenge to existing monopolies, oligopolies and institutions. One such might be Parliament itself.

The advent of the cyber-age appears, therefore, to bring the question of institutional stability into view. As innovations in the political system become more unpredictable in their effect, they go against the grain of existing power practices. For those practices are founded upon a sense of order and discipline in which mavericks can be marginalised, and views aggregated and shepherded into supportive channels. Both Parliament and the Executive fear randomness as well as overload. The established apparatus of representation is nothing if not safe; or, perhaps more precisely, it is capable of deploying a repertory of stabilising mechanisms when it comes under threat. The key question is whether new information and communications capabilities will rein-force or evade the capacity of the political system to shape the technol-ogies that might threaten its stability. Different forms of informatisation will, of course, pose different degrees and kinds of threat to the stability of the existing institutions. Returning for a moment to our ladder of informatisation, we can see that simply expanding opportunities for electronic contacts between individual constituents and their MPs pose no real threat: potentially a more efficient tool for representation, it would not destabilise representative democracy. In fact, it might increase allegiance to the system, and thus add to its stability, by linking the public more effectively to their representatives. Further up the ladder, however, making more information available to constituents may, however, carry more significant implications. This will depend crucially on what is meant by 'information', who controls its know-ledge-frames, and whether constituents, even when standing on the top rung, are able to use it effectively for influencing decisions or for holding their representatives, and through them the government, to account.

Accountability and the role of ICTs: towards open government

This point is an important one. It relates closely to the need to establish a critical understanding of the nature and role of information. It is therefore worth spending some time outlining the information issues involved in the dynamics of political control, since they go to the heart of assessing the contribution to be made by ICTs in addressing the malaise of parliamentary democracy. Processes of deliberation and accountability lie at the heart of representative and responsible govern-ment, and are quintessentially about the shaping of both the channels and the content of information. Walker and Akdeniz aptly observe that representative democracy 'involves most fundamentally accountability to an electorate, ultimately at election time, but, in between elections, it is vital that public opinion can be expressed and can continue to exert an influence . . . Information and comprehension of public affairs are vital if autonomous and free choices are to be made by individual electors. The openness and accessibility of channels of communication and the possibility of participation, either through individual action or, more likely, through involvement in a pressure group or party, are important attributes on which the health of a democracy in part depends'.[11]

Gray and Jenkins link the key process of accountability to the giving and receiving of accounts by stewards and principals. 'To be accounta-ble,' they say, 'is to be liable to present an account of, and answer for, the execution of responsibilities to those entrusting those responsibili-ties.'[12] Codes of accountability—the established customs that govern behaviour—provide the guidelines for the giving of accounts. The code defines the terms in which the account is presented and evaluated. Informatising the processes of accountability would make account-giving more efficient, but it would not of itself challenge the codes; therefore, it would not make accountability more effective in the democratic sense.

Enriching parliamentary democracy depends, at bottom, upon plur-alising, as well as expanding, the ways in which information is deployed and interpreted in the making of political judgements. In this vein, Gray, McPherson, Raffe and Raab offer a view of accountability that highlights the nature of accounts as stories or explanations. These writers go further, however, in focusing upon the significance of how accounts are received and interrogated. 'The legitimacy of a democratic government rests on its claim to be acting rationally, rather than arbitrarily. But while the electoral process is the ultimate crucible of accountability, the concept of accountability can also be expressed in terms of knowledge and its communication. It is about the telling of stories, or the rendering of accounts . . . in order to judge the quality and accuracy of an account, electors must have some means for evaluating it that is independent of government. Moreover, they must be able to force government to give an account of its actions which . . . must include the following: government's objectives, its perception of the situation in which it acts, and a "theory", which explains how the action is to achieve its objectives.'[13]

Thus '[g]overnments must be able to elaborate accounts; citizens must be able to evaluate the accounts and provide other ones'.[14] This presupposes the ability to produce a variety of competing accounts, and procedures for reaching agreement on alternatives. 'Citizens must there-fore have access not only to the accounts themselves, but also to the data and procedures through which the accounts have been constructed. They must have the means to re-define the concepts in terms of which the accounts have been expressed, to articulate alternative perspectives, and to supply these with evidence which may itself be new . . . They must be fully involved in the process of the production of accounts.'[15]

These perspectives on accountability underscore the importance of openness in government. But they show, too, that open government does not simply imply making more information available or providing easier access to the raw data that are collected and processed in government. It also involves accountability in the sense of exposing government's reasons for decisions and actions to active debate, as well as fostering the ability to challenge assumptions and concepts that underpin the data behind the stories—data which are framed in cat-egories that government controls. The manipulation of unemployment and other official statistics provides telling examples of the latter, as do government's risk assessments on the subject of BSE. It follows, then, that the contribution of ICTs to parliamentary democracy will be relatively modest and dull unless they are able to facilitate access not only to a wider range of information but also to information from diverse sources. Questions and accounts could then be framed from alternative standpoints and debates constructed from sources of intelligence that are no longer so closely monopolised by government.

Incompatible agendas?

These matters raise important questions about the ways in which the networks of the second media age will relate to the processes and conventions of the parliamentary form of democracy, or whether, indeed, they would make the latter obsolete. As the great chroniclers of its golden age recognised only too well, the parliamentary form of government requires a precarious and paradoxical blend of popular deference and engagement: citizens' willingness to accept a duty of informed participation in elections, whilst standing back from direct involvement in politics. It requires that they recognise and protect the special legitimacy of parliamentary channels, whilst being prepared to defer to the deliberations of the parliamentary elite. In return, government must be prepared to accept the guidance of Parliament, to believe that Parliament is 'the most effective device we have for scrutinising the work of government and for focusing news, opinion and criticism relevantly'.[16] If this argument still holds in modern conditions, then the question is how ICTs can best be used to restore the aggregative and deliberative functions of Parliament. At one level, this question is simply about adjustments to procedures: about how the formal routines of parliaments and their committees should be reconstituted to take account of new possibilities for expressing views and mobilising lobbies created by electronic networks. On another level still, there are issues about the design of processes within institutions, for it is difficult to see how the extensive use of e-mail to support personal communication and document distribution could simply be plugged into existing ways of conducting business.

However, on yet a further level, it should not be assumed that adjusting parliamentary procedures or opening up new parliamentary channels constitute the limits of reform. As citizens acquire ever more diverse opportunities for formulating and expressing their opinions, their need to use parliamentary channels may decline. Why e-mail one's MP when one can e-mail the minister direct? The virtual groups and on-line communities forming in cyberspace need not rest content with lobbying Parliament when they now have the means of mobilising direct action. For ICTs offer facilities for constituting virtual public spaces that could encourage interaction and debate, not only between stewards (on the inside of parliament or government) and principals (on the periphery) but especially among groups and individuals on the periphery itself. In other words, new political connectivities would emerge, facilitating new linkages within civil society as well as enhanced interaction between elected representatives and those they represent. Where ICTs could assist in forming new groups and mobilising new lobbies, thereby encouraging new kinds of critical activity, the democratic game might indeed be raised. ICTs could, for example, facilitate the circulation of, and subscription to, electronic petitions, with the result that more frequent and immediate pressures would be placed upon elected representatives, demanding more urgent, active response. The use of ICTs for the formation of new social movements, for the creation of new parties or even for the sustenance of factions in existing parties would pose an even sharper threat to what currently passes for parliamentary democracy as new entrants to the arena add to the unpredictability of politics.

Such visions as these should cause us to doubt whether the networks of the second media age should most appropriately be regarded as potential handmaidens of a *parliamentary* democracy. For aficionados of the cyber-revolution, the fundamental point about new ICTs is that they could liberate us from the tired old categories of a failing regime. Whereas parliamentary democracy seeks to re-centre political activity on the narrow channels of representative politics, the infinitely flexible networks of cyberspace offer possibilities for inventing new, more expansive, more pluralised forms of democracy. Not only can humans be emancipated from the confines of geographical space, but in a virtual world, they can also be liberated from the socially constructed categories of race, gender or class. Even identity can be negotiated in the fluid, self-referencing world of cyberspace. It is questionable whether the emerging practices of the second media age can be comfortably squeezed into the service of parliamentary democracy, when it is possible to aspire to even higher rungs on the democratic ladder as society moves on to more direct and pluralised forms which ICTs facilitate and serve. The ladder of *parliamentary* informatisation is not a stairway to the stars.

The networks of cyberspace stand, too, as powerful metaphors for long-wave social and economic change that will continue to undermine the parliamentary form of democracy. Ours is, inescapably and irreversibly, a multi-centric society, with shifting modes of influence and diffuse sources of power. Even central government is no longer supreme. Government now acts through multiple channels forged from complex sets of policy networks. The diversity and complexity of contemporary life goes, too, beyond the structural to the cultural: society is not only multi-centric but multicultural and pluralist in its values. The more this fact is recognised, the more political energies will have to be directed to challenging practices which represent, at best, a patronising tolerance of otherness and, at worst, the exclusion and derision of minority opinions. The processes of parliamentary democracy cannot evade such challenge: attention will increasingly be directed to the cultural provenance of the accounts and stories that are brokered in parliaments. How are they negotiated, and by whom, and whose narratives do they represent? To pose this question is to doubt whether all voices can best be heard and reconciled through the inevitably restricted and highly-managed channels of parliamentary-type institutions. There is at least a possibility that they would be more faithfully articulated through new, more direct, more plural modes of democratic politics.

There is, therefore, a case for arguing that democratic practices must change to accommodate a socially diverse society just as they must also respond to the emergence of more diffuse and complex governing arrangements. The 'explosion of communication' could hold the key to enable such change: technological innovation could have important consequences both for the nature and degree of democratisation. It is by no means clear, however, that the prospect of informatising democracy offers an unambiguously Utopian future: on the contrary, it raises important normative issues. Without new forms of coordination and aggregation, there is a real danger that ICTs will not only reflect but amplify the fragmentation of public space, balkanising politics into multifarious and shifting constituencies that are incapable of being aggregated by any means. Another issue concerns the criteria that should guide elected governments in assessing the outcomes of political debates conducted in the public squares and cafes of cyberspace: what procedures should be adopted, for example, for using new civic networks to seek authoritative expressions of popular opinion, and what public information resources should be made available to support them? Yet another issue concerns the rules of order that should govern the conduct of cyber-politics: whether it is appropriate, for example, to regulate the virtual conversations and bulletin boards of cyberspace, or to set and police the limits of free speech.[17]

The spectre of surveillance?

Or, indeed, covertly to monitor what people are discussing with each other over the networks, for ICTs may also invade the private spaces of citizens. This sounds a further cautionary note about the potential of ICTs, whether in a parliamentary mode or in more direct forms of democracy, one which is perhaps less often heard but is worth discussing. Rulers of old were wont to go disguised into the markets and bazaars of their kingdoms to overhear what the populace was saying. In modern times, under what conditions can participants in electronic political discussion be certain that sufficient confidentiality surrounds their expressions? Walker and Akdeniz[18] are among those who question the extent to which electronic participation in democracy is consistent with the protection of personal privacy, or on the other hand exposes participants to surveillance in ways that are less likely off-line. For example, the addresses of those who log-on may become tradable commodities in possible violation of data protection laws, or in an affront to human dignity. Party managers and government ministers now possess increasingly sophisticated techniques to measure opinion and to tailor and target messages to individuals about whom more and more is known through the mining of large quantities of personal data that are available in public and private databases. The connection between measurement and manipulation may become more tightly drawn in the new media age.

ICTs enable states to collect, store and process enormous quantities of information about the lives of their citizens, and to track their activities and movements. The necessity for public trust in the confidentiality of their information is widely recognised in proposals for the electronic delivery of public services, but the participatory interactions of electronic democracy, in which choices, expressions of opinion, and the concerting of (legitimate) plans often need likewise to be made in conditions of anonymity and confidentiality, if the participants so wish. It is by no means certain that the electronic equivalent of the secret ballot or the protected political communication is available, particularly if on-line discussions cannot be enveloped by anonymity, possibly using secure encryption. The business world is worried about the confidentiality of commercial electronic transaction; so too are many proponents of electronic democracy.

Surveillance may thus cause damage to the very privacy on which a thriving democracy depends. An argument for the mutual dependence of democracy and privacy has been made elsewhere.[19] Privacy is not only a personal value, but is important for social freedom, facilitating association with people, not independence from them.[20] Participatory democracy, and the prospect of better representative democracy through electronic means, both require communication processes that enable a degree of anonymity lest authorship may invite reprisals by those in authority. Civil liberties are central to representative democracy in traditional electoral terms: candidates must be able to communicate freely with voters, who must be able freely to assemble, organise and discuss the information among themselves. The same conditions apply to accountability purposes between elections. Thus the supposed antinomy between individual privacy and the collective processes of democracy and social life is somewhat spurious.

Sophisticated electronic ICTs are certainly not the first media to point up issues of surveillance in human communications and information systems, but the possibilities for invasive practices are now greatly enhanced. ICTs can facilitate political communications between citizens and their representatives, and among citizens who are unable to meet in person, provided they can trust in ICTs' integrity and security against surveillance. It is not Orwellian paranoia to recognise that democratic communications can fall victim to the 'chilling effect' of surveillance unless the ICT infrastructures and systems observe, and are seen to observe, privacy-protection rules, some of which can be built into the technology itself. Contemporary policy conflicts concerning the use and control of cryptography cannot be reviewed here, but they are severe precisely because they engage the relationship between the individual and the state (as well as the economy) in terms of the line to be drawn between the state's 'need to know' and the individual's need — or right — to privacy. They also touch upon difficult questions of how the location of the line is to be drawn — by law, ethical codes, technologies, or some mixture of these — and who should participate in the process of drawing it. Both the wiring-up of parliaments and the wiring-up of citizens in civil society need seriously to embody these wider values of democratic enhancement and civil liberty in implementing ICTs for increasing participatory inputs, improving accountability, and the more frequently mentioned improvement of convenience or efficiency. The temptation of political parties to collect and exploit personal data gained in electronic transactions for marketing purposes and electoral campaigning must be bounded by safeguards of transparency, consent and limitations of use.

Conclusion

Our conclusion, in brief, is that informatisation is almost certainly important and may even be *necessary* for reinvigorating parliamentary democracy, but that it is hardly *sufficient* to deal with either the scale or nature of its problems. This conclusion has been prompted by three main considerations. These are: the deep-seated causes of the malaise of parliamentary democracy; second, the nature, threats and limits of, as well as the opportunities offered by, changes in information and communications capabilities; and, third, the resistance of existing political institutions. It is the way that these three factors are likely to interact that leads us to be less than optimistic that the problems of parliamentary democracy could be fixed with ICTs.

To ask about reinventing parliamentary democracy with ICTs is probably, however, to ask the wrong question. As we saw in opening our discussion, the main reason for focusing on *parliamentary* democracy is that informatisation is most fruitfully directed not at Utopian scenarios but at reforms that are likely to prove feasible for existing institutions. As we have also seen, however, we live in a democratic system that has become both deeply flawed and seriously attenuated. Our most serious cause for scepticism, therefore, is the doubt that informatising Parliament will, of itself, restore its capability of aggregating opinions and holding government to account: in addition, we need to consider how these crucially-important functions can best be developed in the post-parliamentary state. This may require new forms of democracy, ones that are alert both to the innovative possibilities and inescapable dangers of networked technologies *and* more in line with the political and cultural realities of the post-parliamentary age. To mix our metaphors, all else may simply amount to wiring-up the deck-chairs.

1   J. Naisbitt, *Megatrends: Ten New Directions for Transforming Our Lives*, Macdonald, 1984, p. 160.
2   B. Crick, *The Reform of Parliament*, 2nd edn, Weidenfeld and Nicolson, 1970, p. 79.
3   J. Bulpitt, *Territory and Power in the United Kingdom*, Manchester University Press, 1983, p. 83.
4   S. Arnstein, 'A Ladder of Citizen Participation', *Journal of the American Institute of Planners*, July 1969.
5   Report in *The Sunday Times*, 31.1.99.
6   'MPs Move into Information Age', *Government Computing*, July/August 1998.
7   See I. Horrocks and N. Hambley, 'The Webbing of Local Government', *Public Money and Management*, April/May 1998, and J. Taylor and L. Whiteside, *Local Governance in the Information Age*, Glasgow Caledonian University, 1998.
8   C. Smith, 'Political Power in the Information Age. From "Mass Party" to "Leadership Organization" ' in I.Th.M. Snellen and W.B.H.J. van de Donk (eds), *Public Administration in an Information Age*, IOS Press, 1998.
9   OMB Watch, *Speaking Up in the Internet Age: Use and Value of Constituent E-mail and Congressional Web-Sites*, OMB Watch, 1998.
10 The reinforcement thesis is elucidated in K. Laudon, *Communications Technology and Public Participation*, Praeger, 1977, and J. Danziger, W. Dutton, R. Kling and K. Kraemer, *Computers and Politics*, Columbia University Press, 1982.
11 C. Walker and Y. Akdeniz, 'Virtual Democracy', *Public Law*, Autumn 1998, p. 490.
12 A. Gray and W. Jenkins, *Administrative Politics in British Government*, Wheatsheaf Books, 1985, p. 136.
13 J. Gray, A. McPherson, D. Raffe and C. Raab 'Politics, Education and the Reconstruction of Research', chapter 17 in J. Gray, A. McPherson and D. Raffe, *Reconstructions of Secondary Education: Theory, Myth and Practice Since the War*, Routledge & Kegan Paul, 1983, p. 324.
14 Ibid., p. 326.
15 Ibid., p. 326.
16 B. Crick, *The Reform of Parliament*, 2nd edn, Weidenfeld and Nicolson, 1970, p. 5.
17 C. Bellamy and J. Taylor, *Governing in the Information Age*, Open University Press, 1998.
18 C. Walker and Y. Akdeniz, 'Virtual Democracy', *Public Law*, Autumn 1998, p. 504.
19 C. Raab, 'Privacy, Democracy, Information' in B. Loader (ed.), *The Governance of Cyberspace*, Routledge, 1997.
20 F. Schoeman, *Privacy and Social Freedom*, Cambridge University Press, 1992.

An American Democracy Network: Factors Shaping the Future of On-line Political Campaigns[1]

BY SHARON DOCTER, WILLIAM H. DUTTON AND ANITA ELBERSE

Abstract

California's Centre for Governmental Studies developed the Democracy Network (DNet), one of the most innovative electronic voter guides on the Internet. This chapter looks at the motivations behind their key technical choices in DNet's design, and how users of the Internet responded to them. The designed was influenced by conceptions of the citizen on-line, or the 'netizen', and also how the developers believed existing law and policy would apply to this new medium of communication.

Introduction: the design of digital democracy

Images of electronic, tele- and cyber-democracy have generated many utopian and dystopian arguments for (or against) the adoption of ICTs to promote (or protect) more democratic forms of participation, such as the reform of campaigns and elections in ways that move them closer to democratic ideals. Some proponents have argued that electronic communication could improve the responsiveness of political institutions and allow for more direct citizen participation in public affairs. Critics have argued that electronic communication will be used in ways that diminish deliberation, and, thereby, impoverish political debate.

Ithiel de Sola Pool,[2] for example, argued that the inherent qualities of electronic ICTs, such as the microcomputer and on-line publishing, as compared to the mass media, such as television, are democratising. He therefore labelled the new electronic ICTs as 'technologies of freedom' because their design undermined centralised control over communication. This freedom from centralised control has been widely observed in commentaries on the Internet and world wide web. Nevertheless, many have challenged this view, arguing that ICTs are more likely to reinforce existing structures of power and influence, or support more centralised structures of communication. Some argue that emerging media will still further widen inequalities of access to information and other communication resources among the information have and have-nots.

The social implications of technical decisions

The design of technologies arise from conflict and differences of opinion among a multitude of actors. Moreover, technical design features may advantage certain actors while disadvantaging others. Sometimes the conflicts and differences which shape technology are overt, at other times not apparent. Also like public policy, technical advantages can be intentional, or unintentional, with unanticipated outcomes.

Legal models and analogies shaping 'technical' decisions

Prevailing law and policy are often claimed to lag behind technological change. However, existing legal precedents and political-administrative traditions can also guide technological change, often by producers drawing analogies between old and new technologies. Law journals are replete with articles pertaining to how different legal models may be applied to the new electronic media,[3] but little research has been conducted on how the law and legal paradigms shape technological choices. In the US, for example, conceptions of the First Amendment, and how various First Amendment models apply to communication technology could have a profound impact on how the technology is developed and eventually regulated. If producers view a technology as placing themselves in a legal position that is analogous to a speaker in the park, for example, then this could make a difference in what they believe appropriate with respect to controlling content over this system, as compared to it being viewed as analogous to a broadcaster, or a common carrier, or a print publisher. Each analogy could lead to different design choices.

Given the potential significance of ICTs to democratic participation, surprisingly few empirical studies have focused on the effects of tele-democracy (cyber-democracy) projects, or on the social factors shaping the application of ICTs in government and politics. This is mainly because most of the debate over electronic democracy is hypothetical, focused on some future speculations.

This chapter looks at the social forces, such as laws and policies, shaping the design of cyber-democracy, by focusing concretely on the role of a specific application of the Internet to political campaigns and elections in the US. Specifically, we focus on one of the most innovative electronic voter guides under development in the US, called the Democracy Network (DNet). In doing so, our study can advance understanding of how conceptions of the First Amendment in the US is being applied to emerging ICTs, and thereby shaping the design of cyber-democracy initiatives. Our findings are based primarily on in-depth interviews with its key developers that provide an understanding of the evolution of its design and the motivations behind key technical choices.

THE DEMOCRACY NETWORK:[4] The Centre for Governmental Studies (CGS), a non-profit organisation, designed DNet as a means for enhancing the quality of information provided about the issues at stake in political campaigns and elections.[5] Its development was in part inspired by the optimism surrounding interactive TV in the early 1990s. Initial applications were all based on interactive video communication over ITV networks such as Warner's Full Service Network (FSN) outside Orlando, Florida. With the collapse of ITV investments by industry in the mid-1990s, CGS shifted its attention to the emerging media of the day, the Internet and web. DNet's web-site was launched during the summer of 1996.

At its inception, DNet was conceived of as a video voter's guide for the viewers of interactive cable television. It was designed in anticipation of the next generation of public affairs television that would eclipse services, such as the Cable-Satellite Public Affairs Network (C-SPAN). It was to be interactive, community-oriented, and centred on the TV. While it shifted to become more anchored on the Internet and the web, it remained focused on fostering more issue-oriented campaigns and more rational, issue-based voting, by providing improved information about the position of all candidates on issues of the campaign.

Prevailing legal paradigms, particularly concerning the US First Amendment, as well as emerging technological paradigms (interactive TV) and conceptions of the rational voter all shaped designs of this network. In addition, the faltering development of interactive cable TV systems (ITV), accompanied by the explosion of interest in the Internet and web had a dramatic impact on this model for how electronic media can be used to inform voters in the US, which has become a prototype for others round the world.

MOTIVATIONS BEHIND DNET'S LAUNCH: DNet offers candidate and issue-related information, such as candidate's issue statements, biographical data, and endorsements for candidates, and details regarding ballot initiatives (http://www.dnet.org). DNet was designed to create incentives for candidates to participate in the identification of key issues and in clarifying their respective positions. Additionally, it provided a forum for debate among candidates, as well as a medium for citizen-to-citizen and citizen-to-candidate communication, such as through live interviews on the web.

DNet also represented an attempt to counteract the effects of disproportionate funding by candidates, by not charging for the provision of candidate information. The founders of CGS had been involved in public interest efforts to reform campaign financing rules, which bias elections towards those campaigns that can afford more paid advertising time on TV. The Internet seemed to offer an unprecedented opportunity to provide equal time, free from the cost and scarcity of broadcasting.

DNet targeted both national and local constituencies. Users nationwide could access information about the 1996 Presidential race. Along with this national information, users within the city of Santa Monica,

California could access information about local candidates and elections and state and local ballot initiatives. In early 1997, users could also obtain information about local races within the city of Los Angeles and plans were under way for DNet to provide content concerning elections in New York city and Seattle. By the end of 1998, DNet was expanded to provide election information in all fifty states, with extensive information on election issues in nine states, and it continues to expand its reach. Within the 9 states that were a focus during 1998, nearly 100% of the major party candidates participated on DNet.

FEATURES OF DNET'S DESIGN: DNet's design included both a broadcasting component, where communication was one-to-many, as well as an interactive component, where communication was many-to-many. The web-site specifically included six distinct sections. A central broadcasting component included a menu-based system entitled 'On the Issues', where citizens could identify issues of interest to them and compare the issue positions of candidates. There was also a component called 'Candidate Info', which provided biographical, contact, and endorser information on the candidates, and 'Media', which allowed users to read stories in the press pertaining to the elections, by offering links to relevant on-line news.

The more interactive sections included a section on 'Ballot Measures', which provided users with official information pertaining to ballot measures such as summaries of the measures and arguments for and against them. This section was more interactive because users were given the opportunity to post their opinions about the measures and to read the opinions of other voters. A section entitled 'Your Views' functioned much like a bulletin board, where users could post comments and read the postings of others. In addition, chat rooms were available as well as a 'Match Poll', where users were provided the opportunity to compare their opinions and positions with the positions of the candidates. This section also included the capacity for 'live interviews', where users could communicate directly with candidates or with experts concerning the election.

Finally, a section entitled 'Take Action' allowed users to send e-mail directly to the candidates. A form was also provided which allowed users to indicate a desire to contribute to, or volunteer for, a particular campaign. In addition to this interactive function, 'Take Action' allowed voters to find information of value to the election, such as polling places, voter registration information, and a guide on how to obtain absentee ballots. A central component of DNet's design was its Remote Updating System (RUS). Using this system, candidates enter personal identification numbers and passwords to allow them to update information, such as their position statements on issues, and their biographical, endorser, or contact information. Through this system they can also add issues to their election's issue grid, and get on-line help.

THE ISSUE GRID: DNet's 'issue grid' creates a structure of incentives for opening-up the campaign to a wider array of issues. If an issue already appears on the issue grid, a candidate can add their views on this issue. If candidates want to debate or state their position on a particular issue not represented on the issue grid, they can add the issue as well as a statement to the 'On the Issues' section of DNet. A red check mark shows that the candidate has stated his or her position on each issue. The candidates most recently updating or adding to their issue position statements are bumped to the top of the list of candidates, each of which is represented by a row within the issue grid. In this way, new information supersedes old information and old issue statements are archived so that it is possible for a voter or journalist to examine how a candidate's position changed over time.

The issue grid, updated by candidates themselves, was important to DNet. Supporting the philosophy of the founders, the issue grid could hold candidates accountable for issue statements, as well as for their failure to address particular issues. The issue grid, with its red check marks, makes it obvious whether or not a candidate has stated a position on any given issue. In addition, the remote updating of the issue grid made it possible for the CGS to manage a large number of campaigns, despite limited staff resources. RUS enables content to be self-generating, much like content on other Internet discussion groups. It would have required a far greater commitment of staff time for CGS to write, edit and manage candidate information, particularly as DNet expanded to cover elections in other cities and states. Thus, remote updating supported the potential for a small non-profit to manage a nationwide system.

The use of DNet

CGS found that DNet gained the participation of many candidates. A survey administered by CGS indicated that 'candidates liked the system, found participation to be fairly easy, and would have participated more fully using the remote updating system, if the technology had been available earlier in the race.' Moreover, DNet attracted a sizeable number of users, given the very emergent stage of Internet use in campaigns and elections.[6] An independent web-site research and measurement service estimated that DNet attracted approximately 3,000 users in less than a three week period immediately following the launch of the web-site. The most popular section of DNet was the issue grid, 'On the Issues'. The interactive pages of the web-site, such as Chat, Match Poll and Bulletin Boards, also appeared to be popular among users. By the end of 1998, DNet significantly increased the number of users, with the CGS reporting over 5.5 million hits in the November 1998 election cycle.

SHAPING THE DEMOCRACY NETWORK: A variety of social factors shaped the design of DNet. Legal models proved to be important. Also significant were broader conceptions of the kinds of media that would be most useful for reaching voters.

CONCEPTIONS OF THE NETIZEN: Both the ITV and web versions of DNet were created to address problems with conventional media, the intention was to build on the success of innovative public service television in the US, especially the Cable-Satellite Public Affairs Network (C-SPAN). The founder of DNet, Tracy Westen, had championed the idea of creating a California version of C-SPAN and spent five years implementing this project. The result was the California Channel, which broadcasts unedited footage of California State Legislative proceedings via satellite to cable subscribers throughout the state. The California Channel does not editorialise in any way and provides viewers with the opportunity to see their state representatives in action.

Westen was convinced that TV has been the most effective medium for reaching voters. This led him to devote his efforts to the California Channel, and to the next generation of public affairs programming, which he saw possible with interactive TV. One problem with a C-SPAN and its local equivalents, however, is that viewers cannot selectively tune into debate on issues of concern to them at convenient times. Instead, the broadcast of legislative proceedings runs continuously and, therefore, may not be relevant to viewers' concerns at times of the day when a particular viewer is able to watch. CGS built on this problem as one advantage of taking C-SPAN another step so that viewers could actively select from a menu of issues. In this manner, the information could be more immediately relevant to audiences. Rather than passively listening to legislative proceedings, viewers could be more actively involved in selecting the debate which is of greatest interest to them.

Like C-SPAN, the providers of DNet would not provide any editorial content. Instead, the content would be provided by the individual candidates and DNet providers would be more akin to distributors of information. Designers, then, were able to use the emerging ITV industry (and later the web) as a means to correct a flaw with C-SPAN.

AN APPROACH TO INEQUITIES IN CAMPAIGN FINANCING: CGS also viewed DNet as a way to address problems with campaign financing. Westen and other principals of CGS are experts in the area of campaign finance reform. One CGS study into the California initiative process concluded that voters were not receiving the kind of information that they need in order to make informed decisions on referenda. CGS recognised that although there is currently a proliferation of information about politics, the voters remain poorly informed on substantive issues of the campaigns. One reason is that most political communication from candidates to voters, particularly in US campaign advertisements, is in the form of thirty second commercials, most of which fail to address many important policy issues facing the electorate.

Because candidates are forced to spend large sums of money buying television time, they must focus their advertisements on the issue that will be the most salient to the voting public. This practice is the most cost effective means of communicating with the electorate, and a rational strategy in the context of commercial TV. Ironically, this results in voters receiving less substantive information at the same time that more money is being spent on election campaigns. DNet, however, allows viewers to tune in to a broad range of issues. If a viewer is not interested in the issue addressed by the candidate, they can 'point and click' to another issue.

This was another concern behind the design of DNet — an effort to counter the effects of disproportionate fund-raising.[7] In the US political arena of the late 1990s, the candidate that is able to raise the most money gains more exposure with the voting public (because they are able to purchase more television time). This is particularly critical since mere exposure to a political candidate increases the likelihood that a candidate will be favourably perceived. This is one reason why incumbents have such an advantage over challengers. In contrast, with DNet, participation is designed to be independent of financing; all candidates have the opportunity for equal exposure. Even candidates and parties with virtually no financing can get their message out to the electorate.

The failure of interactive television

The design of DNet was influenced also by the technology of Interactive Television (ITV). The promise of ITV emerged during the late 1960s in the US with the schemes for marrying cable and computer technology to wire cities. During the early 1990s, there was a resurgence of interest in ITV, with a great deal of press coverage on the promise of interactive applications.

Communication experts believed that ITV would be the most important new technology to enter people's homes, and that it would be a trigger service for the information superhighway. Industry leaders, such as Time Warner and TCI, along with some of the telephone companies, began laying the structure for fibre optic and hybrid fibre-coaxial cable networks, which would allow for two-way communication and which could potentially provide 500-plus channels of information and entertainment programming. Features such as movies on-demand, home shopping, games, and an increase in entertainment programming could be offered to viewers. Questions concerning the demand for such services were often dismissed in the enthusiasm surrounding new business opportunities.

Given the tremendous capacity available within an ITV system, designers of DNet recognised that information service providers would need to generate great amounts of content to carry over the system. They believed that they could convince the cable companies and telephone companies to carry their services. CGS began creating a prototype using actual candidates and ballot initiatives which would provide an interactive video-voters guide. As discussed above, the principals at CGS liked the idea of communicating political information in video form, as they believed that most citizens would find video programming more compelling than a text-only format. Voters would have the opportunity to see the candidates speaking for themselves, and this would give voters a good sense of the candidates as people. Moreover, the candidates appeared to have a similar conception of the voter, that communicating with voters through video would be more powerful than a text-only format, and, therefore, were willing to participate in ITV projects.

CGS enlisted the aid of a multimedia company to help design a prototype of their system. The original prototype included video candidate issue statements and answers to voter questions for the 1994 California gubernatorial and Secretary of State races. Also included was information pertaining to a controversial 1994 California ballot initiative on school vouchers, creating a system for families to use public vouchers to support their children's education at the school of their choice. Video statements from proponents and opponents of the initiative were included on the system as well as analysis from the State Legislative Analyst. The system incorporated other media as well. For example, a campaign commercial against the voucher was included along with a 'truth box' analysis of the advertisement by a local newspaper. The system was menu-based, so that users could select information that they perceived to be most relevant to them.

When the prototype was completed in the fall of 1994, it attracted media attention, as it provided an example of the way in which the information superhighway could be used to provide public service information. The prototype was mentioned in publications major US newspapers, including the *Wall Street Journal* and the *Washington Post*. Because the project had achieved a public presence, representatives from CGS were able to effectively make contact with the major leaders of ITV projects, including some of the regional bell operating companies and multi-service cable operators, such as Time Warner. At one point, it appeared that there were good possibilities of getting DNet installed in ITV systems planned by PacTel, Bell Atlantic, Nynex, US West, Time Warner, and Viacom. However, by 1995 many companies began retreating from their ITV operations. They discovered that early demand for these services was not as high as initially anticipated, and questioned their long-term profitability. Most of those companies initially interested in the DNet prototype soon lost interest in the system.

One exception was Time Warner. Time Warner decided to proceed with its ITV Full Service Network (FSN) operations in Orlando, Florida. Representatives of Tim Warner remained interested in DNet's participation and went ahead with plans to provide voter information concerning the November 1996 national elections. Representatives of Time Warner suggested that DNet designers work with Time Inc. New Media in New York, which was creating an interactive news channel called the 'News Exchange'. Time Warner suggested that DNet could be included as one part of this news exchange.

CGS began assembling content for the 1996 Presidential candidates. While the initial goal was to have DNet up and running by the key primaries, multiple technical problems with the ITV system prevented DNet from being launched until August 1996, just before the Democratic and Republican Conventions. While some of the information on DNet was out of date by this point, and included statements by candidates who had dropped out of the race, the system was updated to include information about Clinton and Dole.

Despite these problems, designers of DNet viewed its experiment with ITV operations to be a success overall. There seemed to be high participation on DNet by candidates. Even incumbents who are traditionally less eager to take political risks participated in the system. Viewership was somewhat difficult to assess and DNet was not actively promoted. However, CGS recognised that they successfully built the first interactive video voter system, and whenever major industry leaders decide to move back in the direction of ITV, they would have the experience and know-how to participate in the development of this technology.

THE INTERNET AND THE WEB: Despite the success of the Orlando, Florida experiment for DNet, Warner abandoned its FSN. For the near-term, CGS recognised that ITV was not going to provide the wide dissemination of information they had originally anticipated. If DNet was going to reach a wide number of homes, then CGS needed to develop its application for those media available to voters.

By 1996, the explosion of interest in the Internet was in full swing, and CGS began to realise that the web might provide a more viable system for video delivery. CGS began efforts to create a system with the key components of the ITV system and make this available on the Internet, as well as over systems designed for web-TV. Plans were begun to create a system on the Internet that would provide community-based and national communication and information.

The role of technological paradigms

The move from ITV to the web provides an example of the way in which technological paradigms can shape the development of a new technology. Within the scientific community, paradigms provide frameworks that influence how we interpret new information. They provide the analogies and metaphors which allow for the interpretation of new data and the questions that are asked. Researchers concerned with the social shaping of technology have applied this notion of a paradigm to the development of technology. Existing technology provides the model or exemplar within which new technology may be developed. The view that new technologies are based on older technologies suggests that the design decisions of older technologies will be very important as these form the basis for later design choices.

In the case of DNet, ITV provided the paradigm for the delivery of information which was later applied to the web. Originally, candidate issues statements were included on the ITV system and viewers could select which statements they wished to access and compare candidate statements across issues. The original conception of DNet also included ballot information, and press information such as editorials. All of this information is included on the web. Moreover, as the capabilities of the Internet and web have been enhanced, enabling easier access to motion video, CGS has sought to move DNet even closer to its earlier vision for ITV. In such ways, ITV provided a paradigm in terms of both format and content for the web-site. There are some differences between the ITV version of DNet and its web-based version. The original conception of DNet was almost anti-text and key information was offered in video form. Given the textual nature of the web, text is a key component of DNet. However, like the ITV system, designers are working on incorporating more video onto the web. While video currently is available over the web, the video must be downloaded. It takes users approximately 11 minutes to download clips. Efforts are being made to incorporate into the system a faster and more convenient method for users to access the video. In addition, the web, through the use of bulletin boards and chat rooms, offers more opportunity for horizontal communication among users rather than the more one way vertical patterns of communication from candidates to users supported by the mass media. The voter-to-voter applications of the system appear to be among the most popular. Finally, the web offered more flexibility than the ITV system, as candidates could instantaneously update state-ments and engage in debate through its RUS. In such ways, older technology has shaped newer technology.

LEGAL ANALOGIES LEADING NEW TECHNOLOGY: CGS has been led by attorneys with expertise in communications law. One of the princi-pals, Tracy Westen, was a public interest lawyer and professor of communications law with expertise in free speech and First Amendment issues. This background contributed to free speech as well as other legal concerns having direct effects on the design of the technology.

EQUAL OPPORTUNITIES: One legal provision which had an impact on DNet was the equal opportunities provision (Section 315) of the US Communications Act 1934. This provision applies to broadcasters and cable operators, and provides that if a station sells time to one candi-date, the station must provide equal opportunities for all other candi-dates for the same office to purchase comparable time. Similarly, if a station gives time to one candidate, they must give comparable time to all other candidates for the same office.

The equal opportunities provision had a particularly important role for two reasons. First, key developers of DNet had been advocates of the equal time provision in the broadcasting context, because it ensured greater fairness. It was important to the principals at CGS that this equal opportunities concern be applied to DNet, especially since the arguments opposed to equal opportunities in the broadcasting context seemed less applicable on the web. Thus, the structure of the system was built on the provision of equal opportunities for all candidates to participate. If one candidate provides an issue statement, then all other candidates have equal opportunities to offer competing issue statements or to create other issues for debate. Secondly, DNet can offer a system that is even more egalitarian than the equal time provision can be in the broadcasting context, as neither money nor space is necessarily a barrier to participation on the web. As noted above, in the US broadcasting context, the equal opportunities provision applies to both free and paid commercial time. To the extent that one candidate has significantly more funding than another, cost provides a barrier to taking advantage of the equal opportunities provision. With DNet over the web, candidates did not even need access to a computer to participate, as CGS made provision to enter even hand-written statements from candidates onto DNet.

CENSORSHIP: The equal opportunities provision shaped design of the system in other ways, through its 'no censorship' provision. The equal opportunities provision of the Communications Act provides that station owners cannot censor in any way the content of candidate television advertisements. The courts have held that this provision shields broadcasters from liability if one candidate libels another candidate in a television advertisement. As broadcasters cannot control the content of the campaign advertisements, they are immune from liability.[8] The developers of DNet were familiar with this doctrine in the broadcasting context and saw it as applicable to their web-site. They must not control the content of any candidate statements, even if such statements are libellous, as this could open DNet to potential liability.

Creating a system which ensured fairness to all candidates and which imposed a strict First Amendment ethic, in terms of not imposing any censorship, was also of value to the success of the system. It reinforced the developers' commitment to providing a system which was as neutral as possible and which avoided even the appearance of being non-partisan. This was important for a variety of reasons. First, candidates would not want to participate if they perceived that the system favoured certain candidates or positions over others. Secondly, although CGS is a non-profit corporation, it is important that CGS obtain funding to support its activities. If DNet appeared partisan, then foundations and other potential funding sources would not be willing to provide support.

Finally, designers want various government home pages to create links to DNet. However, city governments for example have very strict guidelines and cannot be perceived as sponsoring a candidate or point of view. For instance, CGS originally thought that DNet could be run by city clerks within cities around the country. It soon became clear to them, however, that city clerks were too concerned about doing anything that might appear partisan to be enthusiastic about administering such a system.

THE FIRST AMENDMENT: CGS was influenced also by the type of free speech model which it viewed to be most applicable to DNet. CGS principals, for example, recognised that the system was not akin to a common carrier, because designers drafted specific rules for communication, similar to something like Roberts Rules of Order in the electronic context. In this sense, DNet went well beyond the role of a common carrier.

CGS carefully considered what the impact of particular rules would be. For example, they weighed whether candidates should be able to delete information. They decided that candidates should not be able to delete old information. Once a statement was made it became part of the record of candidate statements. Statements may only be changed or corrected by adding new statements. CGS also decided early on in the development of the system that they were not publishers of information, but distributors. As distributors and not publishers, DNet's developers were careful not to exercise any editorial control over content. By creating a system in which they distributed rather than published information, CGS attempted to strategically position itself in ways that would decrease any risk of liability.

US case law pertaining to electronic communications has established the principle that distributors' of electronic information may not be held liable for defamation, whereas publishers' may be held liable. In *Cubby Inc. v Compuserve Inc.*,[9] a lower federal court held that Compuserve was a distributor of electronic information and did not exercise editorial control over content. As such, distributors of electronic information may not be held liable for defamation unless they '. . . knew or had reason to know of the allegedly defamatory . . . statements'. Another federal lower court in *Stratton Oakmont v Prodigy Services Corporation*[10] held that Prodigy was a publisher of information because it created content guidelines and exercised some editorial control by providing services which instantly eliminated objectionable messages on its electronic bulletin boards. In light of this role, Prodigy could be held liable for defamation.

In 1996, Congress enacted the Communications Decency Act which effectively overruled the Prodigy decision. The Communications

Decency Act states that on-line service providers may not be classified as 'publishers' and, therefore, are shielded from liability for defamatory statements made by users of such services.[11] In June 1997, sections of the Communications Decency Act were declared unconstitutional by the Supreme Court.[12] However, the section of the Communications Decency Act shielding on-line service providers from liability remained in effect. CGS knew that the *Cubby* standard also remained in effect, so that if on-line information service providers are aware of defamatory statements made by users, then they may be held liable for defamation.

More generally, CGS was well aware of this case law and statutory law which applied to on-line service providers and the distinction between 'publishers' and 'distributors' of information concerning liability. They were influenced by this knowledge and recognised early on in the development of the system that they should not take on the role of publishers and, therefore, must not exercise editorial control. Instead, they saw themselves as distributors which provided a menu-based system for content provided by others. In this instance, legal precedent had important impacts early on in the development of the technology.

REGULATING INDECENCY AND OBSCENE SPEECH ON THE INTERNET: The developers were also thinking strategically about how the courts would rule on the regulation of indecency and obscenity on the Internet. CGS wanted to create a system of communication with as much uncensored speech as possible. Thus, the developers decided not to institute a policy where system operators would search for and delete indecent or obscene words. Rather than creating highly moderated discourse, CGS instead moved in the direction of providing uncensored discourse. At the same time, including a disclaimer that system operators may delete speech in order to protect themselves from liability. Along with recognising the importance of a free speech ethic, CGS recognised that they simply did not have the staff resources to institute such rules.

Given these constraints, CGS imposed a '*Cubby*-type' standard with regard to obscenity. Thus, while system operators were not instructed to actively search for obscene speech, if they became aware of obscene speech posted to bulletin boards, they would remove it from the system in order to protect themselves from any potential liability. As a practical matter, this issue was raised in only one instance, which did not require intervention from CGS.

THE REGULATION OF CAMPAIGN FINANCING: Those who designed DNet were initially focused on content issues and liability, such as liability for defamation, but no candidate or voter raised the issue of defamation. Instead, candidates expressed concern about complying with Federal Election Commission (FEC) rules concerning whether participation on the system might constitute an illegal corporate contribution. This became one of the primary legal issues tied to DNet. Whether a candidate's participation on DNet constituted an illegal corporate contribution was initially raised by President Bill Clinton's campaign staff in connection with the ITV project in Orlando, Florida. According to FEC rules, it is illegal for corporations, even non-profit corporations, to provide services to candidates at less than the normal charge. DNet's developers concluded as a voter's guide, the system was strictly informational and, therefore, fell within one of the exemptions to the rules.

The FEC had established standards for determining whether a document constitutes a voter's guide. DNet was familiar with these rules and, as such, the system was designed to comply with the FEC standards. The FEC, for example, requires that voter's guides must direct questions to candidates. There was some question concerning whether or not the candidate's identification of issues constituted 'questions'. Therefore, the system was re-designed so that participation came in the form of questions.

The issue of whether participation on DNet constituted an illegal corporate contribution was again raised by Clinton's campaign staff in conjunction with the web-site. The FEC had ruled specifically that Compuserve and other Internet service providers may not provide free Internet access to federal candidates because this constituted an illegal corporate contribution. When Clinton's campaign staff raised concerns over whether participation on DNet would be construed as an illegal corporate contribution, CGS argued that DNet was sufficiently different from Compuserve so as not to constitute an illegal corporate contribution. DNet did not, for example, provide free Internet access and candidates must use their own Internet service providers to view DNet's web-site. Moreover, DNet did not charge anyone for access. Despite these arguments, the Clinton campaign declined participation on DNet's web-site, arguing that they did not have time to review the legal arguments before the campaign. At this time, the Clinton campaign was already facing charges of engaging in illegal campaign finance practices. Thus, though not originally anticipated by designers, campaign finance rules had an impact on system design and policy.

LAW OUTPACING TECHNOLOGY?:   DNet provides a dramatic example of the way in which technological paradigms as well as public policy concerns can drive the development of technology. Many legal scholars and social scientists assume that law rarely keeps pace with technology. They see the law applied to technology after its development to resolve emerging conflicts and litigation, as in the case of the Communications Decency Act. Issues raised over the conformance of DNet with campaign finance regulations conform with this expectation. However, with DNet, it was more often the case that legal issues were anticipated well in advance of the development of the technology, before the issues arose. The development of DNet demonstrates that law can have an important role very early in the development of technology and therefore challenges more linear perspectives on the law and technological change.

Designers, for example, could have created a highly moderated system for discourse. Yet because designers were concerned about potential tort liability and embraced a strong free speech ethic (for both ideological and pragmatic reasons), they declined to exercise editorial control and encouraged free and open debate in a manner accessible to the American public. In addition, this case study suggests that the legal issues underlying the development of emerging forms of political communication are far from limited to models of content regulation, such as in the applicability of the First Amendment. Campaign financing, liability, and other considerations such as copyright need to be more carefully examined in studies of the social shaping of digital democracy.

THE ROLE OF DNET — THE GUBERNATORIAL RACE OF 1998:[13] CGS wanted to create a system where more meaningful information could be provided for voters, and where candidates could compete for votes on an equal playing field. Thus, DNet was intended to fulfil a democratising function by encouraging more information and issue-oriented campaigns than are available via traditional media.

However, the use of DNet by candidates and voters in the 1998 California gubernatorial primary elections illuminates obstacles, such as the public's interest in politics, that continue to limit the contribution of the Internet to political campaigns and elections. An examination of DNet use before the gubernatorial election in California revealed that usage significantly increased one week before the election. In total 3,431 unique visitors were identified in the one week before the election. These numbers are comparable with usage of other sites with information about elections or political campaigns. The numbers, however, are still limited. This is perhaps not surprising given that DNet is a fairly new initiative on a medium that despite an incredible growth in recent years, still has a marginal reach compared with more traditional mass media. However, this limited number of visitors suggests that DNet's role in the political arena is at the margins.

A potentially more significant finding in the longer-term concerns the way in which voters used DNet. With respect to the issue grid (the most popular feature of DNet), the information most easily available — the first page — was accessed most frequently. In fact, only a small percentage of the respondents that viewed the first pages of the grid also viewed subsequent pages, and the drop-off of users after using the first one to two pages was quite dramatic. This might be an indication of limited interest or motivation on the part of the user to explore a large number of issues, as well as a reflection of more general patterns for surfing the web, which lead users to view only one or two pages of any particular web-site, on average. This suggests that designers of electronic democracy systems may have difficulty overcoming the larger problem of general voter apathy, disinterest in politics, and the fact that most users of the Internet are not avid information-seekers. Thus, electronic democracy systems may become a forum whose primary audience is the politically active minority.

Another relevant finding was that users mainly explored statements expressed by the major candidates. As a result, the minority candidates that in theory could benefit the most from DNet as a way to reach voters, did not do so in reality. Finally, while almost all of the candidates participated on DNet, the debate was dominated by the candidates and issues that dominated the mass media of radio and television. Moreover, the majority of the information on DNet from the four major candidates was derived from other sources of information. However, when compared with television ads, DNet did provide voters with a broader and more in-depth discussion of the issues that played a role in the election.

When comparing the information available over DNet with information available on the candidates' own web-sites, candidates often provided voters with more issue information on their own web-sites than they provided on DNet. Thus, while the candidates' web-sites may have helped provide information for DNet, the web-sites also may have undermined participation. There are several possible explanations as to why many candidates preferred communication via their own web-sites rather than via DNet. Campaign staff perceived that DNet had limited reach and, therefore, did not see DNet as valuable for targeting the crucial swing votes within the campaign. (Yet they sensed their own web-sites to be quite popular.) Moreover, the candidates tended to perceive their own web-sites as increasingly important campaign tools for organising and searching for volunteers, soliciting contributions and registering voters, functions they did not associate with a shared site. Campaign staff viewed the Internet as a tool for communication within the campaign organisation, which may have blinded staff to the possibility of using the Internet to appeal directly to voters.

The use of DNet by voters and candidates during the 1998 gubernatorial primary in California suggests that electronic democracy systems may be pushed in the direction of fulfilling roles similar to traditional mass media. Because users tended to view only the first one or two pages of the issue grid and tended only to examine the issue statements of the four major candidates, designers are beginning to re-examine the presentation of material. Rather than presenting material in alphabetical order, designers are considering providing scrolling issue grids, or allowing users to rank order the issues themselves in order of importance, so that once a user identifies as issue as important, this will appear first. CGS is also moving toward putting the candidates' introductory statements upfront, as a possible way to hold the user. This suggests that CGS may have to take on more of an editorial role in order to encourage greater viewership, just as the traditional media make editorial decisions to encourage greater viewership. Use, then, is reshaping design.

Candidate use of DNet also suggests a convergence of the new media toward the traditional media. Most of the information on DNet, for example, was available other places — either from the traditional media or from the candidates' own web-sites. Efforts to enhance the value of DNet might well move this new medium closer to the more traditional media. Despite this convergence, there is room for optimism about the role of electronic democracy in general and DNet in particular. As noted above, while DNet replicated much information found elsewhere, it did offer a more comprehensive and detailed debate to voters than can be found over traditional media. Moreover, since the 1998 elections, DNet has significantly expanded the number of elections covered as well as the number of users. Since the California gubernatorial primary, for example, DNet has reported a 2,000% increase in traffic from early October until the general election in November 1998. One reason for this increase is technological; the 'Web White and Blue', a US national election awareness site, has helped DNet dramatically increase its visibility on the web. In addition, DNet designers have implemented an automatic e-mail notification system, where candidates are notified via e-mail when their opponents add to or change issue statements. This feature has encouraged more candidate participation because candidates do not want to give their opponents an advantage. As DNet continues to gain a presence, campaign staffers will begin to understand the utility of using this new medium to reach voters leading, in turn, to even greater utilisation. Thus, while DNet currently serves a politically active minority, there is some room optimism that the wider diffusion of DNet could create a virtuous cycle of greater utilisation.

1   The first part of this chapter is based on research reported in more detail by Docter and Dutton (1999), which provides a more detailed set of references to important sources and related literature. See, S. Docter and W.H. Dutton, 'The Social Shaping of the Democracy Network (DNet)' in B. Hague and B. Loader (eds), *Digital Democracy: Discourse and Decision-Making in the Information Age*, London, Routledge, forthcoming.
2   I. de Sola Pool, *Technologies of Freedom*, Cambridge, MA, Harvard U.P., 1983, 5.
3   See generally, L.E. Becker, 'The Liability of Computer Bulletin Board Operators for Defamation Posted by Others', *Conn. L. Rev.*, 1989, 22/203–72; R. Corn-Revere, 'New Technology and the First Amendment; Breaking the Cycle of Repression', *Hastings Comm./Ent. L.J.*, 1994, 17/247–345; T.A. Cutrera, 'Computer Networks, Libel and the First Amendment', *Computer L.J.*, 1992, 11/555–83; E.C. Jensen, 'An Electronic Soapbox: Computer Bulletin Boards and the First Amendment', *Federal Comm. L.J.*, 1987, 39/217–58; E.J. Naughton, 'Is Cyberspace a Public Forum? Computer Bulletin Boards, Free Speech and State Action', *Georgetown Univ. L.J.*, 1992, 81/409–41. H.H. Perritt, 'The Congress, the Courts and Computer-based Communication Networks: Answering Questions about Access and Control', *Villanova L. Rev.*, 1993, 38/319–48, and 'Tort Liability, the First Amendment, and Equal Access to Electronic Networks', *Harvard J.L. & Tech.*, 1992, 5/65; E. Schalacter, 'Cyberspace, the Free Market and the Free Marketplace of Ideas: Recognizing Differences in Computer Bulletin Board Functions', *Hastings Comm./Ent L.J.*, 1993, 16/87–150; M.L. Taviss, 'Dueling Forums:

The Public Forum Doctrine's Failure to Protect the Electronic Forum', *Univ. Cincinnati L. Rev.*, 1992, 60/757–95.
4   DNet is available at: http://www.dnet.org.
5   T. Westen, 'Can Technology Save Democracy?', *National Civic Rev. P.*, 1998, 38.
6   See, A. Elberse, W.H. Dutton and M. Hale, 'Guiding Voters through the Net' in K.L. Hacker and J.A.G.M. van Dijk (eds), *Virtual Democracy: Issues in Theory and Practice*, Thousand Oaks, CA, Sage, forthcoming.
7   Ibid., n. 5.
8   *Farmers Educational and Cooperative Union of America v WDAY*, 360 US 525, 79 S.Ct. 1302 (1959).
9   *Cubby Inc. v Compuserve Inc.*, 776 F. Supp. 135 (SDNY 1991), 141.
10 *Stratton Oakmont Inc. v Prodigy Services Co.*, 23 Media L. Rep. 1794 (1995).
11 47 USC section 230 ©(1).
12 *Reno v American Civil Liberties Union et al.*, 117 S.Ct. 2329 (1997).
13 This section is based on a more detailed discussion of the role of DNet in the 1998 Gubernatorial primaries in California. Ibid., n. 6.

Parliamentary Futures:
Re-Presenting the Issue Information,
Technology and the Dynamics of Democracy

BY BERT MULDER

Introduction

Democracy and information have close ties. In any democratic activity, being informed, together with the ability to participate in open dialogue are both necessities and rights. The ability to express oneself to others, the freedom of the press, the form in which one can partake in or be represented in democratic dialogue, all depend on the structure of information systems, be they technical, financial, legal or social. The democratic process is always realised in media infrastructures. One might say that the quality of the democratic process is determined by the information infrastructure it takes place in. Consequently, changing the media infrastructure will change the dynamics of democracy.

This chapter looks at developments in information technology that are taking place now as the information society unfolds, and at their possible influence on parliaments. In coming years all parliaments will go through the same development as all other organisations in society and renew their information infrastructures. Which infrastructures will the information society use? These new information infrastructures need to be designed to last a reasonable period. How will we establish their design criteria when we do not really know what the next five or ten years will bring?

The treatment of the subject is pragmatic and consists of observations of trends and developments, and questions about the consequences these have for parliaments. It looks at the effects of the developments in the domains of information, communication, coordination and coop-eration. It examines the position of designers of information systems, who, while designing new systems, are faced with strategic considera-tions that have no real answers and little thinking and research done on them. It is not their position to answer these issues, yet in their designs they do so.

The purpose of this chapter is not so much to describe a future with great certainty, although many of the trends may happen, but to try and raise questions at the right level. Ultimately the answers will depend on how one views the role of parliaments in the information society.

Framing the debate

Reflection on parliamentary future from the perspective of telematics has to start with obvious but not trivial questions: what parliaments? what future? what telematics? In order to debate 'parliament' in relation to telematics one needs to use a language that describes parliaments as well as telematics in common language and with appropriate conceptual structures, otherwise one cannot make valid statements about the relationship between the two. With the development of the information society and its growing effects on parliament and democracy, the study that concern themselves with the subject will have to adopt a vocabulary that will be closer to terms like information, dialogue and media.

In considering parliamentary futures in relation to telematics, the term 'telematics' is itself confusing. It might introduce a technological bias that can be harmful to the treatment of the issue. In looking at the coming years we may assume that a strong development of technical possibilities and increasing availability will be the order of the day. That makes today's technology primitive, complex and expensive compared to that of tomorrow. But the real issue is not information or communication *technology*, but information *society*. The immense developments that are taking place right now need to be seen in a far wider perspective than just technology. That distinction is important because it shapes the answers we create. Either we look upon the developments as technical developments that support existing structures and forms of organisation, or we see them as larger transformations that change the way we organise ourselves. The former would leave parliaments unchanged but more effective, the latter would deeply change the role parliaments play in the information society.

In this chapter both viewpoints are used as a framework to describe possible effects of the development of information technology. Firstly, ICTs are treated as functional influences within the existing structures. Secondly, the development of ICTs are treated as developments of an information society, where the transformation is characterised by a deep and widespread restructuring on all levels and at a global scale. Some of the characteristics of this new form of order are flexibility, networklike organisations, dialogue between equal partners and increasing reflection to support this process. In these changes we find telematics play an important role. We developed *telematics as a tool to facilitate wider transformation towards a new society*. Although telematics and change often coexist, it is not immediately evident that the onset of technology *caused* the changes, although it certainly facilitates them.

In considering parliamentary futures, 'future' is another term that needs to be approached carefully. First one needs to consider what period one wants to include. In the area of telematics developments take place so quickly that there will be a great difference between a five-year and a ten-year period. But one may also describe the future not as a period, but as a situation with certain qualities. The future is a society with information and communication networks as a broad infrastructure and basic access for all. At the current rate that may be the case in western societies between five and ten years. Another concern whose future it is we are talking about. Future in this sense may be highly situated and the differences between eastern or western, large or small, low income or high income, young or old may be considerable. The great differences in development create different futures.

Information, technology and society

'Information' as such is of limited use when considering its effects on the future of parliaments. Information is always used to communicate. Communication between partners leads to coordination of actions and when coordination is increased it leads to cooperation. Changing the nature of information will change the way we communicate, coordinate and cooperate. Increasing the use of information and information technology will increase other aspects also.

We can say that the information society will not only provide networks of information, but also create a distributed infrastructure for communication, coordination and cooperation. While the information society can be looked at in terms of information and consequently as the distribution of the means of consumption and production of information, it may also be seen as the distribution of the means to organise, or the means of decision-making. The information society creates a generic infrastructure in which these possibilities will be there for all to use. And that, much more than information, is where parliaments will feel the effects of these developments.

Information

The word 'information' is often used in an almost physical quality. It is treated as 'something' that exists, that can be created, stored, distributed and consumed. Information is considered as a product: it has owners and earns money and does not change. This view is effective in some instances, but information can also be seen as a process. The symbols we use to communicate information do not carry meaning in themselves. The meaning of information is the result of a complex process in which the reader contextualises data and information. Here information is a process and meaning is created every time we contextualise the symbols that are used to communicate. In this process the symbolic (re)presentation is crucial when it acts as an intermediary that catalyses the generation of meaning. For the sake of argument we may say that the representation plays a central role in the issue: representing information *is* the issue. It shapes the perception and the debate. Looked at it in that way changing the [re]presentation of an issue changes the issue.

RE-PRESENTING THE ISSUE: What would the national budget look like if it existed in a new media environment as a dynamic, distributed multimedia hypertext representation? Everyone would be able to access the budget through full-text searches, retrieving small texts customised for the issue at stake. In the frozen version of today, numbers fall into a single category only; a dynamic representation tomorrow would allow different interpretations to coexist. While today the author determines what information looks like, tomorrow readers could add their own interpretations, connecting their own information networks to that of the authors. Spreadsheets would be dynamic and allow users to look at different scenarios. The distributed nature of the information would allow users to start with the overview and then drill down to details, which might reside at the original author's location. Remarks might be added to figures and pieces of text or discussions between several people attached to them. The national budget would be less of a document and more of a process, reflecting changes over time.

This simple scenario uses existing technology and can be created simply today. It raises some basic issues when we realise that the abstract presentation of information actually re-presents the national financial infrastructure which for many parliaments forms the roadmap for their activities. When we change this re-presentation would we lose consistency or increase usefulness? When the national budget as an information system would be open and accessible, and many people would add their own systems of disclosure, tuning the national budget for their specific viewpoint, how could they do so without jeopardising the initial meaning of its original creators?

From the viewpoint of information design, the issue stands as follows: the re-presentation of information plays a crucial role in the presentation of an issue. Stated strongly one might say the re-presentation *is* the issue. Development in information technology will deeply affect the presentation of information, and with that the way we deal with issues. The resulting question would open a field of research: what is the effect of changing representations? How does a distributed information environment affect our deliberation and decision-making?

Today parliaments have their own document staff and maintain their own collection of information. These professional roles will develop during the next few years to incorporate new activities. Parliaments may play a catalysing role because they are central to the handling of information from all governmental departments. Adoption of new forms of information disclosure may have a strong influence on those providing the information: proposed decisions must be consistent and well formed in the re-presentation used.

FORM, STRUCTURE, BEHAVIOUR AND CONTENT: New media designers speak of four different aspects of information which need to be designed: content, form, structure and behaviour. Content and form have been with us for a long time, since they describe the current document-centric way of working. The development of electronic media adds structure and behaviour as new issues. The linear text on paper is replaced by a network of electronic texts pointing to each other and interactive systems invite the user to participate in the experience.

Visual information: The form of information is changing. Parliaments think in terms of documents, mainly filled with text and an occasional picture. With the development of new media, written text can be enhanced to include images, sound and video to create an integrated multi media document. The presentation of information will be more dynamic, more real time and appear more distributed as a (hypertext) network. Using visual material to re-present information will become more usual for two reasons. First, the production and incorporation of visual material in digital documents becomes easier, and second, there is a growing need for an integrated overview of complex issues. In future maps, diagrams, organograms, timelines and photographic material will appear in parliamentary documents. Initially they will be available as ordinary material but later they will be used not only as passive re-presentations but also as active interaction elements through which readers may connect to other material. Analysis of parliamentary material shows that this material will only represent a small part of all available material and as such put no great extra strain on document staff. It will require them to develop a new understanding of the role of forms of information other than text.

Multimedia: The possibility to add digital audio and video will change things. Initially digital audio will be used as an effective means to support the parliamentary stenographers and as a way of distributing audio signals as a broadcast over the Internet, as is current practice in several parliaments. Next the audio signal will be integrated with other available information systems. This will create an information environment where during a speech, important background material may be retrieved immediately. In its developed form it will form an interactive radio station, where audio may lead to an overview of all other material, while documentary material may lead to (historical) audio material. The development of these different stages will be gradual. After the initial ability to put audio real time on the Internet, the ability to integrate audio with other information will be developed, along with the ability to store older material.

The same development will take place with regard to the video-signal of parliamentary meetings. Predicting these developments, although they may seem improbable for some parliaments at his moment, is quite easy. The speed of technological development in these areas will be phenomenal and in a few years the infrastructures and the basic technology will be cheap and easy to use. Adopting these technologies will not require extremely large sums of money; they will become

available as a by-product of the parliamentary information infrastructure requiring little physical work. The consequence is that parliaments will be broadcasting organisations. Will this development be
important to parliaments and secure them a position in the new media
infrastructure of the information society?

Structure — networked collections: The growing ability to link texts
together using Internet technology is basic to the development that
'text', or a document will take on the quality of a network. It will form
a centre containing links or pointers to other supporting explanatory
information or to other related documents. The development has several
results: it breaks down the closed, contained document as we know it
and replaces it with a network of information. How do we manage the
consistency within such a network of information? Can we link to other
information and succeed in keeping these links 'well formed'? Could we
not point to other collections of information outside our own organisations? Could national parliaments in the European Union not refer to
documents kept at the offices of the European Union through direct
links over the Internet, without storing them locally? Could interested
citizens not link to parliamentary documents directly without storing
them at their own local sites? Could we then create a national store of
consolidated legal texts to which everyone could link their own documents whenever they refer to legal texts? Again it is not possible to
answer these questions easily. But it is possible to develop an understanding of what would be necessary to support such developments —
the ability to contain links in documents in a structured way, to create
and maintain links in such a way that they do not disappear or change
over time. The choice to be made here is whether one should strive to
collect all information in a central location and maintain it there or
develop a network of source collections that through a strong and well
maintained linking mechanism over the Internet, could provide a syn-
ergy for all. These developments will start discussion on national level
and play a role in the integration of government information in general.

Behaviour — real time: Digital systems make information readily available and more directly connected to the processes taking place. The
agenda of sessions available on-line will be coupled with systems that
support the management of meetings in the chamber so that information on speakers and their subjects is available as they speak. This raises
interesting issues: today the agenda is a document. It is created, sent out
and archived. But with the agenda maintained in a database that is
accessible to all, what is the agenda? Three weeks in advance? When it
is sent? At the start of the meeting, incorporating the latest updates? Or
just after the start, when those present decided to change it? Or
afterwards? In any of these cases the agenda reflects the situation at
that moment. With the information available on the Internet, the public

is interested in the last minute changes because it tells them what is happening and whether to attend or postpone their visit. Members may also be interested in last minute changes, because it saves them an appearance when their subject is moved off the agenda. The agenda is not a document, it is a process. Which 'agenda' do we archive afterwards? These questions lead to a new set of agreements that will have to be made between the parliament and the organisation responsible for the national archives.

This dynamic agenda coupled with the possibility of distributing digital video images on the Internet will make for a truly interactive television channel. Superior design will create an environment where, while the speaker is addressing the subject, the current information and the historic context of the subject under consideration can be presented. The consequence of this development is that interested parties will follow the parliamentary process much more immediately and many more people can and will check the development of issues more intensely than before.

Communication

Often new technologies are treated in a way that describes more what they are and less what they do. Communication technologies have to do with connection: they either connect or disconnect. The tools that link may bring together what was apart, and may separate what was together. They may create communities or break up communities, they may create an issue or dissolve one, and they may strengthen or dissolve the existing power structure. In political parties this effect is felt as groups of young members use e-mail to communicate, quickly assemble a following that uses the same communication infrastructure and organise themselves outside the existing party hierarchy. Introducing a new communications infrastructure can disturb the existing balance of power in organisations.

NEW PARTNERS, NEW LANGUAGES: In many countries a larger part of the population will come on-line during the coming years. They may come on-line individually or through schools, libraries or community media infrastructures; the effect will be the same. With more diverse groups of people on-line, it becomes necessary to make parliamentary information meaningful to them. Currently parliamentary activity is a highly professional environment in which one has to be experienced to take part: members, aides, legal staff and civil servants all understand the intricacies of the process and its jargon as do lobbyists and issue organisations. Making documents available on-line will not change that. The openness of the democratic process today does not mean it is understandable for all. When parliamentary information is available with such immediacy as described above it might mean that 'openness' and 'access' will be interpreted in a new way and not accepted as it is today.

PUBLISHING HOUSE: On the Internet new technologies to distribute media products are being developed. These make it possible for users not to have to actively look for pages over the Internet, but to subscribe to information that is then sent to them automatically. The information products are defined using standards (e.g. the XML ICE standard for information content exchange) that fully automate the distribution to any number of clients and require no human intervention once set up. It seems a very convenient technology whose result would be that anyone could have an up-to-date parliamentary dossier or agenda on his or her local computer, 24-hours a day. After one subscribes to the parliamentary agenda any change is immediately and automatically updated. After the initial set-up and subscription this requires no extra activity from either the user or the parliament. Updates are 'incremental': only the actual changes are sent over the network, keeping network load to an absolute minimum.

In the future parliamentary information might be structured as dossiers to which interested people can then subscribe. These dossiers are then automatically distributed and kept up to date. With regard to this development there are many things to consider: what should a dossier contain, were it to be effective? What structure should the database have to be able to support this service? If people subscribe only to what they think is interesting, do they not lose a general overview of parliamentary activity? Does one need a general overview? This complete automation of distribution would mean that the dynamic nature of the information system of parliaments makes them publishers, not by choice, but because information systems have that inherent quality. Does a parliament need to support this distributed information paradigm to be able to operate in the information society?

Coordination

The information society is often seen as the distribution of information, but it may also be seen as the distribution of the tools to organise. Parliament itself might be seen as 'a tool to organise' the process of decision-making. With more general distribution of tools to organise, would these interfere with the activities of the parliament?

A MEMBER'S PARLIAMENT: The parliament is an infrastructure that organises resources to support the work of Members of Parliament. One side of that organisation concerns itself with content: the creation, edition, storage and dissemination of documents. Another deals with the process of parliamentary activity: organising and coordinating meetings. In the next few years both of these aspects will be supported by information systems. With the easier availability of ICTs the infrastructure will move from organisations to individuals. Processing power, storage, servers, internet capabilities, and software that searches and retrieves information coordinates activities between teams of people will be available in such a standardised way that its use will be ubiquitous: the means of production and organisation will be distributed. It will become easier for individual Members of Parliament to have his or her own network of people and groups and to maintain it, coordinating research, focus groups, polls and coordinate activities in larger groups of people than is possible today. This will make Members of Parliament more independent from central infrastructure, be that from the Parliament or the Party. They can also more easily organise activities in their constituency.

ISSUE BASED POLITICS: The same capabilities to organise will become available throughout society. Although people in society may feel strongly about issues today, they do not have the tools to organise themselves, express their feelings, get together, deliberate and advance their ideas about it. Parliament is one of the institutions that does that. It is an infrastructure for constructive deliberation. The availability of the means to organise throughout society will change that. It will make it easier for people to make themselves heard changing the dynamics of political debate.

The interest in standing organisations like political parties is waning. At the same time interest in the condition of the local environment is growing. Single issue organisations like those on ecological concerns or on transportation have strong memberships and increasingly catalyse political standpoints. Another good example is the remark of one of the leaders of the Dutch Labour Party, looking at the decline in membership, that political parties should cease to exist and re-establish themselves as a series of conversations. There would be no membership, but they would organise deliberation on issues. Once the issue was over, the conversations would end. It is a reference to the same trend: no standing organisation and issue based deliberation. The question is what the parliament should do to balance these developments and its own activities.

ACTIVE CONTENT: Other technological developments that will stimulate the ability to organise are the standards that allow data to be embedded in documents. New standards like XML have now developed as an open and extensive technology for the exchange of information on the Internet. It allows descriptive data to be added to documents that may concern the structure of the documents, the style with which they are shown, the links they contain, or data that concerns the process they are part of. This simplifies the automated processing of texts into publications, the automated distribution of publications, and the integration of texts into other data collections. Standardised templates would ease the communication between government and parliament. Not only would the format of the text be correct, but control information would make semi-automatic processing possible. Laws could be stored in a standardised (XML) format. When used in that form as a basis for new legislative activities it would allow checks and the automatic formation of new proposals for law when they follow the old text. This would reduce the chance for errors and make the handling of the texts during the process more effective. This not only eases the processing of documents within parliamentary organisations, but also by individual readers, who may now integrate texts into their own information systems almost without any effort.

This 'ease of use' may lead to individual users taking parliamentary documents and enriching them on their own special interest web-sites. Hundreds of people throughout the country will each work on documents that are important to their cause in a way that may be superior to that of parliamentary archivists. The latter work on documents from a parliamentary point of view, while individual professionals in a field may add more pertinent material concerning practical implementation. When a director of a hospital retires he may still be interested in the field of health and devote all his time to the better disclosure of parliamentary information concerning his field. He creates a high quality special interest web-site geared to his colleagues and the public that contains parliamentary documents, his commentary, (inter)national trends and discussion environment. This is just one of many people with lots of time and no cost considerations that devote their energy to parliamentary affairs.

This easy availability of parliamentary documents will lead to a network of web-sites that re-publish and re-present the issues they deal with. How can the quality of information throughout this network be stimulated and maintained? This is different from the information management of a single system which is under our control. It tries to catalyse quality in an *information ecology* that grows and develops and thein which parliament is one of the participants.

TRANSPARENT ORGANISATION: When information on the process and content is freely available, one needs to create a transparent system. It must be possible to not only see the progress of a certain parliamentary process, but also to check its validity. Accountability will be built into the information systems used. To ensure accountability contextual information is available to users so that they may decide on the validity of the information seen. There are different kinds of context that users may require: the necessary and prescribed steps of the legal process, their legal basis, their execution and possible consequences. In real life this means that when a user sees a document, he or she should be able to see the type of document and the process stage the document is in. It is then possible to get different explanations on the type of the document and the step in the process. These will allow the user to determine whether it is still possible to become active in the process or check the status of people compared with the earlier descriptions. In order to be fully transparent the explanations need to be on different levels of complexity, sometimes for different (professional) audiences, e.g. explanatory or instructive. Only then is a parliamentary system truly parliamentary in that it is accessible to the people with whom it is concerned.

GOVERNMENTAL NETWORKS: The standardisation of the exchange of information will make it easier to exchange information between parliaments and other bodies, like other governmental organisations, the European Union or local governments. It will allow better coordination of work and communication between ministries and the parliament. A well-structured exchange of information could diminish the number of mistakes in existing laws that need adaptation, such as in the SGML/XML based legislative drafting and management solutions that some parliaments are working on (e.g. EnAct in Tasmania).

Cooperation

DECISIVE ACTION: One of the aspects of cooperation is shared decision-making. Currently tools for decision-making have been under development in decision support software (DSS) and in group decision rooms (GDR systems). These developments will continue and lead to forms of distributed decision-making throughout organisations and communities on many different levels. They will be used in business and non-profit organisations, but also throughout communities that are not otherwise organised, leading to new forms of decision-making.

This need not directly affect parliament, because its procedures for decision-making have a constitutional basis. But it will influence political thinking when the ready availability of votes on issues in society, generated through an independent and unsolicited process, will change the dynamics of political democracy. It will catalyse people's feelings on issues when they take responsibility and express their choices. Parliament may or may not take results into consideration, just as they do today with lobbyists and petitions. Its possible effect on parliaments is secondary. If this development is to happen, the position of parliament as a strong provider of high quality information might be strategically advantageous. With a superior source of information, even though decision-making takes place in other systems, the source of information might be close to the formal political institutions. Seen from an information perspective, the product of parliament might not only be decisions, but now that decision-making might be distributed, its product might be the re-presentation of the issue as a basis for high quality decision-making.

A good example is the Dutch system called the 'besliswijzer' (decision support), developed by the non-profit organisation IPP (Institute for Public and Politics). It is basically a database driven web-site, where people may be informed on an issue, determine how they will vote, and then vote. It has been used on issues like national infrastructure. To inform the user on the issue the system provides an explanation of different aspects (economic, legal, financial, environmental, social). When one has read through them one may answer a series of simple questions that help one to determine ones standpoint. They are 'forced choice' questions that in themselves are simpler to answer than the whole issue itself. As a result the system returns a voting advice based on the answers given. The system then allows one to vote, using software that provides anonymity and only one vote per participant. The software is the same as that used in e-cash systems. This system is interesting for a couple or reasons. When first used one becomes aware that there is no place in the media where one can go to be fully informed on an issue. Similarly, the questionnaire actually supports the forming of a standpoint in an open and transparent way. Of course the voting is instrumental, but well executed as far as information systems go. The system has no formal status. But when 300,000 people vote 'no' and politicians vote 'yes', they need to have a good story to back up their decision.

STRUCTURED DECISIONS: Decision-making in the information society needs some other remarks: structure and scale. Any decision depends on other decisions: they are always part of a network of related decisions. With information technology these relations can be made explicit and provide a better context for issues under study. Within the European Union more and more decision-making starts at the European level, and national decision-making has the character of an implementation. The relation between the two is often unclear. Availability of that information would in some cases change the debate when participants realise the actual source of legislation is to be found at a higher level. In other cases, legislation is passed to prepare for other legislation. When the network of decisions is available, knowing the specific law under process would help to clarify the debate. With information technology it is possible to make the structure of decisions explicit.

Without hoping to solve it we have to address the problem of large scale distributed decision-making. Today there are no satisfactory systems that support decision-making on a larger scale. In the coming years much research must be undertaken to see if decision-making lends itself to a larger scale distributed architecture and what qualities it must have. If large-scale decision support systems come into existence, what should the relationship be between these and parliamentary activity?

DELIBERATION: Decisions are made on the basis of argumentation. In today's information systems that have documents as their basic element we store great amounts of text and connect them to the issue they belong to. What is in the text is disclosed through keywords, abstracts, full-text searches and links to information on the parliamentary process. During deliberation we do not think in documents or keywords, we think in arguments. While everyone knows this, the argumentation is open only to professionals because they have access to all the information, the different scenarios for implementation and their consequences. Today information disclosure only concerns the textual content of the text, which does not easily allow us to extract the argumentation. Tomorrow's system might store the text as a series of arguments and the relation between them: for, against, supporting, exemplifying, degrading, diminishing, proving, demonstrating. Next to the network of decisions, we might see a network of arguments supporting those decisions. The structure of the rhetoric is as important to the deliberation as the words used to express it. If systems like these are to be used, they will change the contributions members make to the process and hopefully catalyse well formed arguments. It is clear that in different countries, with different rhetoric and debating styles the effect of this development would be completely different.

DEMOCRATIC DIALOGUE: As stated in the beginning of this chapter, I have looked at parliamentary futures through the eyes of a designer of information systems, caught between the necessity of designing systems and the unavailability of good knowledge on the choices described. This is true for the larger effect of systems also: when these technologies stimulate communication throughout society, there is no telling what effect this will have. Enriching communication and making information more widely available is not democratically neutral. Democratic dialogue takes place in a media infrastructure that is characterised by carrier, frequency, language and process. Adding new technologies changes these infrastructures and adds new ones. They change the existing structure of information, participants, their participation and argumentation. The possible influence of the Internet on parliamentary politics will depend on the dynamics of democracy that characterises the environment. British, French, German or Dutch democracies all have different dynamics. During their considerable history they built up their own participants, style of dialogue and role of the press and media. In each nation the developments mentioned above will have a different effect. Then there is the important distinction between older and younger democracies. In older democracies the new systems will force a change in the existing dynamics bringing their own problems with that. In younger democracies the infrastructure of parliamentary information will create and catalyse democratic processes and procedures throughout the nation. It will structure the new democracy. So again, judging the parliamentary future in relation to new technology developments depends on the particular situation.

Parliamentary futures: re-presenting the issue

What will the influence of ICT developments on parliament be? The answer to that question depends on the technical situation in which we find ourselves. Most importantly, in order to answer that question, we must recognise that our answer depends on our way of seeing parliamentary democracy in the information age, or the paradigm through which we explore it.

On technology, this chapter has looked at current developments in information technology and information management and has raised questions about their effect on parliamentary activity. The first argument is that the democratic process is not an abstract concept but expresses itself as a media infrastructure where its conversations, dialogues and deliberations are solidified as documents, articles, and radio and television programs. This chapter outlines a few developments that will deeply restructure that media environment. The second argument is that the development of the information society will change the media infrastructure, which will affect parliamentary activity and change the dynamics of democracy.

On the question of paradigm the chapter has tried to develop its analysis through the basic idea of democracy and parliament as media infrastructures. Addressing the future of parliaments one often speaks using a legal or a political paradigm, sometimes historical or sociological. Very rarely does one talk about parliament as an information infrastructure and look upon democracy as taking place in a media infrastructure. At the same time many people have an attitude towards the influence of information technology that underestimates its power. To understand fully the changes that might lie ahead, it will be necessary to develop this new paradigm and establish its importance to understanding parliamentary activity in the information society.

INDEX

and ICTs, 86–7
  Internet, 84, 85–6
  web-site, 84, 146, 148, 149
Spain, 148, 150
spamming, 114
Sparks, Colin, 58
standardisation of information, 200, 201
Stott Despoja, Natasha, 59–60
surveillance, 169–71

— T —
Taylor, Greg, 47–8
technology
  data standards, 200
  innovations, 41, 161–2, 163, 169, 193–203
  paradigms, 181–2, 186, 204
  social implications of, 174
telecommunications *see* telematics
tele-democracy, 6, 141–2, 174–89; *see also* on-line politics
telematics, 5–6
  in Australia, 49–50
  parliamentary future and, 192–3
  in Slovenian Parliament, 89–101
telephones
  mobile, 18
  in South Africa, 84–5
television broadcasting
  Australian Parliament, 45
  Bundestag, 124
  California Channel, 178
  campaign advertisements, 179
  digital video images, 197
  Interactive Television (ITV), 175, 179–81, 182
  South Africa, 82–3
  Westminster Parliament, 10, 13, 24, 164
Third Way debate (Nexus 1998), 39–40
THOMAS (Congress search engine), 106, 110, 113
Time Warner, 175, 179, 180–1
transparent organisation, 200–1
Trimble, David MP, 39

— U —
UK Citizens On-line Democracy (UKCOD), 39, 40, 161
UN Charter of Human Rights, 14
United States
  California Gubernatorial elections (1998), 187–9

Communications Act (1934), 183–4
Congress, 11, 102–17, 146, 148, 150
Democracy Network (DNet), 174–89
'Irvine School', 76
Minnesota Electronic Democracy Project, 38
political interactivity, 161
Presidential elections, 153, 181
project vote smart (PVS), 152–3
Public electronic network (PEN), 152
updating web-sites
  Congressional, 107, 108, 116–17
  evaluation of, 150
  Frequently Asked Questions, 36
  incremental/automatic, 198
  Remote Updating System (RUS), 176, 177, 182

— V —
video format, 12–13, 19, 22, 87, 110, 180, 182, 196, 197
videotext services, 124
Viggers, Peter MP, 20
Virtual Private Networks, 30
virtual tours, 145
visual information, 195
voting procedures
  Australian Parliament, 44
  electronic, 202
  Scottish Parliament, 19
  Westminster Parliament, 19–20
voting records, 146

— W —
Walker, C. and Akdeniz, Y., 165, 169
Wall Street Journal, 180
Wallace, Jim MP, 69–70
Waller, Gary MP, 14
Washington Post, 180
'web-available' diary, 146
web-sites
  Australia, 46, 53, 145, 148–9, 150, 151
  Austria, 146, 147
  Belgium, 147, 150, 151
  British Columbia, 145, 147, 148, 149
  Bundestag, 118, 122–6??, 151
  Canada, 147, 148, 150, 151
  censorship of, 183
  Congressional, 104, 106–9, 110–11, 111–13, 115–17, 145, 146, 148, 150